Praise for *The Sound of One H*

This beautifully written memoir goes sur[ ]
exceptionally honest. Satyadasa is a talented storyteller and ~~ ~~
funny. The seemingly direct blokeishness of the writing dovetails with layers
of irony. Perhaps the most enjoyable feature of *The Sound of One Hand* is
that Satyadasa takes himself seriously enough to recall and reflect on his
experience, while observing it so honestly that he can't really take himself
seriously at all. Satyadasa [is] unflinchingly honest and subtly aware of the
gaps between the stories – both positive or negative – that we tell about
our lives and their multifaceted and sometimes elusive reality. – **Vishvapani
Blomfield**, Buddhist contributor to BBC's *Thought for the Day*

I really loved *The Sound of One Hand*. Satyadasa's writing is both profound
and moving as well as hilariously funny in places. I know this is an
extraordinarily difficult balance to strike as a writer, and he does it with
great success and skill. Whilst the tale is about the specifics of his life –
being born with one hand and his engagement with Buddhism – it is also
a beautifully written account of the archetypal human quest for meaning.
I recommend it wholeheartedly. – **Vidyamala Burch** OBE, co-founder of
The Breathworks Foundation and author of *Living Well with Pain and Illness,
Mindfulness for Health*, and *Mindfulness for Women*

This is beautifully written. It cleverly weaves together the twin themes of
disability and Buddhism, and does so with humour and humanity, with a
great turn of phrase and, above all, honesty. Satyadasa doesn't whinge.
There are some wonderful details, beautifully observed. We want to get
to know the author; he draws us into his world and keeps us there very
happily, enjoying his company. – **Helena Drysdale**, author

An insightful book of engaging stories from the life of a Western Buddhist
practitioner and meditation teacher, written in a tongue-in-cheek style,
very honest and nuanced, openly exposing the problems and difficulties of
a Westerner grappling with Buddhist ways of thinking, very personal and
yet at the same time deeply philosophical. His sense of irony often had me
laughing out loud. – **Lama Shenpen Hookham**, founder and principal teacher
of the Awakened Heart Sangha and author of *The Buddha Within, There's More
to Dying than Death, Keeping the Dalai Lama Waiting* and *The Guru Principle*

I've just finished the childhood part of your new book, sitting in the car park outside Morrisons, waiting an hour for a taxi! It is absolutely wonderful – there were times when I laughed out loud; it's utterly delightful, very funny, touching, full of gorgeous details and wonderful characters, not least yours! Thank you so much for sending it to me. I also found it quite gripping and moreish, to the extent that when I was supposed to be working on someone else's poems, I skived off and couldn't resist reading you instead. Many congratulations. I loved it, and the way you have plaited the different themes together is masterly. – **Mimi Khalvati**, poet and founder of The Poetry School

Heartening, gripping and thoroughly entertaining, Satyadasa encapsulates the joyful, messy business of encountering a spiritual community (or indeed of simply having to grow up during your twenties) – the ups and downs, the trials and tribulations, the ecstasy. Not only would this book have benefited me greatly at the start of my own Buddhist journey, I'd have been able to buy a copy to explain myself to my Mum! – **Ksantikara**, Young Buddhist Convenor

Satyadasa's memoir shows what a Buddhist life really looks like in the modern urban world. Sceptical, witty, serious, inspired and poignant by turns, his searching exploration is free of the clichés and stereotypes that so often beset spiritual writing. With its wonderfully vivid portraits – including of Sangharakshita, the founder of the Triratna Buddhist Order – as well as its picture of modern Buddhists struggling to find new ways of practising in a contemporary setting, *The Sound of One Hand* is a wonderful introduction to the Buddhist life as it is lived, here and now. – **Maitreyabandhu**, author of *Life with Full Attention*

Satyadasa lays himself bare, revealing struggles, personal and spiritual, that will be familiar to many of us, whilst also providing a truthful and inspiring account of a spiritual community as it matures. I hope this beautifully written and engaging book is widely read.

I found it very engaging and hastened through it eagerly. I especially appreciated his account of the Buddhist movement's troubles and of Bhante, so balanced and fair, insightful and appreciative. He captures people's voices, so that they live in the story. I can imagine newcomers to Buddhism finding it helps them through all the doubts and anxieties of engaging with a sangha, especially one with its past laid bare for all who can Google. – **Dharmachari Subhuti**, author and Buddhist teacher

The Sound of One Hand is a terrific read. Its energy jumps off the page. Particularly enjoyable is the author's wonderful sense of humour, which he's never afraid to turn on himself. Shining through it all is a deep feeling for life, for family, for companionship and for a spiritually meaningful life. – **Vajrashura**, ordained Buddhist and teacher

THE SOUND OF
ONE HAND

SATYADASA

THE SOUND OF ONE HAND

a buddhist life

Windhorse Publications
38 Newmarket Road
Cambridge CB5 8DT
info@windhorsepublications.com
windhorsepublications.com

Cover design by Dhammarati

Typesetting and layout Tarajyoti
Printed by Bell & Bain Ltd, Glasgow

British Library Cataloguing in Publication Data:
A catalogue record for this book is available
from the British Library.

ISBN 978-1-915342-10-2

To my parents, Joanna and our son, Thomas.

CONTENTS

ABOUT THE AUTHOR

Satyadasa David Waterston is a member of the Triratna Buddhist Order. He leads retreats and classes for the London Buddhist Centre and is currently the Buddhist tutor at Eton College.

After studying law at Oxford and a spell as a crime reporter at the Old Bailey, he lived and worked at the Buddhist Centre for a number of years. Since then he has worked as a solicitor in commercial and environmental law, and trained as a functional health coach with the Kresser Institute in California.

His memoir, *The Sound of One Hand*, draws on more than twenty-five years' close experience of the Buddhist community in the UK. It also explores what it was like growing up with only one hand.

Satyadasa lives with his family in East London. He's seen Bob Dylan perform more times than he would advise, and likes to wild swim, or just dip, whenever he gets the chance.

satyadasa.com

PUBLISHER'S ACKNOWLEDGEMENTS

Windhorse Publications wishes to gratefully acknowledge a grant from the Future Dharma Fund and the Triratna European Chairs' Assembly Fund towards the production of this book.

PREFACE TO THE
SECOND EDITION

I've never liked the word spiritual, though this book is probably destined for that shelf. The culture I came from didn't care for it either, so I never had much of a problem until I fell in with some Buddhists. The popular notion that attaches to the image of the Buddha is that a man once found some peace of mind. In the law firm where I trained in commercial property, my manager thought that karma meant calmer. And what is the modern Buddhist supposed to do? Meditate. Just sit there, finding that precious inner peace.

I wrote this book to show things in a more realistic light, as a loose and relatable mythos of how things often unfold: the trepidation of the first retreat, meeting a revered teacher, moving into and out of a spiritual community, feeling devoted and inspired and then rather sick of it all.

What is my claim to this story? I'm not one of the great pioneers, the first generation of Westerners to go East seeking the Buddha's teaching and bringing it home. However, my family, my Buddhist teachers and my own living memory together span the main arc of Buddhism in the West. My grandfather was part of the generation of earnest seekers after the war, when a new kind of universalism opened up and words like Zen and the Tao entered the lexicon. It bored my mother to tears.

The journey I've tried to describe goes from my birth just south of London to a second birth inside an igloo-sized clay monument on an old Moorish terrace in the mountains of southern Spain. Our personal myth, which is a precious thing to reflect on, intersects uneasily with the wider world in all its tumult and uncertainty. As I look back on the burst of inspiration and imagination that flared forth when Buddhism first came to the West, I feel a sense of confusion and possible loss. What will have become of all this, three generations down the line? Nothing stands still. The beat generation put away its rucksack. Free love and the mind-expanding mission of the sixties now looks like a wide-scale breach of health and safety. The *New Scientist* tells us meditation is scientifically justifiable, pending further data, so we take time off work to go on retreat to de-stress, detox and feel our feelings. It all works, sort of. I've not set out to fathom the past or the future but simply to lay bare one journey from one perspective: my own. I hope that through this glimmers some heat from the fire started by those early pioneers.

I'm delighted that Windhorse Publications has published this new edition. Writing a memoir is a daunting process, not least because of all the people who might justly be annoyed by it. Before I started I also had the handicap of thinking I was good at writing. That notion soon came apart, and without the help of several key people, I wouldn't have got as far as draft two, let alone draft nine. Firstly, thank you to Helena Drysdale for her honest impressions and much-needed encouragement. Maitreyabandhu has been a steadfast friend. Having him cast a poet's eye over my attempts was both funny and terrifying, writing being an exposing task in ways never intended. As with many endeavours in my life, his influence was the sine qua non. He would have crossed that last sentence out.

My wife, Joanna, read several drafts. She has an uncanny way of getting to the heart of things. I stand in debt to her wisdom, patience and kindness, which she brings to many people besides me, though I get the lion's share. I am blessed by our union. In fact, after this life, I have vowed to pursue her into the next one if that proves possible, so we can be together again.

Finally, two special thankyous, which I wish I could have given in person. Bhante Sangharakshita died in 2018, not long after the events in this book conclude. I wrote this book, in part, to honour what he made possible for me. Earlier the same year my mother died. During the awful year of her illness and decline we had some touching conversations where she recalled details from her childhood that she knew would give my account colour. My uncle Howard helped in this respect too. I dearly wish I could have shared the results with my mother. I hope she would have found it partly explanatory, mostly funny, and forgiven the rest.

Nowadays I lead classes at the London Buddhist Centre. There we all sit, silently, in rows, developing awareness. Sometimes I open an eye and take in the oddness of it, and the goodness. Modernity is everywhere squashing something in us, technology outgrowing us. We need more than mere peace of mind. We need greater wisdom, courage and connection to the cosmos, and a culture that encourages and magnifies that endeavour. It's not really here yet, not as far as I can see. Perhaps the spiritual adventure of Buddhism coming West is simply a tale that is going to be much longer in the unfolding than a few generations. It's not proving easy to raise up the image of the Awakened One, which is not a man or a woman, not merely a myth or an archetype, but the transcendent ideal of human Enlightenment, mysterious and attainable, far away yet at hand.

STUMPED

Something was missing from the start. Dad bumped into another expectant father in the hospital corridor.

'What news?' said the man.

'We have a lovely baby boy,' Dad replied, 'but . . .'

The midwife had introduced me to the world by thrusting my arm in front of Mum's face.

'. . . but he's not got his left hand.'

The man had whiskey and poured them both a glass.

Everyone was doing their bit. Dad's father, a farmer, broke from his daily rounds to shout some words down the phone to his son: 'Never mind, we'll love him twice as much.'

Ten years earlier the drug Thalidomide had caused multiple limb deficiencies in thousands of children, so while Mum was sedated I was examined for ailments more sinister than an absent hand. Every blemish was a harbinger of possible problems ahead. Mum's parents, Grandpa and Nanna, were only allowed a quick look in. As they sat in the waiting room a poem came to Grandpa, which he wrote up on a nurse's attendance sheet:

His small grave face but twelve hours here
Bears mysteries stranger than the seas,

In hieroglyphics more austere,
And older far than Rameses.

Setting events against a mythological backdrop would surely help.

After nine days the doctors confirmed it was a congenital birth defect, which is a fancy way of saying they didn't know what caused it. My parents took me home, filled with overwhelming love and anxious sorrow. At the primary school where he was deputy head, Dad found himself repeating 'He's a lovely baby boy, but . . .' to a stream of colleagues expecting happy news. Mum was a classroom teacher at the same school. They didn't want the whole thing to be about the hand, but . . .

As for me, I fitted right in. Newborn babies can't do much however many hands they have. We lived in Banstead, Surrey, in a steep row of semi-detached houses, with tight little porches and bay windows. Our Cortina sat out front on the crazy paving. My awareness grew from the milky, undefined realm of supermarket trolley seat and playpen to include reference to a 'little hand' which accompanied my journeys around the house. I expected to see it there, not realising it was different or any less than a person might want, even though my younger sister had popped out with two.

My little hand became part of the family, a feature like Dad's chin dimple which one could poke through his beard, or Mum's long, dark hair which was hard to straighten, or our Labrador's big, brown nose. In truth, 'little hand' overstates things a bit. There are small nodes across where the knuckles would have been but these are only fingers in an archaeological sense, like the worn away remnants of an iron age fort. Stump would be more accurate, but who the hell wants a stump?

When I was able to sit up my parents took me to a photographer on the High Street. In my fluffy cardigan it was hard to see that my left shoulder, upper arm and forearm were smaller than their opposite number. They agonised over whether the little hand should be visible. Mum rolled up my sleeve, like she did every day, repeating the little trauma of exposing it to the world. Was it okay to want to cover it up? In the one they chose to frame, I looked adorable: roundish, blue eyed and blond. The stump fell out the bottom of the picture.

At the age of four I had an operation at Roehampton hospital. It was exciting to be in pyjamas somewhere different. I clicked open my miniature suitcase and tipped some toys and my favourite stones onto the bed. The plan was to cut free a semi-sprouted digit which had melded with the rest of the stump, or little hand, whatever it was. After the sleeping medicine, a nurse read *Bambi* and the other kids fell asleep. They put a gas mask on me, saying I wouldn't be able to count back from ten. I gave it my best shot.

Bumping across a courtyard on a trolley afterwards, I looked down at the clump of bandages. For weeks after, whenever Mum put on a fresh one, I had a moment to admire the V-shaped nook cut in the stump, which was a simmering goo of blood, pus and skin grafted from a spare bit of flab near my groin. When it finally scabbed over I was left with a sort of thumb. No proper nail and no bigger than a baby carrot, yet still, a genuine opposable digit to aid my evolution. Thanks to the thumb-thing I was the first in my class to tie shoelaces, although in fairness to my classmates they weren't being advised by a consultant paediatrician.

On visits to the hospital he prodded and poked, searching for underlying bone structure, which on X-ray looked like the top of a tiny catapult. I was proud I had a special object to present, something out of the ordinary.

'Can you go like that?' he said, holding up a closed fist and waggling his thumb. I managed a tiny back and forth motion through about twenty degrees. He tied his own shoelaces with one hand clenched. Then it was my turn.

'First wrap the lace round the little thumb. Make a tie . . . that's it. Now press down on the tie with your thumb and keep it firm.

'Now make a bow with the big hand. This is the tricky bit. With your big hand now, press the tie down and with the thumb pick up the other lace and lift it over . . . under . . . and through the gap. That's it!

'So now you should have two bows. The big hand takes the new bow and the little thumb swaps over to the first one.'

Velcro was easier.

I felt special, the way a child should feel at that time when we're cushioned by a consciousness which hasn't yet fully separated from the universe of things, and so is not prey, not yet, to the bleaker potentials that arise at full self-consciousness. I pleased people. I thought the teachers beamed smiles at me because my maths and spelling were excellent. I must have been as irresistible as an Andrex puppy with a missing paw. And I tried hard at things. At recorder class my stump could stretch across three holes so I could get bottom D okay, however the hole below that was a big one and though I tried to spread the stump over it, stumps don't spread well, and I made mostly squeaks. The music teacher said brass might suit me better because the clever bit is done with one hand. So began a loveless march through a world of spittle and numb lips. First tenor horn, then a big-belled euphonium in a case which banged my shins on the way to school. The higher goal was the trombone, though I had no idea why it was the goal, or if it merited fifteen minutes a day puffing through dismal tunes from my wonky music stand that always fell down.

The upside of a stump

Fact is, not much needs all ten fingers. Mum hacked mittens down to size and sewed over the holes. The thumbthing helped me yank wheelies on my BMX. Dad switched the back brake cable to the right-hand side because relying on the front brake to stop risked me flying over the handle-bars. Cutlery was set for me the same as for everyone. I had a leather strap to hold the knife to my wrist, though if left to my own devices I preferred to pin sausages down manually with my thumb-thing, or just shovel food in wholesale. The consultant gave me a fork-cum-spoon-cum-knife which was useless. Too much pressure cutting down on a hard potato and the plate flipped. Baked beans could be herded to the edge, then what? None of this was at all traumatic, though to this day I have a mental block over which way round knife and fork should properly be laid.

No-one could teach me precisely how to do things. In sewing class my teacher could only watch as I turned the stump into a big thimble so I could cross stitch super-fast, buffering the needle into the hardened skin while racing around the alphabeted edge of my sampler. I could do tricks too.

'Look at this,' I said to Warren, a skinny kid with glasses.

I pushed a needle under the surface of the skin on the palm. The needle slid along a few millimetres and out again, clamped in a little tunnel of skin. I dangled it in front of Warren.

'That's wicked!' he said. 'Can you do the thicker needle?'

'Yeah, I can get three in. Look.'

'That must hurt,' Warren said, gazing in admiration. 'Is it numb?'

I never understood why anyone thought it might be numb. *It feels like a heel feels*, I'd say. Heels are tougher than hands and I showed Warren how hard I could punch the wall. The fat padded area of the stump absorbed the shock better than Warren's knuckles and he ended up bawling into his glasses. I'd win at arm-wrestles too – the whole forearm was several inches short so getting leverage against it was tricky.

Although cutlery and zips and practical stuff didn't bother me, it was essential to be able to catch a ball. When Dad got back from work I would demand throws in the garden. He was a headmaster now and the beard was gone. A ball thrown to the right was a cinch. His underarm high balls I'd trap against my chest. To the left was harder, however an acrobatic leap twisting the big hand round so it faced out was usually do-able. A high ball to the left was hardest. Things bounced off the stump and into the bushes. I'd have carried on catching into the dark, but at some point one of Dad's high balls would go over into the

neighbour's garden and he'd take that as a convenient cue
to pack up and go in.

It must be harder to have a child with a disability than
have a disability yourself. The business of getting on with
being me gave me adequate remittance from awareness of
a missing hand. But as my parents stood on the touchline
on Sundays during rugby matches they were surely more
continuously aware of my deficit than me. Mum looked
bedraggled and unhappy when I glanced over. (Her needs
only came first when *Dallas* was on – Sue Ellen's perms
had made sense of hair that was difficult to straighten.)
They couldn't know that at rugby a stump was very handy.
The row of curtailed knuckle could burrow into rucks
where ordinary hands could not. I'd jemmy it between a
clutched ball and an armpit then lever my elbow against
the opponent's rib cage until he yielded the ball. It could
deal out bony jabs. The worst torture for an enemy flanker,
or my sister if she was annoying me, was to grind in the
thumb-thing. The bony gristle clunked at each rotation and
no-one could endure it. I was small, but with a ball under
my arm, hard to stop. Player of the Year, no less, aged eight.
Maybe the other boys let me through more easily? Maybe.

The first difficulty came when I started at middle school.
Personally, I didn't find my little hand weird or dislikable
but in the playground I tucked it behind my back or I hid
it up my sleeve, which was easy because my sleeves were
often too long. However much I'd roll them up, they'd
roll back down. Break times were points of danger, more
so on warm days when we were allowed to play in the
copse next to the cricket field, where various gangs built
and defended encampments under the oak trees. Our gang

leader was Ian, an ugly, spindly kid with a lattice of purply blotching on his legs and fat purple lower lip. He was the tallest, though, and he was my friend, about half the time. Our encampment needed resources.

'You've got to steal their rubber tyre,' Ian said. 'Bring it back and we'll decide if you can be in the gang.'

'No way. I got the metal pole yesterday. It's someone else's turn,' I protested.

'Do you wanna be in the gang or not?'

I sauntered to another camp as if ready to defect, acting friendly and asking to see their bit of tyre, admiring it. Once it was in my hand I ran off and handed it over to Ian.

'You knob, we fooled you,' he said, wobbling his lip. 'One-handed slugs can't ever be in the gang.'

Other gang members agreed that one-handed slugs couldn't be in the gang. I wasn't big or bold enough to smash anyone's face in and assume command of gang membership criteria. The factual basis for my ostracism stunned me into silence. On quite a lot of days, whether or not I could be included in the gang was the main activity of the gang. Without me there wouldn't have been much formal business. I bore with it for a couple of years, not realising how much I hated school until many years later when I passed the school and hated it. I kept my problems private from Mum and Dad. Escalating up to that level would have made my situation more real, much worse I thought, flooding the whole of my life with what was confined to the playground.

My disability wasn't mentioned much at home, which was how I liked it. In the summer we took tents and dinghies to the south of France, returning blonder and browner. In the winter snows, neighbours came out to hurl snowballs at each other and toboggan down our hilly street. While deep in activity I lost self-consciousness. Steadying my notebook, climbing a rope ladder, or launching into a teetering handstand, I was as happy as the next boy. We all hated the freezing dash from the changing room to the over-chlorinated outdoor pool, but once in the water I was content enough, splashing around trying to swim straight. The trickiest times were when the little hand was hanging around in mid-space with nothing to do. I felt exposed. It wasn't long enough to reach the security of a trouser pocket and it couldn't twiddle or entwine with the other hand to cover over the embarrassment of an idle moment.

I don't remember hoping or imagining or believing that one day my little hand would grow into a big one. However, I do remember the morning, the precise moment as I approached the school gate, when I realised I had a problem that wasn't going away. It wasn't a practical difficulty that could be solved with a bit of smart thinking about doing up buttons or braking my bicycle. It was a problem with no solution on the horizon. I stood watching the others run past me into the playground, in a deluge of self-consciousness.

2

THE BREAKFAST TABLE

My grandfather had unsolvable problems too, like whether or not the breakfast table at their house in Cheam actually existed, and in what sense.

'Do you think the table exists, Grandpa?' I said.

It seemed important to get this clear.

'Well, it appears to exist, provisionally, one might say,' he replied, sitting down at the table and easing off his fingerless gloves with neat little tugs on the finger stubs.

'What does *provisionally* mean?' I asked.

'It means the breakfast table we see doesn't exist, ultimately speaking, as a table,' he said, while arranging un-finished Hamlets into the notches on the rim of his ashtray and lining up a few lighters. The table had a worn green velour cloth, covered at Grandpa's end by an edition of the *Sutton and Cheam Advertiser*, which alternated as his writing mat and dinner mat.

Grandpa was usually upstairs when we arrived on Sunday afternoons. I'd help my grandmother Nanna collect a bucket of coal from the chute, squatting down to look as scoops went into the boiler. Sandy, our Labrador, was let out into the garden with Kim, my grandparents' Alsatian. Then we sat in our allotted chairs at the breakfast table, waiting for Grandpa to finish preening his neat white beard or whatever he did up there. Eventually he entered the breakfast room in a regal way exclaiming 'Aahaaa!' as if it was a revelation to see us gathered and he'd only come down as luck would have it.

Once pleasantries about the amount of traffic on the strip of dual carriageway through Belmont were over, the conversation could go anywhere. I didn't know what ontology was. No-one did except Grandpa and Howard, but it often popped up. Uncle Howard was a few years younger than Mum, a bachelor of divinity with dark swept-back hair and large sideburns. In fact, a dead ringer for Soren Kierkegaard.

'Yes, David,' Howard said, continuing the theme, 'you see when we say 'table' or 'cup', for instance, it is rather an arbitrary delineation of the forever fluxing substrate about which we know nothing for sure.'

'The table is Thus,' Grandpa demonstrated, thumping it through the *Advertiser*, as the first plume of creamy smoke swirled up to the ceiling.

'How do we know anything more than that, was Kant's question.'

'You always seem to know,' said Mum.

'My dear girl, what one knows is that one knows very little. Other people *think* they know. The man on the Clapham omnibus is quite sure of himself. I have more kinship with the simple gardener.'

Mum frowned and shifted in her seat.

'What about Jim Brewer from the adult school?' she said. 'He's a gardener. You said him and his wife were as banal as they come.'

Nanna came struggling in with a tray of cups, saucers, cakes and a pot of tea under its woolly hat. Mum jumped up to help as Nanna had only recently had her gallbladder removed.

'Good news! See how much better Nanna is now,' exclaimed Grandpa.

'Very good news for some people,' Mum replied.

Domestic services had been resumed. Grandpa gave his napkin two swift flicks in his right hand, always two flicks, before wedging it into his collar. He did it like that every time and every time it drove Mum potty.

'Grandpa, do you think there's no table then?' I repeated, keen to get everyone back on the important matter of the table.

'I didn't say that,' Grandpa said, looking at me through a moving shape of smoke.

'Is it still there when we look away?' I asked.

Although I was merely repeating an issue that had arisen on a previous visit, I could tell Grandpa was pleased with my question by the way he pressed his fingertips together below his nose.

'Heidegger asked a more fundamental question,' he said. 'Why is there a table at all, whatever it is, rather than Nothing at all?'

I briefly imagined us all not there, a little gap in the middle of Cheam.

'Be a dear, David, run into the pantry for the biscuit tin,' Nanna said, gently circling the teapot.

Maybe my missing hand helped me relate to Grandpa's fundamental doubt about the status of things in the world or sharpened my awareness that the appearance of a thing is not necessarily the reality. For whatever reason, I loved to listen to Grandpa, who never rushed to give away the deeper reality of the breakfast table, which it seemed only he could comprehend.

Nanna kept more to the surface of things.

'Now let me see . . . it must have been a Tuesday.'

Tuesday was when she first met Grandpa at an optician's in Seven Kings before the War. She was a striking brunette with high cheek bones, working reception, greeting customers, fitting glasses and keeping the books.

'Yes, I'm sure it was a Tuesday because our boss Mr Levenson was on his day off. This dashing young man came in and tripped over by accident and would you believe it landed on the floor right in front of my desk. I dashed round to help him up. It was Don! It was his first day at the office.'

Mum's verdict: it may have been a Tuesday, but it certainly wasn't an accident.

Gladys endeared herself to Donald by giving him a first edition of T E Lawrence's *Seven Pillars of Wisdom* for his birthday. A telephone romance ensued between reception and the junior optician's testing room. However, one fateful day, almost certainly a Thursday, Mr Levenson got a cross-wire on his phone and overheard Donald lampooning his 'bloody Jew' boss. Gladys stayed quiet and kept her job, but Donald was summarily dismissed. He got his revenge by marrying Mr Levenson's loyal receptionist and taking her away.

Mum's memory of a cold childhood was no mere metaphor. The absence of central heating meant the regions beyond the breakfast room were dash-through

rather than live-in. The same climatic conditions survived
to my childhood, but I enjoyed venturing into the cooler
regions. In the vestibule two fox heads hung on the wall,
grimacing down with small sharp teeth, surmounted by
crossed rapiers. Running past them, I came to the hall
lamp made from a curled snake and a grandfather clock
which Grandpa regularly reset to the radio pips. The chilly
air made things stand out sharper, both then and in my
memory now.

Bounding up the stairs in twos or threes, I came face to
face with a thin brass-coloured Buddha that sat on the upper
landing table next to a fat-bellied, ivory-white Chinese
Buddha, which was crawling with babies. The floorboards
bounced a little under the carpet, causing tiny squeaks from
the wardrobe in Grandpa's dressing room, a room which I
felt permitted only to glance in, not enter. Doubling back
across the landing was a room bare of furniture and any
known purpose, referred to as the Meetings Room. Who
met in there I could not say – ghosts probably. I ran on with
them at my back into the bathroom, with its huge jar of
purple Epsom salts, blue china tiger and an iron bath with
a rectangular drainage hole so huge my sister and I feared
it would suck our feet down on the rare occasions when
we stayed over and needed a bath.

One such stay over was Christmas. While Grandpa
napped after lunch, Howard, by nature a mild man, pres-
ided over a game that involved family electrocution. With
elbows resting on the breakfast table we joined hands so
that a current could flow between us. Mum and Dad took
up the positive and negative batons of a coppery device to
complete the circuit.

'Okay, ready, it's going up,' said Howard, ramping up the amps and the tingling feeling. When someone broke the circuit they were out.

'Okay, hands together . . . ready? . . . up again.'

My little hand had no fingers to tingle but the sensation drilled into the bones of my wrist.

'Okay, up a bit more, here we go.'

The game usually ended with me and Dad in a face off. He seemed oblivious to electrical energy and always won.

When it was time for presents, Santa Claus would appear in the vestibule in a cape and a garish plastic mask, which made my sister cry. She cried even when she was old enough to query why Grandpa always came back downstairs minutes after Santa had left, saying how dashed annoyed he was to have missed him again. On Christmas night my sister and I slept in the same attic bedroom where Mum had fought as a child to maintain her core temperature. Once the old thick mattresses were warm with body heat we were happy as anything wedged in a ravine of fat cylindrical pillows. For night-peeing it was either the chamber pot or a perilous journey down a level, past the Buddhas, to the toilet with a massive square wooden seat, unworkable chain and shiny non-absorbent toilet paper; then a fleet-foot back to bed before all body heat was lost.

The only person higher up the family chain of being than Grandpa was Nanna's father. My sister and I called him Great Big Grandad to mark his unsurpassable ontology. We were counting down the years until his letter from the Queen. A couple of times a year we crammed into the Cortina to visit him at his house in Ilford. Grandpa sat in the passenger seat next to Dad, with Nanna, Mum, my sister and me in the back. One year they changed the law about seat belts.

'Belt up you lot,' Dad said, turning around.

As there were only three belts in the back, Mum volunteered to be the one who would fly through the windscreen if necessary.

'Mum, Grandpa isn't wearing his seatbelt,' I said as we started off, looking at the distance between Grandpa and the windscreen.

'He doesn't want to,' Mum said.

'*He* doesn't need the state to interfere,' Grandpa said.

Great Big Grandad was born in 1888, long before everything was invented. A working-class man, the foreman in a paint factory, he was in the Royal Garrison Artillery behind the trenches in the First World War, packing guns with explosives and firing shells across no-man's land. Nanna's birth gave him home leave, which meant he missed the worst period of the Battle of the Somme. 'Only three men in my battalion survived the whole thing,' he recalled for us, more than once, while cleaning and tamping his pipe.

Great Big Grandad had outlived his wife by four decades and sung to himself in the mornings in a warbling tenor. It was a special event to see him at the head of the table in his black-rimmed glasses, big sagging cheeks gobbling through a plate of prawns, veiny hands trembling with the effort of de-shelling. Prawns were a chance for me to abandon the pretence of cutlery, though his empty cases piled up faster and higher than mine.

On the way home through the Rotherhithe tunnel, I was still looking at Grandpa and the windscreen every now and then, wondering if the state was wrong or right. It seemed marvellous that Dad didn't even mention Grandpa's failure to wear a seatbelt, until later that is, when we got back to our house and he said Grandpa was a silly fool.

Let there be ghosts
The existence, or not, of ghosts was our family's proxy for religion. Apparitions had a firmer ontological footing than God, who definitely didn't exist, or the breakfast table, which existed only in a manner of speaking, though I never did get clear in which manner that was. Ghosts held out the hope that life might be more than meets the eye. Christianity is chock full of mysteries and strange occurrences and maybe in another era it would have interested me for that reason. But no-one I knew cared about Christ's story and no-one cared that no-one cared. Mum professed atheism and Dad had been baptised and confirmed in the Church of England, so he thought about God even less than Mum. People fell into two camps: those who ignored the clergy, and a much smaller camp who *were* the clergy, like the friendly Baptist minister four doors up. Religion was a sort of virus that attached itself to less fortunate people.

At school we were force fed it at the sleepiest point in the week, somewhere about 3.10pm on a Tuesday afternoon. My memory is that we never really did anything in that lesson. The teacher just handed out a sheet about a Sikh festival or something and then we all went catatonic. If I found myself in a church, I knew when to stand up, when to look down, when to mumble. *Someone born of someone came out of the land of such and such and said unto so and so . . .* We never prayed, except in the ordinary sense that people are praying all the time – whether they know it or not – for things, for happiness, for life itself. The time a beetle got tangled up in the bedroom carpet and we all watched on our knees as Mum unpicked each fibre with a hair pin and tweezers without pulling off a single leg, we certainly looked like a family in prayer.

Anything my parents couldn't explain interested me. One evening, while I slept in my cot, Dad fell through my bedroom ceiling. He'd missed his footing on the attic beams and stepped through the plaster floor down to his waist. While he hauled himself back up Mum ran in to check on me. This story was full of unexplainable elements. My bedroom door had slammed shut and the handle had rattled violently as if someone was inside trying to get out. A sudden updraft created by the hole Dad had made in the ceiling? No, Mum said, definitely not. The door was too solid to rattle and too tight to the carpet. I assumed these strange forces were about me.

The other bedroom mystery was the smell. Before sleeping I sometimes called Dad up to investigate.

'It's back,' I'd say.

'Yes, it is,' he'd agree, starting a sniffing tour of my bedroom. It was a musty smell. It wasn't me, he'd checked, or the bedroom lamp or a dead mouse. Sandy was ushered in for a sniff and found nothing unusual. In my mind the smell was connected to a presence over in the corner of the room, so we agreed to leave the lamp on to counteract whatever it was.

For Nanna, ghosts were de facto, she'd seen them. For Grandpa, debates about their existence or non-existence were carried on at a rather trivial level of understanding and he wouldn't be drawn in. For Howard and the rest of us, their ontological status was more troubling. In the most exciting game, only rarely played, we tried to communicate with them. *The Glass Game*, a version of *Ouija*, linked us back to a mysterious, now extinct, group called the Theosophists. An upturned glass was placed inside an alphabet circle and pressed down with one finger from each participant. At one game some years before my birth there had been categorical communication. Nanna must have convened proceedings as she always did, by swirling her free hand over the board in a gypsy flourish.

'Is there anybody there?' she would ask.

Apparently the glass moved to 'S' then paused.

Dad started guessing Steve or Stan or Susan.

'Wait a bit, give the spirit more time,' said Nanna.

The glass always trembles, making you think it's thinking about which letter comes next. Spirits are notoriously slow spellers.

Then it decided, pushing anticlockwise a short distance to P then across to E, then . . . N, C, E . . .

'Or Spencer,' Dad said.

'Or Spence,' said Howard, breaking the circle.

A Mr Spence had owned the house before them and he was dead. No-one was prepared for such a definite answer, so they turned on Uncle Howard and accused him of cheating. He protested his innocence, though over the years the matter was raised so regularly that he became worn down and eventually confessed. Unfortunately he couldn't reconstruct his crime when asked how exactly a single finger could move a glass which is being resisted by several other fingers. His was an unreliable confession and doubt still reigned. Theories about collective consciousness were mooted, but the demons and ghosts won an ontological reprieve to lurk throughout my childhood. I was happy about that. The certain non-existence of ghosts would have taken a lot of the fun out of family life.

Doubt wasn't even dispelled when I saw a real live ghost at my other grandparents' house. The Bedfordshire farm where Dad grew up had always been a relief for Mum. No-one discussed whether the breakfast table existed. People lived with a looser set of ideas, more mud and manure. Mention of Heidegger or Hegel might have been taken for a new type of rotavator. Dad had graduated from go-cart to tractor before Mum was allowed to turn on the radio. After Grandad retired they moved across the village to a fully heated house with a generous garden. On arrival my sister and I would tumble out of the Cortina after wrestling free of seat buckles. I'd sprint a few laps around the perimeter of the house to announce myself, leaping over familiar slabs and cracks in the paving, then slide along the hallway in my socks and into the kitchen for food. There was no doubt about existence here. The sun was sunny, the rain rainy, and the soft tarmac on the driveway smelt of pure tarmac.

Grandad, born in a farming family in lowland Scotland, had bandy legs, a large reddish nose in a weathered face and a teary wheezing laugh. Men on the farm feared his gruffness, which I witnessed in flashes. There had been a run of suicides in his family that Grandad didn't talk about. His father had done the deed in his sixties by feeding exhaust fumes back into his car, while his paternal uncle and aunt had killed themselves in a joint pact a decade or two earlier by driving into a loch. 'You are a silly man', Grandma used to say in an affectionate way.

Grandma was a plain-looking woman, tanned by the outdoors life, with a large flat mole on one cheek. She was resigned to a kind of cheerfulness about life, maintaining buoyancy with such sayings as *Well blow me down* and *I'll go to the foot of our stairs*. On Easter mornings while Mum and Dad had a lie-in, she took us to church. Our object was to get a chocolate egg from the altar, which was afterwards stored in Grandma's magnificent larder of Bakewell tarts, shortbread and R White's lemonade on friendly reachable shelves. Grandma's technique was to ask if I wanted a second or third helping of toad-in-the-hole a split second *after* dishing it onto my plate. Edges, cuts and scrapings all came to me. Mum likened me to a human dustbin, but she had no jurisdiction at Grandma's.

One day Grandma told us about the old lady next door who had lived in one room for so long that a tree had grown through the other part of the house. Now she had died and the house was being renovated. The workmen felt eerie presences, Grandma said, and they disliked working alone on the site. The new doors and windows hadn't been put in yet, so Grandma said we could go over for a look when the workmen had gone. When evening came my sister watched from behind the fence as my parents and I picked our way over the building rubble, across the lawn towards the empty house. The dare was to get to the top landing and back.

Dad walked briskly towards the porch. I lagged behind, alarmed by his levity. I was sure the hollow-eyed house would yield more debatable proof of ghosts. Dad started patting the lintels and admiring out loud how well they'd redone the porch, scuttling backwards a few feet at the sudden noise of Mum treading on a Coke can. Through the porch, into the screed hallway, Dad had begun approximating the cost of construction materials, when suddenly a spray of stones came skittering at us down the concrete stairs from the top landing. Mum now led the run back across the front lawn towards the fence, Dad and I chasing for second. As we were scrambling over I turned and caught sight of a figure in the darkness at the rear of the house. Surely this was the final proof. Seconds later Grandad emerged from the shadows, bent double on his walking stick, red-faced with laughter. He'd crept round and thrown some pebbles through an upstairs window. After the excitement there was only time for one game of Scrabble before bed. As he often did when losing heavily or getting irritable at how long we were taking, Grandad brought the game to a conclusion by flipping up the board. He then tried to win back our favour by deliberately letting his false teeth drop out.

The real ghost appeared on another visit. I'd woken early and the sun was already bathing my bedroom in warm light. I looked down and there was a man kneeling on the end of my bed with a serene face, closed eyes and hands pressed together at his chest as if in prayer. I looked at him for a couple of seconds and then attempted one of those cartoon exits with pedalling feet, straight into my parents' room. Dad wearily gave me his spot and went to sleep in my bed. Ghosts didn't bother him, apparently. In the morning I poked my head round the door and saw a pile of bedclothes heaped up where the ghost had been. I suspected Dad of arranging the bedclothes into the ghostly shape I'd described. I was eight and I'd seen the man very clearly. To allay my nervousness my sister was moved in to sleep in the same room. Unwelcome apparitions could go for her instead.

Big little mind

I am four. My ceiling, replastered after Dad's legs came through, has a kind of painted over crack. After long jumping into bed to avoid bad things underneath I gaze up at it. Sometimes there's a spider there, an old friend. Sometimes, looking up, it feels like I am marvellously big, as if I fill up my whole bedroom. Either that or I feel vanishingly small, a speck in a big wide room. With experiment I discover I can flip between the big experience and the little experience. I called it my 'Big Little'. Little worried me because I felt no more than a pinpoint receding somewhere behind my eyes, at a vast distance from the ceiling and the spider. Big was much better. I encompassed all the things in the room, including my spider friend, but it was odd because I didn't seem to have edges.

The closest I got to meditation in my childhood was a few years later, on trips with Dad to Banstead Woods to spot owls at dusk. We'd stand on one side of an open stretch of field silently watching a distant line of oak trees, steadying our binoculars on a fence post. The little patch of silence between us was more memorable than conversation. Owl readiness meant keeping alert, moving one's point of focus from tree to tree at the same time as a keeping a broad awareness of the whole wood. Owls could come from anywhere. When the trees became blotchy and indistinct in the dark and my attention drifted away, a hoot or a flutter would bring me back to my senses. Once a nightjar swooped past. Probably a nightjar, we agreed to agree. I'm not sure if we categorically identified anything; after all, it was dark. Somehow the owls were more vivid when we didn't see them.

One light summer evening I was supposed to have gone to bed, but I wasn't tired so I propped my elbows on the window sill to look down into our back garden. Dad was wheeling a barrow along the paved path which ran up the middle towards one of his two sheds. My BMX was crashed on the lawn next to Sandy, who was intently grinding his back teeth on a stick next to a little pile of wood chips. Suddenly it seemed like the final scene in a film which turns into a sepia print. A page turns over to reveal *The End*. My parents would die, I would die, my sister would die, Sandy would die, the garden path would die, along with the bike, the sheds and the conker tree, and the breakfast table in Cheam. For a few days, maybe a week, I shed tears under my bed covers. Then I forgot about it.

The first to actually go was Sandy. We buried him in a flower bed at the end of Nanna's garden. Dad dug a hole, only to find more of Kim the Alsatian still there than expected. A mental note was made not to bury a dog wrapped in a plastic sheet. We stood round in tears as Dad clumsily but gently lowered in the stiffened and curled up yellow body and then quickly shovelled earth over his companion of three thousand walks on the common.

3

ONTOLOGY

I was an athletic, spotty teenager squeezed into Levi 501s. One day Grandpa tried to teach me meditation. He was in his seventies, with a trim white beard and woolly cardigan, testing my eyes in the chill of his study. I sat in a high-backed antique chair opposite a chart on the wall as he raised his old ophthalmoscope up to each eye in turn. I found it thrilling to have him search a light into the back of my eyeballs, his magnified eye coming in and out of view and his long exhalations wafting down onto my lap.

After selecting a lens from among the convex, concaves and cylindricals neatly lined up in his wooden trial case, he cleaned it with his handkerchief and slipped it into a frame. Then I went through the chart again. My vision was always 20:20, top score in the family. I regretted not having eyes which needed more testing. Before I left he motioned out of the window and said I should label things as I passed them on the street, so my attention was less scattered and more present. Just things ordinarily visible in the eastern fringes of Cheam. I looked out at the smooth, creosoted gate and the front garden, walled round with privet and London plane.

'So I see the hedge and I say "hedge"?' I asked.

The idea didn't grab me.

Still, I listened carefully to Grandpa as we sat round the breakfast table on Sunday afternoons with our tea and biscuits. Mum got annoyed, especially if Dad appeared to be taken in by anything her father said. I chipped in whenever I could. My gift was remembering things people said and then repeating them back when they said something which contradicted what they'd said before. Grandpa seemed to like that.

Mum struggled to admit anything good about her father, but in many ways he was ahead of his time. He wasn't interested in politics or nation states or racial difference. He was a man of universal values. In 1947 he had written in the *Sutton Herald* about how he looked forward to a time when the 'bloody pursuit of fox, stag, badger and hare' was recognised as a 'savage pastime' and banned. Homosexuality, in another letter to the editor, should be legalised. Over in the *Epsom & Ewell Advertiser* he asked why Christian prelates wouldn't oppose the immoral form of slavery known as conscription. He backed the anti-British Jewish resistance movement in Palestine and opposed sanctions against German citizens living in the UK. Other contributors to the *Wimbledon Guardian* hissed and spat at his lack of patriotism. He countered: 'Until man learns to feel emotions on behalf of all mankind, war and enmity and the childish squabbles . . . of which history is but one long dreary chronicle will surely continue.' He never mentioned in the newspapers how he put eyedrops in before his war conscription medical to make sure he failed the eye test.

After the War Grandpa's journey into books and ideas began in earnest. Free of religion he was free to seek the truth. For the first time in history, ideas from all round the world and across time were easily ordered from a book-shop. The fleeting nature of this life and our certain date with death was a problem. Grandpa said most people block out these facts by burying their attention in the series of pointless hobbies which constitute normal life. His search was to become an obsession which dominated and dictated the lives of his wife and children.

His enquiry started in the 1950s with rationalism and early Western literature. The children were settled in bed with Homer rather than Rupert Bear, but they liked the stories just as well. Then in the late 1950s Grandpa went East, beyond the dry worldview of rationalism. He read everything he could on Buddhism, on the Tao that cannot be named, on the Vedas. The *Optometrist* magazine rejected an article he submitted for publication about 'Sight As Religious Metaphor' on the grounds it was un-Christian and, presumably, not actually about eyes. Eventually he quit full-time optometry and lived on rent from houses acquired with help from his banker brother, in order to devote more time to the study of the true nature of being. In addition to the *Daily Mail*, Nanna read whatever he read: Nietzsche's *Gay Science*, Huxley's *Perennial Philosophy*, and the house Zen favourite by Douglas Harding, *On Having No Head*.

The basic trouble with Buddhism

For Mum, as a young girl, the basic trouble with Buddhism was that its scriptures didn't, it seemed, actively encourage birthday presents or family outings of her choosing or any nice things at all. Just a line or two in the Pali Canon about that – dealing with birthdays and how important they are – might have really helped. Instead everything lined up around her father's routine, like the pencils lined up in his desk drawers (if ever she dared to look) or the napkins meticulously folded and returned to their holders, or the screws he oiled, sized and sorted into tins, that were themselves then arranged according to tin-size in the tool shed. The family terrier often ran away from it all. On his return, Grandpa shut him in the tool shed too. Mum was upset at the thought of him in there with the nail tins, clueless as to the nature of his offence. At least he was safe there from the dog inspector. Grandpa refused to pay the dog license fee (seven shillings and sixpence), causing the family to live in fear of a knock at the door.

The Buddha's denial of the creator God caused a particular hardship for Mum. She wasn't allowed to join her friends in the Christian school assembly, adding to the loneliness she felt at home, where friends almost never came. Her father was a source of great embarrassment. At a parents' evening he had reprimanded her bible studies teacher for re-heading her class book 'Religious History' to get round his objections to Christian dogma.

She did try, once or twice, to fight him on his own turf. One afternoon, for example, while playing bat and ball with Howard, an overarm smash cracked a pane in the garage window. Her father was angry, so to avert a growing crisis Mum decided that, as he'd been lecturing them about a philosopher who argued that 'cause' and 'effect' are merely created by mental associations, she would contend, therefore, that there could be no proof that either she or Howard was responsible. There was a ball and a broken window, but no objective way of showing how exactly one thing caused the other. The causation was all in her father's mind. He ignored her.

Most days Mum was confined to the breakfast room, which at least had some heat. The table took up half the space, with an armchair squeezed to one side next to a coal fire. Howard sat at her side, father adjacent; behind him, a chiffonier with shelving banked to the ceiling with casserole dishes and square china plates. Outside the window, a stone birdbath and a washing line. Nothing in the house ever changed, except the colour and size of the family dog. For hours they sat with their father while he read. Every time he turned a page he blew a jet of air up the inside spine to get rid of dust, a procedure which punctured Mum's boredom with irritation. Sometimes he paused to make a note in the margin, or write a haiku, like these two 'English Senryu' which he later published:

In the blackbird's cry.
Not a trace
Of Monday morning.

In the small hours,
The lavatory cistern
Demonstrates its character.

After lunch the really dull part of the day began. Footstool and blanket came out and the armchair became a bed. Soon he was snoring, with the terrier at his feet. Howard and Mum got the meagre heat that radiated through those two. Silence was to be kept for an hour and a quarter. Nanna found it easier to endure this part of the day by going to bed and just lying there, awake. Mum sometimes resorted to copying out names on the spines of her father's books with her calligraphy set.

In the mid-1970s Grandpa's spiritual tectonics shifted again, this time with a drift back West, to the greats of Western philosophy. He had deplored the 'spiritual whore-mongering' and 'guruphilia' of the 1960s. Every Tom, Dick and Harry thought they could meditate now, and they had soiled it all with their tawdry aims and materialistic, machine-like attitudes. He admitted that the 'heady nectar of the East' was very tasty, but now thought that taking up an Eastern religion is, to borrow from TS Eliot, to 'follow an antique drum.' The great mysteries of life are best approached through the richness of one's own culture, not by pretending to be a Tibetan.

Grandpa was not a Buddhist.

'Not as such,' he clarified.

Mum grew her hair long like Joan Baez, qualified as a teacher and married Dad at a civil ceremony at the cricket club, leaving Grandpa free from daily contact with his more awkward child. She saw too sharply the incongruity between her father's words and deeds. How did all this wisdom marry up with the domestic frustration, anxiety and near despotic pettiness? If he was so spiritual why did he compare her to a losing horse – an 'also ran' – when she missed the top maths stream by one place? She couldn't even borrow a rubber from his desk. He'd only had children because Nanna insisted, he told her. They agreed on one thing: they didn't like each other.

Grandpa was now conceiving a new 'Way' which united the direct approach to the mind typical of Eastern religion with the subtlety of Western philosophy. He had gathered a good following at the philosophy and meditation classes he offered at the College of Liberal Arts in Sutton. Students signed on for course after course and asked to see him afterwards for more instruction. They enjoyed his autocratic yet charming way of setting straight their mistaken assumptions about meditation. They wanted a book which described his approach and his scheme of practice, so they had something to go by when he wasn't around. So Grandpa sold the rental houses for not much, airy terraced dwellings in Islington and the East End. Schopenhauer required concentration, not gas regulations and leaky taps. Selling them was the only way to get to grips with Heidegger's *Being and Time* before they got to grips with him

Nanna typed up manuscripts, did the household chores and all the shopping, apart from pork chops which Grandpa liked to collect himself twice a week by bicycle. Social contact was strictly forbidden for Nanna. She wasn't even allowed to visit us on her own because if the house was left unattended it might be burgled, meaning if she went out then Grandpa couldn't. Mum seethed about this and Nanna fought back a little, with rows and door slamming, but no-one mounted an effective rebellion.

Then there were the women in his life and the suspicions. In his beige safari suit with four pockets and a sash belt – the only item of clothing he ever splashed out on – he would walk with Mary on Epsom Downs, probably reciting to her lyrical poetry from memory. Grandpa always walked at a steady pace, upright, making the most of his small frame. Or he would give wise counsel to Jackie over tea at her house. Carol, who lived opposite, had a husband who didn't take kindly to Grandpa's afternoon explorations of ontology with his wife. The intimate whispering chats with female students on the hall phone must have hurt Nanna.

Grandpa didn't try to allay suspicion. In one poem, which he included in a little volume for free distribution, he describes his meeting with a young female student from his meditation class at a cafeteria. Nanna would have learnt, from the poem, that they parted after a kiss 'with tongues entwined'. The sixty-year-old poet then walks home wondering why her 'moist mucus membrane' made him feel 'better than a thousand sermons of wisdom'.

'Don't tell me that poem is metaphorical,' Mum said. 'It's disgusting.'

His main method, though, was to teach his students to meditate so they could experience what he called 'ontological modes' – rarefied states of being by which the keen meditator could edge closer to ultimate reality. Through persistent existential questioning of the 'frames' through which we see the world, Grandpa's scheme would then liberate the meditator from all worldliness.

For three more years Nanna typed and Howard reviewed. Grandpa had a heart attack and had to hold court for a few weeks in his oily pyjamas. He slowly recovered thanks to his own prescription of blockers, thinners, duck fat and cigars. In keeping with his orderly approach, he had advance purchased a burial plot in a local cemetery. It was rather more generous than usual in that it was family sized. The idea of it disturbed me. I'd mentally stack us inside: Nanna down there next to Grandpa presumably, Mum and Dad on the next layer, top layer for my sister and me. Horrendous.

The all consuming effort went on. Mum reluctantly agreed to do the illustrations on meditation posture. Grandpa rejected a publisher's suggestion of a more handy layman's guide. In the end he printed it himself in a tiny font, reminiscent of the lower rows of his eye chart, and invited his most loyal students to the launch. *The Philosophy and Practice of Meditation: An Existential-Ontological Approach to Contemplative Experience*, by Donald Henry Huckle Martin, codified in a single volume Grandpa's 'reckoning as to the way of all things'. Grandpa had gone from scientific West to spiritual East, circling back to the jewels of Western philosophy. All without ever leaving Cheam. He never went further east than Margate.

The book set out a schema for spiritual practice that was so erudite, so carefully poised, so mindful of using language in a way which does minimal damage to the 'ontological' reality beyond words, that Grandpa had to give birth to fifty words entirely new to the English language. Handy words such as ontenescient, ontorogation, ontoplenum, intraception, transmonadance and onticalization. In Grandpa's world this was speaking to Westerners in a language they could understand. Keen though they were, most students never got through the book. It contained no jokes and some students still felt they needed Grandpa in person to explain what it actually meant. The inscription in the copy he gave Mum offers thanks for how she contributed, 'without overmuch curiosity as to the why and wherefore of it all'.

I was only ten, but I remember the day Grandpa proudly told us that a copy had been sent to the British Library. I felt proud too. Whatever Grandpa knew was now preserved in the library vaults at the British Museum, for the benefit of those who would come later. Dad's verdict was swift, merciless and not delivered to the author: 'Unreadable'.

Being and time in Purley

Ontological issues didn't plague our home life. We moved to Purley in south London, to a larger semi with a bigger garden for Dad's expanding collection of old farm implements, ploughshares and wagon wheels, and more room inside for Mum's antiques. A pitchfork and a sheep dipper hung on the kitchen ceiling. It was like living at the Mill on the Floss. When the neighbours got a new Fly-mo, we got a barley hummeller.

My little hand expanded slowly into its teenage years, keeping rough proportion to the rest of me. I didn't want any adjustments. I wanted to win games without concession, giving my victories an extra layer of congratulation. Scout leaders marvelled at how I pitched my tent faster than the other patrols. I didn't think it was that astonishing, but I took their praise. I read the instructions, listened to the scout leader, observed the fundamentals of ground sheets, dollies and sod cloth, then went at things like a terrier. Being the best and quickest at things gave me a sense of being normal.

According to the family myth, I'd inherited Grandpa's intellectual streak – a comparison with her father which Mum didn't seem to mind because a big brain is always good news. At the local boys' secondary grammar school I used it to turn the tables on an old tormentor, whose major weakness was a weirdly triangular head. I'd stop him in the playground, armed with my ruler, and give a public demonstration of how the square of the hypotenuse between his chin and the crown of his head was equal to the combined square of the flat of his face and the top of his head. His head would be useful if anyone forgot their protractor, I declared. He couldn't deny the shape of his head, so I won. Being at or near the top of the class was a position worth cheating to defend. With an English translation hidden below the desk on my knees, I'd do live Latin translations of some minor moment in Virgil's account of the Trojan War, making enough deliberate mistakes and hesitations to allay our teacher's suspicion. My friend Roberto saw me doing this once and we were sent out into the playground for our unstoppable laughter.

Roberto was Italian English, and more gifted than me at both Latin and English. Girls were drawn to his dark curls and olive skin. He had an eccentric grandfather too, an old mariner-like fellow with a ragged beard who forayed around the house with a strange shuffle-hop, as if his legs were tied together at the ankle. He examined his dinner with a magnifying glass and slept in the attic surrounded by piles of empty Gaviscon packets.

He only spoke to me once. I'd pressed the doorbell and, peering through the pearled glass of the front door, I could see him shuffle-hopping towards me. I hoped in vain Roberto would intervene before he'd covered the length of the hall, but no. Our eyes met.

'Fuck off, you don't live here,' he said.

For Christmas one year he gave Roberto a single pound coin wedged, with sellotape, into a hole he had cut in a piece of cardboard. Roberto showed it to me with wide eyes and hanging jaw, looking for confirmation that this was not normal behaviour. I enjoyed my role as arbiter of normal and corrective to Roberto's habitual doubtfulness about life. Roberto's dad wasn't too normal either. I only saw him a few times in all the years visiting their house as he stayed mostly upstairs. When Roberto and I arrived back after an arduous one-day competition hike of forty-five miles across mountain and moor, his father didn't greet us or ask how we had got on. He had already told his son that hiking wasn't a 'relevant activity'.

'Is that normal, Dave?'

One morning Roberto bicycled round to our house to announce that Grandfather was missing. He'd gone to the post box – the outer limit of his shuffle hop – and now he was nowhere. Roberto was almost ecstatic. The mysterious disappearance made him temporarily less doubtful about life. We roved around Purley on our bikes looking for him, hoping he wouldn't turn up too soon. He didn't. Late in the evening the police called from Derbyshire. Grandfather was in a pub telling stories and the locals didn't know what to do with him at closing time. Grandfather had shown a sign of normality. He'd pretended to post a letter, and then shuffle-hopped onto a bus, then a train to London, then a Tube, then the intercity, then taken a taxi all the way to his childhood village.

Apart from the behaviour of grandfathers, not much needed explaining in Purley. My early love of ghosts and mysteries had ebbed away. Life was W H Smith, bus stops, railway lines, trees set down every so many yards, a leisure centre with two pools. Things worked. From the way teachers and everyone spoke I sensed there was an agreement, so obvious it wasn't worth stating, that we were the lucky generation. At long last the sea of superstition had been crossed and now our job was to accumulate and guard the right kind of knowledge. The shopping centres and ordered civic amenities of south London were touched with a kind of truth. A rather dull sort of truth perhaps, but workable and undeniable. By some good fortune the culture I'd been born into was on the right track.

Until I heard Bob Dylan's guitar and rasping voice I assumed nothing important was missing from life in the post-God London suburbs. Listening to *Bringing It All Back Home* on my walkman on the bus home it was obvious something had happened in the 1960s which was way more important than what was happening in the 1980s, especially in Purley. Roberto and I recorded albums tape to tape like it was contraband: *Highway 61*, *Blonde on Blonde*, *Nashville Skyline*. My own musical career had reached its higher goal: the trombone, a suitable instrument for me apparently because all my stump had to do was pin the damn thing against my neck. Roberto played the trombone too, although as his Dad thought musical instruments were not a 'relevant activity', Roberto had to practise in secret. Trombones are not easy to practise in secret. They don't readily attract girls either. In fact, I agreed with Roberto's Dad that trombones were completely unnecessary.

To be more like Bob, Roberto and I went to parties with harmonicas and hip flasks stowed in our long dark coats. I would hide the stump under a sofa cushion or casually behind my back. I didn't find girls as easy as folding a fly sheet or fiddling Latin homework. Sounding clever with Bob Dylan lyrics didn't help. It wasn't as simple as diving sideways to catch a ball. Or maybe it was, I never tried. I was convinced that girls wouldn't want to be touched by a stump. Sometimes they were forced to hold it at a group dance or in an exercise which required holding hands in a circle. Less timid girls grabbed it directly, others gingerly held my wrist or clutched my elbow, as if the stump might confer disease. To be fair I doubt I would have wanted to hold anyone's stump either. However, I never met anyone like me.

The stump was an odd companion, an unpleasing partner that no-one acknowledged. Concealing it too obviously would draw attention to it, but subtly hiding it was obviously obvious too. I smudged the whole problem in my mind by believing it wasn't a big deal. The fact that no-one said anything about it confirmed to me that they must think the same. Maybe they didn't even think about it. With girls I wasn't top of the class. I wasn't a total failure, but, to borrow the phrase teachers used to make pupils revise more in the run up to GCSEs, I was 'heading for a polytechnic'.

My first proper brush with ontology

One day I ran into a mirror. The phone was ringing. I was in bed, jet-lagged and confused about where I was. I'd just come home from a World Scout Jamboree in South Korea, where I had represented Surrey. The ringing noise was clear, but it evoked no connections in my mind. My parents were out, so it rang for some time before the concept of 'phone call' attached itself to the noise. I leapt out of bed and lurched towards a glimmer of light from the landing, which turned out to be a reflection of that light in my full-length Victorian wardrobe mirror. I went into it at full tilt, shattering the thick glass with my knee, elbow and forehead, before reorienting and running downstairs to the hall phone. It was a friend calling to swap GCSE results. Blood was dripping onto the phone book, the carpet and, horror of horrors, I'd smudged it onto the Laura Ashley wallpaper all down the stairs. Mum would be furious. I apologised to my friend for bleeding and hung up, calling instead our neighbours, two elderly spinsters, who suggested they call their friend who was a homeopath. Homeopathy works. Just hearing the word triggered a survival instinct and I asked them to call an ambulance.

A few weeks later the stitches were out and the bruising nearly gone. I was lazing in my bed during an afternoon lull at the back end of the summer holiday. Dad had cricket on the radio downstairs. Then something happened. I had no interest in Grandpa's schemes for categorising mental states or labelling hedges, but I noted this experience precisely because I couldn't categorise it. It had nothing to do with succeeding at school or with girls or with any thoughts about my life.

Out the window I caught sight of a plane moving silently through clear blue sky. I watched it disappear behind the branches of an oak tree which stood set back in our front garden. What happened took place the moment the plane re-emerged on the other side of the tree. Its sudden, silent re-appearance into the blue sky took me by surprise. I felt a surge of non-separation from the window, the tree, the plane, the pilot and the passengers. The front and back dropped out of my experience and for an instant everything was shot through with everything, right to the heart.

In my final school year I was made school captain by votes from the staff. I wondered if the stump was a swing factor in staffroom discussion, but I figured there were enough facts confirming my actual merit. I basked in the wonderful thrill of inner power uniting with outer recognition. Whatever the lower boys made of their one-handed overlord, they got out of my way. Success was compensating for the dent of difference I felt and the dampener in my relationships with girls. If I could get into Oxford, all self-doubt would finally be laid to rest. Roberto and I sat the entrance exams. He wanted to read English, which I liked too, but I wasn't as good at English as Roberto and my priority was to get in. Someone, I forget who, said I'd be good at law. Maybe it was me who said it. It was agreed I was clever enough and cleverness was required for law. I envisioned myself as a barrister doing something ennobling.

Grandpa never went to university and had little to say about it. He was writing a 'late trilogy' of essays, what he assumed would be his final thoughts on the human predicament. Angina, kidney problems and gout were worsening. On visits we would find him in the breakfast room in his dressing gown, with dishevelled hair and a pained look. Once he pulled off a sock to show us a black crack caused by gout on the arch of his foot. I'd not thought about Grandpa's feet before.

One day, as Nanna cleared the table for lunch, he said he was thinking of 'haute fenêtres'.

'"High Windows", you mean, by Philip Larkin?' I said.

'That's my boy!' he exclaimed. '"The sun-comprehending glass, and beyond it, the deep blue air, that shows Nothing, and is nowhere, and is endless."'

My knowledge of Larkin's bleak poem confirmed the bond we had. He was indifferent to my decision to study law and indifferent when I was accepted at Oxford.

Despite his physical troubles he was still lecturing on philosophy at the local College of Liberal Arts. Roberto and I went along once and I felt proud to see members of the public listening respectfully to his remarks about the limits of the knowable. It was a better audience than the breakfast room.

The following spring he stopped his lectures and eventually had to go into hospital. On visits we stood around his bed as he charmed the nurses and told doctors what to do. When the shuffling and fluffing of pillows was done there wasn't much to say. He complained we would drive away while he was stuck there to die. No-one disagreed or argued back. He was at the sharp end of ontological-existential enquiry, beyond the reach of books, marooned between hospital sheets with tubes disappearing into his pyjamas. Maybe he and Nanna had some tender exchanges, I don't know. Visits from his favourite 'student' complicated matters and it took careful logistics to stop her and Nanna bumping into each other.

Grandpa's condition worsened on the night Dad had booked us tickets to see Bob Dylan. Mum stayed home, but for me there was no question of not going. By some miracle Bob was going to appear in physical form at the Hammersmith Apollo. As he walked from the behind the drum kit towards his guitar, eye contact, albeit one way, was established with a character from another dimension. Even Bob had to walk onto a stage, like a person. I strained to see how he picked up his guitar, his slight stoop, how he moved. He mumbled in a nasal whine but it didn't matter because I knew all the words by heart: 'Desolation Row', 'Tangled Up In Blue'.

Thanks to Bob I'd had at least a thousand girlfriends before I'd had any.

In the small hours that night Grandpa died. A day or two later we gathered at the house. As he had stipulated, he was to lie for a few days in an open coffin on the desk in his study, a cold room well suited to its final purpose. Nanna was struggling, Mum more business-like. She asked my sister and I if we wanted to have a look. We were ushered through the hall, past the fox heads with their fangs and crossed rapiers and into the study with its glass bookcases and optical charts, edging forward until a familiar beakish nose came into view, an ashen face and yellow-grey cigar-stained fingers. For a minute we had the uncomfortable luxury of examining Grandpa's features without him examining back. It was imponderable on a different level to speculations about whether the breakfast table did or didn't exist.

I felt a stab of shame at the thought that Grandpa's studies had been a waste of time. The ideas which defined him now had no mind to be thought in. They were congealing in his brain cells. The lack of any forward story from his dead body seemed to diminish the meaning of his life. His careful study of philosophy, his meditation, even his book – so what? An infinite extension of nothing lay ahead, no matter what vague things people said about floating off into the ether. In his final moment in the night how had he faced such thoughts? How could anyone face that? I didn't want to end up dead in a library, surrounded by a family full of chilly memories. We backed away from the coffin and went for tea.

On the funeral day the undertakers carried Grandpa away from his beloved library. They were exactly on time and the grandfather clock in the hall began a sequence of eleven chimes as the coffin passed. I heard every ratchet and ding in slow motion. At the graveyard chapel there were students, people I'd never seen, but no-one who seemed like a simple friend. No-one wept. Nanna had taken some valium. Flowers from the 'other woman' were kept out of her view. Uncle Howard led the service and I read from the *Book of Ecclesiastes* about how there is a time to be born and a time to die. Grandpa liked poetic bits in the Bible.

He wanted 'Memento Mori: Remember, you too must die' on his headstone. Mum said it was revenge against us for still being alive. Anyway, it seemed a little gratuitous for a graveyard setting and something else was chosen.

Months passed. Manuscript copies of *The Philosophy and Practice of Meditation: An Existential-Ontological Approach to Contemplative Experience* settled into dusty boxes. The book was owned by maybe one hundred people, read by somewhat fewer. Anyway, Mum must have assumed she'd never be bothered by Eastern religion again. She didn't reckon I'd go one further than Grandpa and ordain as a Buddhist in a remote mountain retreat, changing my name and apparently my identity. Nor did she hope, I'm sure, that forty years after her father led his first public meditation class, I would lead mine.

4

OUT OF MY HEAD

Before I left for college, Nanna gave me a book from Grandpa's library which had a small, fat golden Buddha on the front. *The Book On The Taboo Against Knowing Who You Are* by Alan Watts cut things down to the essentials. Humans were like tubes and however we decorate our particular tube, however many appendages we have, beneath social conventions all tubes are in the same basic predicament: vulnerable, finite, and making it up as we go along.

Although I was very drawn to this book, the surface of things cuts pretty deep. I felt my difference and nowhere more so than at the college disco. There's something irreducibly uncool about taking a disability onto a dance floor, but of course everyone is polite and no-one says a word about it. A stump deviates from the pattern, and noticing deviations is an evolutionary thing. I pass loads of people with ears while out shopping but I don't register any ears at all. An ear that is not there however, that shows up at twenty yards. The urge to look is irresistible and a quick glance feels justified, almost biologically necessary. I don't always catch people in the act of sneaking a look at my stump. Noticing things while being unnoticed must be another skill from the prairie. I waft my eyes at a shop display or something in their general direction and then bring a quick focus onto the missing ear. Yuck. I'd definitely be wearing a hat.

Congenital limb defects are unnerving for everyone. Unique in their aberrance, they bend at a funny angles, bifurcate into twiggy digits, or end in a fleshy mass with tiny polyps like tie-ups on a balloon. Yuckadee. I found my way onto the dance floor the same way I get into a cold pool: put my head down and go. It was alright once I was in. I grooved away in long, floppy sleeves to spare everyone, and myself, the odd communication from my pollarded limb. A nice clean amputation is better. One can imagine a normal limb was there before the shark attack or the threshing machine incident or some other romantic happening. I saw a professional dancer on telly with a half-arm amputation. He was springing about like Rudolf Nureyev, but to me at least, his fancy moves just looked like an elaborate effort to distract attention from what wasn't there.

After Alan Watts, a small collection on Zen themes from archery to motorcycle maintenance grew on the bookshelf in my college room at Oxford, wedged between volumes on constitutional and administrative law. Zen reasoned things out on a more fundamental level than the judges at the Court of Appeal. In Zen Buddhism there is a koan: what is the sound of one hand clapping? The dull thud when I applaud is not the answer. Koans are questions which offer no solution on their own level. They force the student into a deeper type of awareness, pushing him or her up against more ultimate issues. I understood this koan had something to do with our normal experience of the world being twofold: self on the one hand, other on the other. The basic human problem is being trapped in this feeling of separation, while hurtling towards death. To really hear the sound of one hand clapping is to be free from the prison of self-reference.

The stump was always there at the boundary between me and everything else. Hands are for making connections, pointing things out, pioneering over the boundary of self, towards, with any luck, a desirable other. Stumps are very hopeless explorers. The only thing they point out is themselves. They create a mood of unease like border control. I don't know, maybe the discomfort was all in my head. I never made light of it or alluded to it myself, so no-one else had permission to jump the divide. At the college bar, little blips of heightened self-consciousness came round like the cold repeat of a lighthouse beam.

A blip as I notice it exposed on the bar . . .

Another blip as I clutch bags of crisps and two pints to my chest . . .

A big spike as I wipe a line of beer froth from my shirt . . .

My thoughts about all this remained my own. They piled up in the hinterlands of my awareness, like the layers of reflection in a train window which one never quite sifts one from the other. I was only half-conscious of their content, but they formed a reality around me as real as the walls and the floor.

I took a deep breath and sat down next to my favourite lawyer, with whom I was besotted. Her dyed blonde hair was tied back, ready for an all-night session in the library.

'That Zen guy Alan Watts I was telling you about, he says ordinarily we're no more than tubes who put things in at one end and let them out at the other.'

'You're not calling me a tube are you?' she said.

'No, not you – he means people in general, and lawyers I suppose, generally.'

'Carmen sucks things up like a tube. She's sucking up to you know who. She's already done her estoppel essay and started on Unfair Contract Terms.'

I loved my fellow lawyer too sincerely and she wasn't grabbed by the tubes idea. Mystical Eastern observations did not increase my allure. She had charms against my charms, even when I resorted to directness rather than Taoism. It took me a long time to face the fact that I wasn't the right type of tube for her.

Gradually I begun to realise that in the overall scheme of the universe, law was a shockingly narrow focus. I fell in with the English students, revelling in their chatter about James Joyce's long sentences and Andrew Marvell 'annihilating all that's made to a green thought in a green shade'. Hell knows what that meant but it sounded good. I wanted to break out a bit. I sellotaped a thumb pick to my thumb-thing and restrung a guitar, which was immediately more promising than a trombone. And I made friends with Adam, a chemist who did real things with actual stuff in laboratories. He was stick thin with a shock of blond hair and nostrils so long and cavernous they needed no caricature. One evening, after 'microdots' had been procured and nervously washed down, I ended up lying with my head on his girlfriend's breasts. It felt good but I knew it wasn't right, so I sat up. There was no-one there. I'd been lying on a pair of trainers. There was a helicopter outside in the street making the curtains move. I needed to let the others know.

Then time slid somewhere.

Outside now, a man passes Adam a hotdog. Adam looks at me wide eyed and confused, nostrils at full flare. A gust of wind and he'd have taken off. We try to make sense of what just happened: Adam passed the man a piece of paper and then the man passed Adam a hotdog. We couldn't believe it. The hotdog man had lost out, big time.

Back indoors now, I pat a balloon to Sam, an immensely tall anthropologist, and he pats it back and I pat it back and he pats it back. For brief blips we are unanchored from the normal constraints of a situation. Sam appears to understand this and I want to talk to him about it but for some reason I can't. Talking about the balloon we are tapping has nothing to do with tapping the balloon, which is miraculous and inconceivably odd.

Time slides again.

Where is everyone else? How can I get out of this bathroom? How did I get in here?

Later, out in Port Meadow, there is a cow. We all see it: half a ton of pure cow being a cow right there in the meadow. We find this unsurpassably funny.

Time slipped on, and when it stopped slipping the walls condensed back into an ordinary terrace house, and we condensed back into our various names and personalities. I lay on a sagging sofa in the kitchen feeling metallic and spacey. Adam, naked from the waist up, was frying eggs, his blond hair flattened stiffly up one side of his head. To my relief things were steady again. The pan sizzled, like pans do, and no-one was saying anything profound or hilarious about eggs. There was lots to think about.

'Nothing is fixed then?' I said.

'Nope,' said Adam shaking the pan. 'Things tend to wobble, don't they? This egg is well fixed though, want one?'

'No thanks.'

'Budge up,' said Adam coming over with his plate. 'Did you hear about Sam going to the toilet and getting chased down the street by his own turd?'

'Yeah. And what were you and Steve doing sitting in front of the mirror? That was a bit intense,' I said.

'Er, yeah, that was weird, you can see yourself getting grey and wrinkled if you try to . . . it's a bit freaky.'

'Do you think things are as they are now or how we were seeing them last night?' I asked Adam.

'It's just chemicals,' he said.

'It didn't feel like chemicals.'

'Guess it's the brain altered by the chemicals, then. Take it easy, it'll be all gone from the system in a few days,' he said, polishing off his egg and readying for college.

I was amazed. Up to then I had taken for granted that my normal perception of things is how things really are. I knew the mind interprets the senses. Grandpa liked to show us the drawing of a beautiful young woman who suddenly appears to be an old hag with a big nose and then you can't get the pretty one back. But I'd assumed my senses mirrored how things are, more or less. Okay, earthworms sense the world in a very different, much more wiggly way, but they are just earthworms. Last night my assumptions about reality had at the very least been wobbled. However,

I was too well brought up to let the un-fixedness of the Universe impede my studies. Law requires no intuitive leaps or theorising about reality. Neither was having holes blown through my fragile sense of self something I longed to do every weekend.

The other discovery I made around this time was that self-consciousness of disability on the dance floor vanishes entirely with ecstasy, along with the need to make comparisons and dwell on differences, and all the envious or competitive thoughts which can set even friends apart. I didn't do this much either though. I replaced a worry about dying of dehydration with a more middle class worry that recreation of this ecstatic kind would blow all my carefully stored happy capital and set me up for a lifelong comedown on low interest rates.

Just watch your lip

Friendship with Adam and adventures in class A drugs were opening me up, but I still felt locked in myself, screened off from other people. My experience was too much in my head and not enough anywhere else. I had a sense of what Zen was driving at, but without my old schoolfriend Roberto I may never have got beyond tube theory. At the end of our first year Roberto was unable to settle to his studies. His college was down the road and several times a week I'd bolt through the grey arch of the Porters' Lodge and up a worn wooden flight of stairs to find him in his room.

'Dave, this is absolute shit.'

Roberto spent as much time fretting about not having done his reading list as it would have taken to do all the reading. For many students this was part of the standard bluster: to talk about one's miseries while actually being quite happy about them. I read a line or two of his inky scrawl on Critical Literature Theory, a subject so horrendous it made me glad to be a lawyer. Lawyers just had to read the reading list. English students needed flair. They sat up half the night in suede jackets smoking roll-ups, then plucked something brilliant and incomprehensible out of the ether between breakfast and the tutorial. Some of them did anyway. Roberto had this type of style but he was weighed down by a very low opinion of his efforts and an Olympian expectation about scholarship that I couldn't relate to. At the end of our first year he went on a free Buddhist retreat in Wales. When he came back he was in a clear frame of mind and I was impressed by the change. I supposed it had to do with the meditation – ten hours a day, he said.

A year later I booked on the same retreat, hoping for a similar boost.

Grandpa never went on a retreat. He thought there was something suspect about wanting to get away from it all. The true sage, he said, could live a fully conventional life. 'In the world but not of it' was a phrase he liked. He retreated no further than the meditation stool in his dressing room. If children barged in, he remained still, eyes closed, until they went away. In his book he wrote that with enough concentration 'the orange over there ceases to be different from the observer of the orange in here'. He tried to teach this to Mum and Dad, but they proved no good at meditation. Mum was deliberately no good on principle, no doubt. Dad's attention, I imagine, was too heavily weighted towards the orange as potential food to appreciate the 'vast, plenary orange-ness' of oranges that Grandpa was pointing to. My parents learned to live with the insinuation that they may be the family representatives of the bovine mass of humanity who, Grandpa said, flailed around with emotional problems and wasted their lives on banalities.

I was sure I could do better than Mum and Dad, and I was excited to find out what it was all about. On the bus to the retreat, somewhere near the Welsh border, a student with a dark bob and lipstick invited me to her birthday party in Cardiff that evening.

'You can stay over if you like,' she offered.

'Er, I'd love to, but the retreat is ten days.'

'Oh, come on then, you'll only miss one day.' I suddenly wanted to miss the whole thing.

'But the silence starts this evening.'

'Well, if it's silent you won't miss much, will you?'

The retreat centre was a collection of single-storey buildings and a couple of paddocks surrounded by open countryside. As the sun went down I pitched my tent in the middle of a new and silent world. At 4am a long, low chime intruded into my sleep. I groped for tracksuit bottoms and somnambulated towards the meditation hall. The front rows were for experienced meditators. I selected a few cushions and settled down halfway back, crossing my legs. One knee wouldn't touch the floor, so I put a cushion under it. When everyone was wrapped in blankets on their little mat islands, a tape started up with an old Burmese man chanting and giving instructions like:

'Concentrate on the sensation in your upper lip and around the nostrils. Feel the air touching your skin in that area. Stay focussed on that. If your mind wanders, bring it back to these sensations.'

I accepted the challenge and set to feeling my upper lip like a soldier on watch duty. Just watch your lip. No more clever-clever. After an hour we had five minutes to walk around the dusty paddock, the sun still fat and weak on the horizon. Then the bell called us back for another hour.

'Just feel sensations on the upper lip, and notice how they change.'

Then another walk, then breakfast, then a wash, then more meditation. Instead of transcendental bliss, I got a cold. When I sniffed the meditator in front of me tutted. What a bastard. Did he expect me to let my nose stream like a snotty child? Maybe he did. Later on someone, I assumed the tutterer, put a box of Kleenex on my meditation mat. Blowing my nose into the silence of fifty retreatants was just as bad. Even wiping with a tissue caused a cacophony of noise, like boiled sweets at the cinema. I rationed my sniffles as much as I could. When the cold started to clear, my head caught a musical virus.

'I really really really want a Zig a Zig Ah.'

It played on a loop, followed by subsidiary thoughts like:

Why do I want a Zig a Zig Ah?

What does it mean?

Which Spice Girl do I fancy most?

My distractions were all low brow. For short periods I could fix like a laser on tiny sensations multiplying on my upper lip. At times they became so intense that I brushed my face to check there were no spiders on it. I had to move every ten minutes or so to ease the pain in my hip and let blood back into my calves. I rolled up my socks and jammed them under my ankles. The tutterer disapproved of my shuffling. Erasure started up with '*Oo oo oo sometimes . . . the truth is harder than the pain inside*'. In between sessions I rummaged through rejected cushion-ware at the back of the hall for a wedge of kapok or a square of foam.

After a few days Scary Spice gave up singing and the ordinary concerns of my life were relegated to deep background. I was a warrior on guard duty, alert to the slightest tingling in my nostrils or coolness on my upper lip. As the retreat intensified, instead of sympathy and understanding, the Burmese master on the tape advised us not to move at all, not so much as waggle a finger. We were told to scan attention through our whole body. Pleasant waves of energy flowed down from my scalp. The sides below my ribs were dull, but they said dull was okay too. Painful, pleasant, dull, nothing, anything was okay. These guys had one answer to every experience: it will change. My response to the idea of change, changed:

That's obvious. Next thought please.

This breath is exactly the same as the last one.

Ring the damn bell, my knees fucking hurt.

It has changed . . . this is bliss . . . I want to cry.

Apart from Grandpa's fleeting instruction to label things in the street, in sixteen years of educating my young mind, no-one had given me a simple means for observing my mind or even suggested this might be something to do. Yet these Buddhists, that's all they seemed to do. It was simple and mostly enjoyable, bringing attention to this or that part of my body. The Burmese master, who reminded me of a big, contented frog, explained in a pre-recorded video that by observing physical sensations without reacting we were training our minds and purifying negative habits. Discourses ended with his deep and drawn-out chanting: 'Be ha-peeeee, be-ha peeeee, be ha-peeeee.'

One morning I noticed the sunlight mingled with steam rising from the bowls of porridge. I felt quietly very happy. I could be aware of thoughts. Thoughts arise in awareness, like sounds and smells and wisps of steam. I was usually stuck to my thoughts like a fly on flypaper. Now I was out of my head, enjoying the space, without any drugs. Paying attention seemed unreligious and practical, yet it was mysterious too and without any obvious end point. The other retreatants grew more agreeable, even the tutterer. We'd been asked not to make gestures or wink at each other or even look directly at each other, so I knew them instead by jersey or sock, by how they stood in the meal queue and how much they heaped on their plate.

On the morning of departure silence ended and we swapped tales of bodily pain. Everyone had assumed they had more than everyone else. One man asked how I came to be missing a hand. It wasn't often someone asked. None of my college friends had. If you leave it too long before asking a glaringly obvious question it becomes embarrassing that you've never asked.

'I was born like that,' I said, regretting no longer story.

'You must be burning karma,' he said.

I didn't ask what he meant. It sounded like it was a good thing and that was enough.

Meditation rocks
Back at College, as the Burmese monk had recommended, I tried to do an hour of meditation in the morning and an

hour in the evening. Before breakfast I set myself up on two volumes of the *Shorter Concise Dictionary* surmounted by my pillow. Soft back law books tended to squidge and slide, but A to Markworthy and his companion to Z were ideal. I didn't manage two whole hours even once. A more easy-going meditation group met in a church hall nearby. It was run by an English guy who turned up in a suit after work. He taught a different technique, varying the length of each breath. I loved hearing him repeat the simple breathing instructions over and over again. At one-to-one meditation reviews he asked how I was getting on and pointed out unhelpful ideas I'd picked up, like what I thought I should be feeling.

One morning, a few weeks after the retreat, I was walking to the law library when I suddenly felt turned up a notch. It was like driving out from the carwash and suddenly realising how dirty the windscreen had been. I knew immediately my relationship to the world had subtly changed. The cut-off feeling and a protective, slightly cynical streak had abated. To mark the new me I shaved my hair close and got an ear pierced. Before auditioning for a role in a play or talking to a someone I fancied I spent a moment feeling the tightness in my stomach, or watching self-defeating thoughts pass along. Self-conscious stump-awareness was no longer an all defining reality. There was more space to allow in how other people were aware of me. This new sense of inner freedom and flow, thanks to ten days of mindfulness of my upper lip, soon brought me a leading role in a play and a girlfriend, short-lived though that affair was.

Roberto's life post-retreat went quite differently. He rusticated (Oxford lingo for taking a year off) to a room in north Oxford, where he did lots of yoga and consumed masses of seaweed and Chinese tea. He was thinner, paler, with hair growing long and lank. He said his father had made him feel like a lodger as a child, as if his bedroom and belongings were not really his. So he sent everything associated with those days, including all his furniture, back to his father. One day he left a note asking for help deciding where to put a new armchair he had acquired. What is he on about, I thought? I jogged over and found him in a state of great indecision. I suggested where to put the chair and I left before being offered lunch from one of the jars of things pickling on his window sill. It was just something eccentric English students do, I supposed, like when he came to our college dining hall in pyjama bottoms.

One Saturday, we went together to Purley for a family discussion about his situation. He said he wanted me there to witness how nuts his family was. His father was upstairs doing something unspecified. As we sat in the kitchen with his Mum, Roberto explained why he couldn't go back to college and that things weren't right.

'You never listen, Mum,' said Roberto.

'You're always fussing,' his Mum replied.

They made no advances on their stated positions in two hours. In my umpire's role I thought they were both right. His father didn't come down once, even to say hello, which was considered so normal as to not merit a mention. Roberto and his Mum continued their argument in the car on the way back to the train station.

Then something happened. I didn't see the exact moment. We were waiting on the platform. It was Roberto's blank look that scared me into paying attention. I'd never seen

a look like that from anyone. It wasn't 'fussing'. Soon
he'd pulled a woolly hat over his face and said nothing all
the way back to Oxford. After getting off the coach we
stood on a kerb of the High Street. It was past midnight.
Roberto wouldn't go back home and he wouldn't go with
me. He picked up a stone from the road, a gesture I found
disturbing. Something bad had happened and it scared me.

When I suggested we go to the hospital, he nodded.
I gave the duty nurse his details. I got his date of birth
wrong but rather than speak Roberto handed me a note
saying 'Early birthday present this year?' An hour later we
saw the duty psychiatrist who agreed Roberto should stay
in for observation. I was anxious for this outcome. I had
no idea what we would have done otherwise. At 2am we
were sent to get some food while a bed was arranged in
another hospital. A tinny radio belonging to a cleaner was
playing 'Mr Boombastic' to an empty hospital canteen. We
sat at a table.

'They've got lasagne,' I said. 'Do you want some?'

'I don't know. I don't know,' Roberto said, staring at me.

'*Say me fantastic . . .*'

'There's nothing else on.'

'*Says I'm Mr Ro-mantic . . .*'

The lyrics added to the mood of horror.

'Are you hungry?'

'*She says boom boom boom . . .*'

I asked the cleaner to turn the music down. She refused.

Rob looked straight at me: 'I don't know. I don't know
if I'm hungry. I don't know if I'm hungry.'

He was definitely not fussing. At 3am an ambulance took
Roberto away. I was in tears with the shock. The next day

a doctor told me Roberto was having a 'psychotic episode'. He said it was common in young men. Hopefully it would be a one-off episode.

Most days I went to the ward. It was like Roberto had been pushed out of his life. I wondered if the retreat was to blame for his breakdown or if it had accelerated something that was going to happen anyway. He wanted it kept secret from his family for as long as possible. When they did find out, they blamed him for fussing. After a couple of months his loveable, doubtful self started to glimmer back and he began a long period of recovery which would eventually allow him to return to college and complete his degree.

In the run up to my final exams I gave up meditation in favour of cramming case law into any remaining plastic brain space. As I stepped outside after the last exam, the cobblestones and sunlight through the trees trickled back into my awareness and the mental wall of case summaries dissolved in bliss and champagne. I felt as happy as I'd ever felt in the company of my heroic friends. It felt wrong to end college now, when exams were out of the way. This should be the good bit starting. I wanted us to all move to a big house in the country and carry on. Despite brave words about continuing togetherness, I feared this was the high point in our friendships and now we would scatter to the winds.

5

A LONG WAY TO GO

Most of what goes through my mind has nothing to do with how many fingers I have or what anyone else thinks about it. When the stump changes up the gears on the motorway and takes control of the wheel it doesn't occur to me to wonder what my passenger might be thinking. In the summer after college Adam and I met in Florida. A whole continent was in front of us, with long straight roads and the fantasy of freedom. Gas was a buck a gallon, the air con an open window. Mum was convinced our plan to drive to California would end with death in a roadside ditch. It was useless promising it wouldn't or pointing out that a gear stick on the righthand side makes driving even easier for me. Death by over-eating seemed more likely. In Louisiana I nearly exploded at an all-you-can-eat catfish bar. Despite his beanpole appearance, Adam managed a 50oz steak in Texas.

Meditation had taught me how to be more involved in life and more active in relation to my thoughts. But Adam showed no interest, so it wasn't part of our routine. I meditated in snatches here and there. In New Mexico I sat with a skinny guy at a hostel who had matchstick legs and claimed he could sit in full lotus for two hours. I could get one foot up on the opposite thigh, but with my rugby thighs it was so tight I had to roll backwards to escape. By Colorado, Adam was sickening for his girlfriend back home. While he flew back to reunite with her, I camped with a woman from a Buddhist college. We'd have travelled together across the Badlands but I lost track of her car in a mile-long queue of recreational vehicles in Yellowstone Park and never saw her again. She was six foot tall and smoked menthol cigarettes.

These moments of vaguely Buddhist connection were larger in my mind than they were in actual time. Adam flew back to join me and we drove down Utah and across Death Valley to San Francisco. His girlfriend was still pining, so she flew in. You couldn't wedge a dime between them. When dormitory beds ran out, I was not invited to kip on the floor in their private room. I grabbed my gear and huffily announced I was off. I'd had the hump with all their humping.

Towards dusk a coach dropped me on the far side of the Golden Gate Bridge. Two Swedes I had met in Borders bookshop, where I was free-reading *The Dharma Bums* by Jack Kerouac, had told me about a hostel in Marin County. They sketched me a map. I dashed across lanes of traffic to the other side of the bridge and found the track over the Marin Headlands. It was wild and windy and there was no-one about. The map was essentially a rectangle and a squiggly line. I'd found it convincing at the time it was drawn but as darkness fell I regretted leaving town.

I turned inland and came to a long, dark, road tunnel, un-indicated in the Swedish drawing. I scurried through like a rodent. Finally, from a track on a long ridge, at last I saw light down in the valley. All that stood in the way was a long sweep of gorse. After trying up and down the road for a route I decided I had no option but to push my rucksack into the spiky branches and plough straight through and down. Twenty yards in I felt panicky, thinking about snakes and racoons. Were there bears? Was it flap your arms, play dead, or do the hokey cokey? I turned round and pushed quickly back up onto the ridge, glad no-one had witnessed my feeble attempt. What would Jack Kerouac have done? Probably sit out all night drinking whiskey and writing a poem to the beauty of the scene or any old crap that came into his head. Then in the morning he'd stroll back to town, pick up a girl and a large breakfast on the way, then write a poem about that.

I sat down and tried to think. It was nearly midnight and the full moon was out. Maybe I hadn't tried hard enough to get through the gorse. Once I got halfway down it would be as painful to retreat as to carry on. I ploughed back into the tightly packed bushes until branches were over my head, talking myself onwards. Then I got tangled in a barbed wire fence which some bloody Yank was using to delineate his particular patch of impenetrable gorse. Thrashing to un-snag myself pinned me in more securely. Now what? I was desperate to escape the fauna now surely closing in on the English idiot frantically tearing himself out of his shirt.

Not cool, not Kerouac.

Then the bright ball of moon caught my eye and I remembered my breath. I felt a sharp edge of air through my nostrils, running fast and fine as silk. A wave of clarity and joy came over me and my body went limp. Calm now, I unhooked my shirt and trousers and pushed back up to the ridge road. The joy was still with me and my feet so light on the ground, that I started to run. I ran on and on, my rucksack weighing nothing, like I was an inch away from taking off. Eventually the road doubled back down the valley and towards the lights, to the hostel where the Swedish cartographers were sitting around a bonfire. They handed me a beer and I told my tale like Jack would have done. Pretty cool to get caught up in gorse like that.

The next day I went back to San Francisco to patch things up with Adam and visit the full moon festival in Chinatown. On the sidewalk an old man with wispy hair sat painting. He wore a blue smock and must have been about eighty years old. He didn't appear to notice me watching and I couldn't see what he was painting. Maybe a bamboo thicket or distant mountain peak like the others behind him. He drew with his little fingernail by dipping it into the ink and conducting strokes straight onto the canvas.

'How old are you?' he suddenly asked, looking up and smiling.

'Twenty-one,' I replied.

'Such a long way to go,' he said.

I stepped closer to inspect his drawings for I knew not what, and then walked on. His words felt familiar, like how a previous night's dream can suddenly echo up into daytime activity, though this was deeper than a dream echo. I had a long way to go. . . Surely he didn't mean I'd get older and become a lawyer and then die. He must have meant another type of long way to go. The idea was exhilarating.

I returned to Borders and my well-thumbed copy of *The Dharma Bums*. Kerouac was fired up with Boo-ddha and

Beat Zen, a kind of hungry commitment to Now without authority or rules. Grandpa had a touch of Beat about him. 'The true art of chastity,' he writes in his book, 'is the art not of abstinence, but of waiting on the body's own sensitive ripeness . . . lust [in contrast] is just goading my genitals into unripe activity.' That's the sort of thing Allen Ginsberg might have said. Grandpa had dispensed with religious authority too, but in Ginsberg and Kerouac you could feel a kind of reverence for life, a sense of holiness and humility. Grandpa waxed lyrical about the mysteries of life, but those other ingredients were missing.

That evening Adam and his girlfriend were still occupied, so I went to a wine bar and met a young woman with a shaved head who announced out of the blue that she was a lesbian and did I want to go with her to the best place in town to see the moon? We bought a bottle of wine and entered the lobby of a skyscraper. On the twenty-seventh floor she pushed through a door marked *Alarmed* assuring me it wasn't. I followed her onto the lower roof and then up a ladder onto the very top.

'We can drink the wine here. Let's look over the edge,' she said.

The moon glinted on the low rail which ran around the edge of the roof area at about knee height. My right hand is smallish but strong. It does the work of almost two hands, the stump pitching in on a need to basis. I try to even out the jobs, opening doors and picking stuff up et cetera, but inevitably my left arm does less and is not as strong. Looking at the rail and its location I wanted two hands to hold on. I decided to lie flat on my stomach to take in the glassy drop to the downtown financial district.

Kerouac wouldn't have been such a sissy about it, but then again he's dead.

The flight back to London gave me a stopover day in New York. I lugged my rucksack and guitar to Greenwich Village and had a blueberry pancake in an empty restaurant down from Cafe Wha, where Bob Dylan used to play. It was a long way short of interesting and the 1960s seemed like a fairy tale, though I ate my stack as if it had been made by Pete Seeger and served up by Lenny Bruce. It felt wonderful to have a long way to go.

Back in the real world

Back in London in late autumn I was sharing a house with some dope-smoking punks in Finsbury Park. I didn't know what to do with my life. I tried busking with a friend, strumming to one of her esoteric ballads about her boyfriend's habit of sitting on their fridge. A passer-by borrowed my guitar and earned us more in twenty minutes than we'd earned all day. I took a job selling Christmas hampers on the telephones at Harrods. One poor customer cried when I insisted it was not possible to parcel up a package of pheasant and veal and leave it 'by the door' for her husband to pick up. After a fortnight I quit.

The punks painted the walls purple, blue and black, even the toilet, and spent most of the day skinning up in their respective rooms. I met up with friends here and there about town, but sixteen years of schooling had not prepared me for such a drop off in community and common purpose. As soon as I could I moved to a house-share with an old friend in Whitechapel. Our garden backed onto a tiny pub owned by the bare fist boxer 'Mean' Lenny MacLean, a well known figure in the fading East End community. Grandpa's great uncle was the first publican at the Blind Beggar pub just round the corner, famous for the gangland shooting of George Cornell by Ronnie Kray in 1966. That little family connection didn't persuade me to go into Mean Lenny's.

My next job was as a post boy, opening letters and delivering mail around a huge building in Pall Mall. Post came in twice a day so in between deliveries I parked my feet by my empty in-tray and read. I was halfway through *The Brothers Karamazov* when the post manager approached me with a complaint from the assistant post-room manager.

'Alan's bothered that you're reading and not doing the work. You'd better stop,' he said.

'I don't mind if Alan reads, could you tell him that?' I replied, taking my feet down.

'I don't think Alan wants to read,' the manager said, quite correctly.

Alan only ever reads envelopes, I thought. He was a peevish man of many years' service who spent the quieter periods of the day shuffling boxes of rubber bands and straightening bits of paper. He walked in and, turning scarlet, blurted:

'He just sits there with his feet up while we work!'

'I'm happy to do all the post on my own so long as I can read when there isn't any.'

It was a sincere offer, calculated to expose my enemy's real position.

'That's not the point,' the manager said.

I knew it wasn't the point. I was learning the workplace rule about never admitting there's nothing to do. The 'snooty young man' quit and finished Dostoyevsky's masterwork on the dole. Once a fortnight I had to sign on at the Whitechapel Job Centre, a building resembling a large rabbit hutch. It was winter and the pavements of Whitechapel were trodden with a semi-frozen mulch of cardboard and Asian vegetables from the street markets.

'What sector are you interested in?' asked the man behind the desk at my Job Seekers Allowance interview.

'Journalism maybe,' I replied.

'Okay. What about advertising?'

'I don't think so.'

In my book, advertising was a small step up from land mine manufacture.

'You have a law degree I see . . . okay. What was your last role?'

'I worked in a post-room.'

'Okay, what were your main tasks?'

'I opened letters.'

'And what skills did you pick up?'

'Opening and sorting letters, I guess.'

'Okay,' he said. I couldn't make out what he was noting down, but I assumed it was 'can open letters'.

'Any other skills?' he went on.

'You can mark me down for karaoke if you like.'

'Okay, I meant computer skills.'

'I can do all that Microsoft Windows and Office stuff and type at forty words a minute.' Forty was pushing it. The thumb thing is only reliable for Shift, Caps and Control and occasional forays into mid-keyboard.

I didn't mention my hand, as I didn't think it was relevant. I didn't use it for conscious effect, to sway the JSA man into giving me a few extra weeks without having to take a crap job. Surely he would intuit the brilliance he was faced with that morning and reckon the hand as nothing much. Brilliant *despite* my hand, that was the story I'd grown up to enjoy. If we'd been squaring up for a fight, then I might have let the JSA man have a good view of the stump. A couple of times in my life I've made sure someone threatening me sees it, so they have time to reflect on just how good it would feel to duff up, or be duffed up by, a disabled person.

Was I a disabled person? I didn't think of myself as one of them. I never claimed any living allowance or registered with any agency or applied for parking stickers. I didn't tick boxes on any form which asked whether I had a disability. It brought up an image of myself I didn't have. I wasn't annoyed or embarrassed about being asked if I was disabled, I just didn't think I was, technically, in that horrific category. I assumed there'd be a legal definition somewhere which would exclude me. I certainly didn't like to think that my inability to have a clear and confident career strategy had anything to do with my missing hand or some unresolved issue to do with that. Maybe it did. Maybe that was obvious to the JSA man. I remember I was shocked when a fellow apple picker on an apple farm one summer suggested I was picking apples because I was having trouble finding work *what with your hand*. He was being sympathetic. I was more amused than anything. I was bagging up as fast as anyone. Two-handed people dither. But I suppose I could see that picking apples wasn't a great choice of labour for a person with one hand. I'd be better off as a grape treader.

My assumption was that the JSA man saw me as I saw myself: a successful young man who was currently unemployed due to every job in the world being demonstrably and observably crap. Did I want data entry for a high-profile media company in the West End, 37.5 hours, £6.90 per hour? Having no career plan, this was the sort of thing that came my way.

The word 'career' heralded an indefinable loss. At college I'd flick through the law firms' brochures that inundated my pigeonhole, gleaning information about my future from photos of attractive models looking over each other's shoulders at important documents in a focussed yet relaxed way. The subliminal message was the promise of understated power, control of my destiny, and sex. Maybe I read in the sex bit. Or maybe not. Application forms asked why I wanted to be a commercial lawyer, why at Cobblers, and how did I see my career progressing? The student applicant knows to stress an interest in corporate finance and show awareness that Cobblers is a 'leading player' in the European private equity market. The real answer:

I haven't got a clue what goes on at Cobblers and I don't know what private equity means. I'm extremely clever and believe that this job will allow me to exercise my swollen brain, without which relief I'm worried I may become ill. The people at the firm seem roughly like the people I'm at university with, just like the hundred other firms I'm applying to. Above all it's a job where I can get a qualification and a big salary and then I'll decide what I want to do with my life because everything will hopefully be clearer by then.

Between temping jobs, I volunteered on letter-writing campaigns at Amnesty International. The injustices meted out against people kept locked in cells were real problems which I did not have. Friends were moving to first-rung management jobs in provincial towns or running errands on third-rate TV shows. I arranged my photos in an album: the final college parties, everyone hugging everyone else, Adam and me cooling off in the Rio Grande. To perk myself up I started joining my flatmate on his daily jog through Stepney towards Victoria Park. One day we ran past a large red brick building on the Roman Road. I noticed a modest sign indicating *London Buddhist Centre*.

I made a mental note to come back and check it out.

6

BUDDHISTS IN
BETHNAL GREEN

As I dashed to the cloakroom to flick off my shoes before a lunchtime meditation class, the receptionist called out that Sangharakshita was taking the class today.

'Really?' I said, coming back to reception in my socks.

'Could you help him set out the cushions? You're the first in.'

I lingered by the shrine room door feeling doubtful. How I should greet him? What should I say? What would he make of me? It felt as if I was about to set out cushions for a giant.

It had been wonderful to discover hundreds of people just up the road from where I lived also following their breath in and out. They did it a bit different to how I'd learned, focusing on the natural breathing pattern, whether it happened to be long or short, rather than breathing to a particular depth. In the few months I'd been attending meditation classes I'd yet to catch sight of Sangharakshita. He had a flat upstairs, I'd heard. I was surprised he was taking the class as it was usually led by a Scottish woman with a soothing voice and long dark hair. She had a difficult name too. Like everyone, she mentioned Sangharakshita a lot. When someone asked her what they should do if they couldn't stay focused on the breath she said: 'Well, you know, Sangharakshita, he says that the object of meditation isn't to have a good meditation but to transform ourselves. So maybe don't worry too much. No-one can do meditation perfectly, it isn't like that.'

Everyone and everything referred back to Sangharakshita. At an evening talk on Buddhism and the Beatniks, a handsome oldish guy with a silver ponytail who claimed to know the Zen poet Gary Snyder, said: 'Sangharakshita tried LSD when he came back to London in the 1960s. It was okay. He called it a smash and grab raid on the transcendental. It's more important to change our lives from the ground up than have far-out experiences.' He also mentioned that Allen Ginsberg had popped round to visit Sangharakshita at the London Buddhist Centre in the 1980s. There was a picture of them standing on the roof terrace above, looking out over the shabby surrounds of Tower Hamlets. Mythic events had converged above my head: Sangharakshita knew Ginsberg, Ginsberg knew Dylan. I wanted to go up on the roof and just stand there soaking in the facts.

The Buddhist Centre was a five-storey redbrick Victorian fire station, rebuilt from a ruin by some of Sangharakshita's more enthusiastic followers in the 1970s. I soon picked up the back-story. Sangharakshita didn't come from the Land of the Snows or anywhere glamorous like that. He came from Tooting in south London and his name was Dennis. Dennis was a skinny boy, a voracious reader with round glasses and a wide grin. One day in 1941, while browsing the second-hand bookshops in Charing Cross Road, Dennis found a copy of the *Diamond Sutra*, one of the most difficult texts in Buddhism. After gulping it down he realised that he was and always had been a Buddhist. It was unusual to be a Buddhist in England, very unusual to have read the *Diamond Sutra,* and extremely unusual to have understood it. Dennis was sixteen. Two years later he was conscripted into the army as a signalman and sent to India. After the war, rather than wait for demobilisation he started to journey around India. He didn't plan to go home. Having arrived by such good fortune in the land of the Buddha's birth he wanted to stay there. Ripping up his passport and renouncing his identity as Dennis, he adopted the name Dharmapriya, the 'Lover of the Buddha's Teaching'.

Along with a friend he travelled long distances on foot, sleeping in ashrams and caves. They possessed no more than they could carry. They met the radiant Hindu sage Ramana Maharshi, in whose silent presence devotees sat, soaking up a transcendent and wordless communication of the Divine. They met lesser-known seekers too, like a woman who had vowed twelve years of silence in a four-foot square underground chamber. Sangharakshita's memoirs tell how he saw her surfacing for a call of nature and a little food; she smiled sweetly at him and stroked his cheek before jumping joyfully back down to her austerities.

Buddhists were harder to find. Buddhism had been wiped out in India a thousand years before. The few they met seemed less impressive than the Hindus. Some Buddhist monks even disapproved of these two earnest young men who were doing what the Buddha had recommended by going forth from possessions, money and status and begging for food. Eventually their ardour took them by foot all the way to the site of the Buddha's death in Kusinara, in the northern state of Uttar Pradesh.

There at last they found a senior Buddhist monk willing to oversee their ordination into the Theravadin brotherhood, the oldest surviving form of the Buddhist community, known for saffron robes and shaved heads. Dennis was given the name Sangharakshita, which means Protected by the Spiritual Community.

Shortly after his ordination, his teacher took him to a hill town in the Himalayas called Kalimpong, and told him to stay there and work for the good of Buddhism. He stayed for fourteen years, keeping up a frugal and happy monastic life. He befriended many Tibetan exiles who'd fled to India after the Chinese invasion. Some became his teachers and initiated him into new meditation practices, visualisations and mantras. Perhaps to them the English monk from far-off mysterious Tooting was rather exotic. From his little hermitage, with its panoramic view across wooded valleys towards the snowy peaks of Mount Kanchenjunga, Sangharakshita penned articles to Buddhist journals and Buddhists the world over. Film stars, politicians, princesses and lamas dropped in for tea. When the Buddhist revivalist leader Dr Ambedkar died in 1956, Sangharakshita went on a whirlwind teaching tour down in the plains, giving public talks to hundreds of thousands of newly converted ex-Untouchables, consoling them over the loss of their leader and rousing them to practise Buddhism.

My temping jobs had no prospects but the regular hours allowed for several visits a week to the Buddhist Centre. The teachers had an attractive friendliness about them. Another alluring woman with a mellifluous voice taught me the five-stage meditation about loving kindness called Metta Bhavana:

'In the first stage wish yourself well by recognising that deep down we do have that wish for ourselves. A heartfelt wish, not just an idea. . . Sangharakshita says we must be careful not to get alienated from our experience when we meditate, or look coldly at ourselves, as if from a distance.'

It felt weird to wish myself well, but there was sense to it. If I couldn't wish myself well, how could I wish anyone else well?

'In the second stage direct the feeling of warmth and well-wishing towards a good friend.'

That was easier. The third stage went further by radiating friendliness to a 'neutral' person, such as the clerk at the post office, to whom we have no strong feelings of like or dislike. A sleepier stage usually. I sometimes woke up in the forward fall known as meditator's nod. The fourth stage was for the 'enemy', or a person we found difficult and would rather avoid. I didn't have any enemies, but my rugby-playing medical student housemates often irritated me with their total lack of existential quandary and by regularly vomiting beer and wine into the bathroom sink.

'Sangharakshita says it's better to be in touch with our negative emotions if that's what's there. Then we can work to transform them.'

The final stage was loving kindness for all beings, beginning with those in Bethnal Green, then extending out in all directions across the cosmos, including animals and whatever sentient life there is.

Whenever Sangharakshita was mentioned I listened, harder than I did to Bob Dylan. He had encouraged students not to do a meditation practice similar to the one Roberto and I had done at the Wales retreat, on the grounds it could lead to what he called 'alienated awareness'. The instructions were to observe whatever comes up, see it as impermanent, and 'let it go' again and again. 'Heady' young men in particular took these instructions as a cue to ignore or suppress their emotions, from which they were chronically cut off. Sangharakshita said some had even ended up in hospital after practising this version of meditation too forcefully. That, I knew, was true. On my retreat there was an Eastern European guy who sat unmoving and bolt upright. I thought he was a pro. It's easy to assume someone is meditating well because they look good doing it. After powering up on a meditation, he'd speed around the exercise yard like a deranged comet. If he was eating at one table, I instinctively chose the other.

I wondered if I was alienated from my emotions. Maybe Sangharakshita was talking about me too? I could relate to the idea of not liking myself very much, though I always cried when *The Snowman* came on the telly at Christmas, so I guess that made me okay. I started doing the loving kindness meditation every other day. I wasn't overflowing with love and was still a bit vague about what Metta was and whether I felt it, but when I met the people I'd put in the various stages I felt less judgemental and more happy to see them.

Sangharakshita's memoirs carried a charge, like an electric current. I followed his journey as if, in some way, it was my own. I pictured the small eccentric community in his hermitage. I met his Tibetan masters and was there when he received initiation into the practice of Green Tara. I imagined myself exchanging letters and visits with fellow seekers such as the German explorer Lama Anagarika Govinda and his mystic wife Li Gotami.

By imagining himself into the sandals of Buddhists across history, at the age of just thirty-one Sangharakshita published *A Survey of Buddhism*, the first book in modern times to draw together the major phases of Buddhist history into a doctrinally unified account. The book argued there was really only one Way, though it could take many, many forms. Early Buddhism, known for discipline and rigorous psychology of mind, was not a 'Lesser Way', as the later schools had suggested. The Mahayana, or the 'Great Way', was not a new religion, but a renewed accent on the altruistic and imaginative aspect of the spiritual journey. Tibetan Buddhism and the esoteric rituals and practices of the Tantra flowed from the Mahayana, yet embedded in all Buddhist schools were the earliest teachings from the Buddha himself, as set out in the Pali Canon.

Above all, the *Survey* emphasised that practising the Dharma, the teachings of the Buddha, led not to a blank nothingness as many early Westerners had believed, but rather to a joyful and ever deepening state of wisdom, compassion and energy. Sangharakshita was among the first Westerners to immerse himself in the actual practice of the Dharma under a Buddhist teacher. Rather than just one, he had an array: a monk from the early monastic school, a Zen-like meditation master of Chinese Chan tradition, and various lamas from Tibet.

Bringing it all back home

After eighteen years in India and with blessing from his Tibetan teachers, Sangharakshita returned to the UK. The trustees of the Hampstead Vihara had invited him, as Britain's most senior monk, to live and teach at their premises in London. It was 1963 and Buddhism in the West was still a niche thing, of academic interest for the most part. When Grandpa took a trip to the Watkins bookshop just off the Charing Cross Road he could see at a single glance most of the books on Buddhism then available in English. But there were no Buddhist centres, no temples, no retreat venues and the Beatles hadn't yet sat cross-legged in front of the Maharishi.

When Bob Dylan arrived in Greenwich Village about the same time, he was exactly where he needed to be, almost by accident. He knew traditional folk music inside out and played his variations in the bars and cafes. But after a while Bob had inner urges that didn't fit with the folk genre of protest songs and finger-picking guitar that had made him famous. This weedy looking guy with cool hair was to become the channel for something new. The pivotal moment was in 1965 when Bob ditched his acoustic guitar and 'went electric' at the Newport Folk Festival. The fans of 'real' music moaned about the blare of amplified instruments, while others said Dylan was re-working folk into a mould which properly expressed the craziness and raw energy they felt. 'How does it feel . . . to be on your own . . . with no direction home?' Basically, they dug it. Dylan's electric sets were boo-ed throughout his UK tour the following year. At a Manchester town hall gig someone in the audience yelled 'Judas'.

'I don't believe you. You're a liar,' Bob replied.

Bob's genius was to go with the inner urge to change.

Sangharakshita was also steeped in tradition, and for him, too, there was no direction home. He didn't quite belong in the East or the West. At first it had all gone well, swishing around London in his robes. He tried to unite

London's two tiny Buddhist groups, the Hampstead Vihara and the Buddhist Society. The Vihara took a traditional view of Buddhism, as exemplified by the Theravada, into which Sangharakshita was himself ordained. The Buddhist Society, on the other hand, was a sort of BBC for Buddhism, dedicated to impartial and sober study of the whole Buddhist tradition. Its founder was High Court judge Christmas Humphreys, whose interests centred on the Zen style typified by Alan Watts. Sangharakshita found both organisations a dispiriting contrast to the vibrant, imaginative world of the Tibetans. Some attendees at the Buddhist Society summer school were apparently a little alarmed when he proposed a Buddhist ritual with candles and incense, though many turned up to see it.

In the genteel world of British Buddhism, Sangharakshita's Judas moment was growing his hair an inch or two over regulation. To the trustees of the Hampstead Vihara such laxness was a snub to the monastic establishment. He also started hanging out with close male friends and not always wearing robes. Though the trustees never directly accused him of breaking his monastic vows, homosexuality was still illegal in Britain and even the suggestion of it was intolerable for a conservative Buddhist organisation. Sangharakshita started to wonder if monasticism was helpful if it encouraged the idea that robes, baldness and celibacy is what makes you a real Buddhist.

In 1966 the trustees wrote to Sangharakshita saying that he was no longer welcome as the incumbent monk at the Vihara. Folk were fired up, both for and against him. Reflecting on it years later, Sangharakshita wrote that the dispute had nothing to do with the length of his hair or even with sex. It had to do with his desire to stop a hardly born British Buddhist movement sinking into a quagmire of religious formalism, middle class morality and the kind of monk worship he'd seen enough of already.

After being called Judas, Bob turned to his band and told them to 'Play it fucking loud'. Sangharakshita played it loud too. He made a resolution to start a new Buddhist movement. Quite a lot of Buddhists boo-ed. It's not kosher to start up new Buddhist lineages willy-nilly or mess about with tradition. Under whose authority was he acting anyway? Like Dylan, Sangharakshita was driven by inner impulses not really within his control. Thankfully there was a motley and potentially unpromising collection of hippies, some of whom may well have been at the Newport Folk Festival, who were not boo-ing. They were captivated by his lectures and his demeanour. In addition to long flowing hair and mutton chop sideburns, Sangharakshita wore robes of more colours than Joseph, rings on all his fingers and a semi-cured Afghan coat soaked in patchouli oil to block out the sheep smell. He looked like a shaman Jesus: revolutionary, intense and energetic. His urge for personal change intersected with a social dynamic which reflected that urge beyond the personal level, an eruption of new consciousness going on. And he gave up celibacy. Who wanted to be celibate in the Summer of Love?

His vision of a new Buddhist movement arose in him at the peak moment of the counter-culture revolution. In 1968 he founded the Western Buddhist Order with a ceremony in the basement of a gift shop in Covent Garden. Twelve men and women were ordained. The Order didn't exist on paper and there was no membership fee.

It was to be a network of friends committed to practising Buddhism. It was hard to classify along traditional lines, as Order members weren't monks or lay people. He drew practices and rituals from across the Buddhist tradition to suit the needs of his students and distilled the key principles for new ways of living and working together. Dharma teachings geared to Westerners poured out of him, as if a dam had burst.

Sangharakshita believed that for Buddhism to take root, social change was necessary. Importing an Eastern variety of Buddhism was unlikely to work, just as Tibetan plants probably won't grow in an English back garden. How could a traditional Eastern Buddhist understand the West's culture of individualism and consumerism, its history of gender politics, or appear anything but naive in a culture which debases and deconstructs mythology and religion? Western thought has also filtered through a hundred years of Freud and Jung's ideas about unconscious motivation, which came after a thousand years of Christian ethics and theology. All this needed some weeding out. You won't get genuine Buddhist culture in the West by buying in naff art from Sri Lanka or pretending that you actually believe the Dalai Lama is the fourteenth reincarnation of a transcendental uber-being. A bit of explaining needed to be done. And when all the good questions have run out, Westerners have plenty of stupid questions which need answering as well.

Most of the original twelve Order members quickly drifted away. For a man now leading an Order consisting of just three or four active members living in squats, Sangharakshita must have had a lot of self-confidence. By 1978, with the Order grown from a handful to a bus full, Sangharakshita opened the London Buddhist Centre on a downmarket corner of downmarket Bethnal Green. The hippies communally bodged their way through several years of renovation hell, making the old fire station habitable upstairs and beautiful on the ground floor for the public classes. An artist sculpted two large plaster of Paris Buddhas and painted a river-delta mural in the reception room. Mounted outside on two red gates was a wrought-iron Dharma wheel on top of two deer, symbolising the Buddha's first teaching in a deer park in Varanasi 2,500 years ago.

And now my part in the story was about to begin: I had to put out the cushions. I stepped through the shrine-room door overloaded with self-consciousness, heart thumping. There he was. A small man in a chair at the back next to the wall of meditation cushions arranged in a brickwork pattern. He looked about sixty-five, thin and a bit hunched, physically not very prepossessing. Was he nodding off? I started setting out cushions and mats. Stirred by the squeaks and creaks from the wooden floor, he got up and came towards me.

'Hullo,' he said, smiling at me with crooked teeth. 'What's your name?'

'David.'

'Good. I'm Sangharatna I'll be leading the class today.'

R A T N A. I breathed a sigh of relief. Wrong guy. Buddhist names were very confusing.

7

VERY STRANGE, VERY OKAY

Ultimately I wasn't hanging out with the Buddhists because of Bob Dylan or because some Chinese man in San Francisco painting with his fingernail had pointed me on a mystical journey. Nor did it feel as if I was going there to compensate for having one hand with the solace of religion or because my grandfather had written a book about meditation. It involved a kind of overall pointlessness I didn't feel at the Buddhist Centre that I did feel everywhere else. The teaching, in practice and in theory, made sense to me. At Oxford, philosophy professors batted papers back and forth, quibbling over esoterica such as how to derive an ought from an is, or if the sentence 'I can move my arm' has any meaningful content. The search for truth was reduced to statements about statements, all clever sounding, but no-one appeared brave enough to point out the underlying purposelessness of the whole philosophy department.

The more immediate reason, however, for my becoming a regular happy face at the Buddhist Centre was because on the morning of day four on my second retreat I dropped into a totally new state of mind.

I was one of eighty retreatants on a ten-day retreat held at a school in rural Oxfordshire while the children were on summer holidays. I nearly didn't go. Thoughts about how hard it is to sit without budging all day and about the post-graduate course in journalism I was soon to start had begun to dominate my mind. Just in time someone from the Centre told me that on this retreat they did only four sessions of meditation a day, the wake-up bell was as late as 6.30am, plus there was a swimming pool and even time to chat. It sounded like a retreat for softies, which suited me fine as I fancied a holiday.

The retreat was led by Maitreyabandhu, a thinnish man in his late thirties with a chiseled jaw and short dark hair, greying above the ears. He fizzed with friendliness. Before devoting what seemed like his whole life to meditation and retreats, he'd studied art at Goldsmith's, in the same year as Damien Hurst. Hurst had since worked out how to arrange a cow in a tank of formaldehyde, while Maitreyabandhu had worked out how to build a four-sided Buddhist shrine from a pile of stage blocks and leftover bits of scenery in the middle of the school's theatre. There were plenty of cushions, and Maitreyabandhu went out of his way to make sure we were comfortable sitting. On this retreat there were to be no hours of intense focusing on our upper lips, and battling with the changing sensations of agony in the knees was not considered a prerequisite to progress.

There were different methods. On the second day I was paired with Maitreyabandhu for an exercise where we sat opposite each other, knees about a foot apart, looking into each other's eyes. I found this very awkward at first, almost shocking.

'No need to stare,' said the woman who was co-leading the retreat.

'Just take in the person in front of you . . . a conscious

subject just like you . . . a whole universe in there . . . and allow them to look at you.'

The bell rang after a couple of minutes and we stopped to have a chat about what it was like. Then, to my dismay, we were instructed to look at each other in silence again. Maitreyabandhu gazed at me in a quizzical and insistent way, still friendly but seeming more serious this time. I looked at him as unguardedly as I could manage.

'Keep breathing and stay aware of your body.'

Maitreyabandhu's features started to kaleidoscope. I focused on one of his eyes, then the other, then softened my gaze, remembering to let him look back at me. One side of his face was bright and welcoming, the other looked older, more shadowed and sad. For fleeting moments we seemed to meet each other at a midpoint. It was hard to know. I kept falling back into an embarrassed sense of 'me'. On the fifth and final round he broke into a wide, clownish smile and soon we were both belly laughing. After this fairly excruciating but energising exercise the retreat came alive, with everyone making more eye contact generally. Maitreyabandhu warned us not to try this exercise with people on the train.

Twice a day we did the metta meditation: wishing each other well, wishing people we hated well, wishing the stranger in the next dormitory and all other creatures well. I was doing that when the new state of mind arose. It began with my body seeming to expand. It felt as if I was filling up like a balloon, light and upright.

'This must be wrong,' I thought. Like a good Zen student I let the thought pass like a cloud in the sky. It was just a thought.

I have seen adverts where a woman sits on a beach in perfect lotus position, in order to convince us that going to Mauritius is the same thing as a perfect state of mind. I was now in that place. The expanding feeling steadied into a warm upswell of bliss bubbles, like an inner jacuzzi. My normal lumpen form seemed to disappear. It was very strange and very okay. No-one would not want this feeling. I opened my eyes to check nothing odd was occurring. There was a cast-iron radiator on the far side of the hall. Space seemed full up and complete. Nothing was missing. I closed my eyes again. The incessant radio commentary babble of my mind ceased and I was left in a field of surround-sound love. It was like discovering a warp drive; the heavy weight of ideas about myself, expectations and comparisons with other people were all left far behind. No more lurking sense of not being okay and needing to make myself better. No more vague sense of being disconnected. I was already okay and already connected.

After, at breakfast, I watched people munching their toast in quiet rows, like a stable of horses. Happiness was pouring off me. We were all okay, even if we didn't know it. If a mass murderer was on the retreat, would they be okay? I couldn't see how the feeling of universal well wishing that had flooded through me that morning would waiver a millimetre even if Stalin was opposite me, motioning for someone to pass him the Marmite.

Even the absurd lines of thought going through my head were quite okay.

A woman I'd made friends with seemed to know what I was experiencing, because she was experiencing it too.

'Have you . . . ?' I said.

'Yes . . . amazing, isn't it!'

We giggled like schoolchildren.

At my meditation review that afternoon I described the whole thing in great detail to my meditation mentor.

'It sounds as if you got into dhyana,' he said.

I was pleased it had a name.

'Maybe it's second dhyana, I don't know.'

'You mean there are more?'

'That's what the tradition says. They come and go under the right conditions. There are eight in total. I wouldn't worry about which it is,' he said.

I wasn't worried. If a UFO replete with little green men had landed in the school playing field it wouldn't have worried me. It would have constituted a smaller and more ordinary revelation about how things are. It's pretty obvious there must be little green men somewhere in the universe. What's less obvious is that consciousness has depth. This new state of being gently ebbed throughout the day, without any come down or paranoia or worry about burning through my store of happiness. It didn't feel like a store of anything, just how things are.

Later on Maitreyabandhu and I did a triple loop of the school rugby pitch. He walked with a slight stoop, listening and nodding as I gabbled away. I could look at him openly now. As we rounded the goal posts, I told him how much I agreed with Buddhism, with everything Sangharakshita had written, and with everything that he, Maitreyabandhu, said.

'Maybe you are a Buddhist,' he said, with a hesitant, friendly frown.

I'd snookered myself into agreeing I was a Buddhist.

'What are you, Grandpa?' I'd asked Grandpa more than

once. Sometimes the whole family joined forces to try to pin him down to a single religion. 'Are you a Buddhist?'

'Aha, indeed – very good – what am I. . . indeed?' he'd reply, sucking at his cigar and looking up into his own thought bubble.

'Atheist,' Mum put in.

'Ah, no, that merely tells you what I'm not,' Grandpa said.

'A Taoist, you always said Taoism was the best,' Nanna said.

Grandpa cackled with the fun of it. Strands of smoke accumulated from the ceiling, building downwards towards us. 'Nietzsche said after coming into contact with a religious man he felt he must wash his hands.'

'If you're not any of them you must be an Agnostic,' Dad said, trying to conclude the discussion.

'Well . . . not really,' said Grandpa, brushing off Dad and Agnosticism.

By now a yellow cigar fog was drifting lazily at head level.

'Are you a Krishnamurti-ite, Grandpa?' I once suggested.

'My dear boy, you may be getting nearer.'

Krishnamurti, a high-caste Indian with huge eyes and a mop of silver hair, was popular at the Cheam house. When he spoke at nearby Wimbledon Town Hall Grandpa corralled the family into the back of his beloved 1939 Wolseley, named Flo, to see him. Mum described Flo as a sort of mobile icebox with freezing seats and awful fumes. Grandpa once used glue and black paint to disguise cracks in the tyres to get Flo through her MOT test, which caused a row at the garage. Krishnamurti escaped being labelled or bracketed by any religion from East or West by cleverly cornering the Un-labellable part of the spiritual market.

He dismissed all religious authority, including his own, although one couldn't help be struck by the extraordinary sense of personal authority with which he dismissed himself. In his ponderous style he said things like:

'The truth [big pause] . . . is [bigger pause] . . . a pathless land.'

Individuals of this generation were free at last from the power-mongers and hypocrites of Church and State, free to inquire directly into the wordless mystery of life. Grandpa used to drive the family to another man he thought quite sage, who ran a sweet shop in Worcester Park. Sages can be anywhere. Mum and Howard would sit hoping for sweets as her father and his friend rejoiced in each other's strident denouncements of conventional thinking.

I hadn't set out to be labelled a Buddhist any more than I'd set out to be labelled disabled. Buddhism is apparently noted for being free from dogma, so I could breath easy on that score, but the act of calling myself a Buddhist was going one big step further than Grandpa. Maybe if I'd had this experience in a church I'd be going around telling everyone I had felt the Holy Spirit and was now a Christian. There was a 'New Age' bloke on the retreat who hung around the tea urn in stripy trousers trying to nobble thirsty retreatants into agreeing that all religions are One.

'The Buddha, Mohammed, Jesus and the Sikh guy . . . Wassisname . . . are all basically the same, I reckon.'

'Er . . . yeah . . . s'pose so.'

My universal love for all beings was being tested. From what vantage point could he be sure all religions are One? Who was he exactly to lump all those sages together? God?

I didn't want to hear about the teachings of Wassisname. They didn't seem the same as the Buddha's teachings at all. New Age people seem to float above religious labels not by identifying with *none* of them, as per Krishnamurti, but by identifying with *all* of them. At a stroke all religions are kind of neutralised and made equally not much.

I finished the walk around the rugby pitch a self-labelled Buddhist and happily so. I wasn't being told to believe anything. I'd had an experience which made it seem plausible that after the growth from babyhood to adulthood, there is more growth to Buddhahood, whatever that may be. The intuition was more than merely a new state of mind. I didn't know what it was exactly because it had no form I could see or touch or adequately put into words. It flowed through the retreat in how everyone related to each other. I'd stumbled into a whole world of colour. It felt like magic right there in the sensible fields of middle England.

We'd had no news from the outside world and I didn't think about it much until one morning by the tea urn I overheard a woman whispering 'Diana' to another retreatant. She'd been walking down in the village and had heard a radio coming from a parked van. We were supposed to be in a silent period but whispers were going round. In the tea break Maitreyabandhu broke the silence to tell us that Princess Diana had been killed in a car crash. We felt the shock of the news. We had no tv channels to turn on and we didn't need them. The image of Princess Di crumpled up in a car was sufficient. A few people were in tears as we sat silently, finishing our drinks before going into the meditation hall for the afternoon sit.

8

CULT

A week after the retreat, still glowing with the occult knowledge that I was okay, I moved to a terrace house in Sheffield. A large branch was strung with baubles in the living room and the walls were covered with identification charts for mushrooms and spiders. There were three guys living there – a Tibetan Buddhist-cum-carpet fitter from Leeds, a Frenchman who did the pre-match juggling at Sheffield Wednesday and a carpenter whose bedroom was deep in wood shavings and paint pots. The Frenchman, in regular bouts of ennui, would knock on my door and say 'Pardonez moi, I am *bor-ing.*' We'd get a few balls going in the hall, me chucking one in then catching one back as fast as I could manage.

Kate lived opposite. We met at the induction to the journalism course. She was a slim redhead with hazel eyes, who wore tight denim and had an appealing way of pouting her lips. Every day we raced each other at short-hand and started learning how to turn dull local events into the lecturer's yardstick for a good story: what Grandma repeats to a neighbour over her garden fence. Kate had a boyfriend but I never met him and after a few weeks he evaporated. I made my interest clear then sat back and let things unfold. I was feeling okay. A few days later I was lying in my bedroom on my mattress, which I'd set on packing pallets, listening to the Mamas and the Papas, when Kate appeared. She sidled in looking a bit shy, slipped off her shoes and sat on my bed.

'I don't know how you've done this,' she said.

I had a few ideas.

I had learnt that doing less is often doing more. The mind is usually in the grip of what they call the mental hindrances: craving, aversion, restlessness and anxiety, mental sloth, bodily torpor, doubt and indecision. The hindrances both cloud the mind and restrict access to the higher ranges of consciousness, the way clouds obscure the blue sky. On that retreat morning when things became deliciously okay, the hindrances stopped pushing and pulling at my attention, like sails slackening after a storm. My almost non-stop, mildly doubtful, inner burbling abated. Into the open calm came feelings of warmth and expansion, then a vivid, energetic presence. A month later this presence was still with me to some degree. All I had to do then was, well, not much really.

I was in love for sure. The autumn leaves obliged by burning slowly in the sun right through to December. Sometimes we'd skip shorthand class and drive out into the Peak District in Kate's Fiesta or lie in bed listening to Neil Young. Other days I'd go picking mushrooms or drinking real ale with the carpenter or sit underneath our living room tree talking Buddhism with the carpet fitter, who was the real thing, a genuinely happy middle-aged man, very generous with his time and possessions. Twice a week I borrowed his bike and peddled uphill to meditation classes at the Sheffield Buddhist Centre, another centre of magic and friendliness behind a hairdresser's shop.

It was hard to put my feeling for Buddhism into words. It related to what or who I already was and what I could be. A brief dip into higher states of consciousness gave me confidence the Buddhist tradition wasn't all make believe. Before meditation sessions we chanted the ethical precepts of Buddhism in Pali and English, or recited a salutation to the 'Three Jewels' – the Buddha, the Dharma and the Sangha – to evoke the beauty of the ideals towards which we were striving. At times our chants were underlain by more powerful roars blown up on the wind from the Sheffield Wednesday football stadium down the hill. The feeling I couldn't put into words was like that more powerful incantation coming from the crowd, a swell underlying my to-ing and fro-ing to meditation classes. The more I read about meditation the more amazed I became: higher, more pleasurable states of mind were well trodden terrain. If the meditator works more subtly with this new sense of inner bodily spaciousness, it was said rapture can arise, which can further intensify into a profound mental happiness known as sukha. Sukha can deepen into unshakeable equanimity, which itself can deepen further into states which are hard to refer to anything we experience on a day-to-day level.

One Saturday, October 27, 1997, Kate came over with the papers for us to read together on the sofa, like good trainee reporters. Kate was looking rather pleased. She handed me a copy of the *Guardian*'s weekend supplement. On the front cover was a picture of Sangharakshita. The article was headed: 'The Dark Side of Enlightenment'. The strap line read: 'Sex and suicide scandal haunting Britain's Buddhists'.

The story inside detailed Sangharakshita's homosexual relationship in the 1970s with one man and the psychological abuse meted out by a leading Order member at the Croydon Buddhist Centre, which the article said had devolved into a personality cult and was the 'major cause' of a young law student from Oxford University committing suicide. He had felt he couldn't leave the community for fear of being labelled a spiritual failure. I took a deep breath and read the article again. Kate snuggled up next to me. She pointed out how well 'sex', 'suicide' and 'scandal' alliterated and how along with 'haunting Britain's Buddhists' the journalist had succinctly conveyed everything one's Grandma would need to know.

I was shocked. I wasn't sure whether to doubt the Buddhists or doubt the *Guardian*. Was all the friendliness and warmth a sinister front? No-one had tried it on with me, but maybe the 'oppressive authoritarian' homosexual cult was going on somewhere else. Surely I'd have noticed something? It said the London Buddhist Centre was a 'nerve centre' for bases all over the world. Crikey O'Reilly! I'd been meditating in a nerve centre! The photo of Sangharakshita was simply a photo of a man with glasses, yet somehow in this context it seemed to scream 'sinister and manipulative, old gay Buddhist conducting events from the centre of his Evil Empire'.

The journalist's fact base seemed plausible enough. She acknowledged that no-one in the Order was hiding the fact that at some point in the 1980s the culture at the Croydon Buddhist Centre had become unhealthy, unhelpful and cult-like. The Order did not appear to deny that the ex-law student had been badly affected. The article said he'd joined the Buddhist community after becoming 'increasingly disenchanted with careerism and materialism'. He did sound rather like me. The article also detailed Sangharakshita's sex life, as told to the journalist by a former lover.

'It says he "rubbed himself against" the other bloke,' said Kate, who was delighted by the whole thing.

'That seems a reasonable description of sex,' I said.

'"Twice a week" it says . . . he's less demanding than you.'

My coffee had gone cold by the time of the third or fourth reading. It turned out the law student had killed himself three years after leaving the community and shortly after losing a job. I wondered if we should blame his employer, or society in general for letting him down rather than the Buddhists? If Roberto had killed himself after the retreat, would we have blamed the Burmese Buddhist master, the Chancellor of Oxford University, his parents or the spiritual loneliness of modern life? When Sangharakshita was made aware of the bullying, I later heard, he gave the protagonists a bigger blast of wrath than you might expect from a Buddhist. They left the Order and the Croydon Buddhist Centre returned to normal. It's bad enough in Croydon without cults.

I thought about Kate reviewing our sex life in the *Observer* in twenty years' time: *He used to go on about Buddhism and spirituality, but every night he'd just lie naked on the bed, sort of waiting. His funny hand made me feel awkward, but I felt as if I couldn't say anything or he'd get really touchy. Sometimes he ordered me to get undressed . . . there were these knickers he liked to see me in . . . then. . . he'd rub himself against me.*

We laughed about all this, but the article made me very uneasy. I didn't want it to be true. An unnamed 'leading Buddhist' said that Sangharakshita peddled a 'quixotic ideology'. And Stephen Batchelor, a well-known Buddhist whose writings I'd read, was quoted as saying it was a 'potentially totalitarian system' and that 'they operate as a self-enclosed system and their writings have the predictability of those who believe they have all the answers'. Social activist and Buddhist Ken Jones said Sangharakshita's was 'a deviant form of Buddhism'. Were the positive feelings I'd had merely a sign that I was already fully indoctrinated? Was this exactly what people feel when they're in a cult? The leading Buddhist said most people can't tell one Buddhist group from another, in the way they can (to take a totally neutral example) tell Catholicism from the Moonies.

Taken by the Moonies. I remember that phrase as a child. The adult son of one of Dad's colleagues was *Taken by the Moonies*. During the brainwashing process Dad relayed how the Moonies followed the young man into the toilet, so he didn't have a single sitting to think for himself. His parents, to whom he refused to speak, eventually hired someone to kidnap him. Dad's tone of voice left no room for alternative constructions of what was going on. A cult was the worst thing that could ever happen.

A few days later I got a postcard from Maitreyabandhu enquiring if I'd read the article and offering to chat if I wanted to. Hmmm . . . a postcard . . . how creepy. The cult reaching out its tentacles? Should I check my toilet pan for devices?

I was now a partially haunted, *Guardian*-reading British Buddhist. The journalist had sounded every note in a perfect chord of disgust. I didn't believe it was quite right, but my favourite newspaper (up to that point) was clearly implying that no right thinking person would associate with this nasty little outfit. It made me think then, what do I really believe and am I prepared to carry on and stomach being considered dangerously gullible by wider society? Sangharakshita had refused to comment on any of it.

I carried on bicycling up to the Buddhist Centre twice a week.

'You going up to the cult?' Kate would say, smiling sweetly.

Sounds like a commune

One morning towards the end of the journalism course we lay in bed, sun filtering in through the orange drape that hung across the bedroom window. We had to discuss the future. I wanted to devote the future to my twin loves – Buddhist practice and idling in bed with Kate.

'Surely someone else can be relied on to keep a stream of news flowing to the public,' I said.

'What, so you can go and live in the commune?' Kate said.

'It's not a commune, it's a community.'

'And work at the organic vegetable shop?'

'It's got nothing to do with vegetables.'

'Buddhists are good at vegetables.'

'Ha ha. It's an ethical gift shop.'

'And you want to live in a commune with them.'

'It's not a commune, it's a community!'

Kate was more pragmatic. She was soon to start as a junior reporter on a weekly paper in Halifax. I had a pragmatic streak too, but the Buddha had appeared and mucked it up. I felt guilty for wanting to ditch a second career before it had begun.

'We'll be miles apart,' I said. 'You'll get onto a regional, then a daily and in a few years you'll be writing nicely balanced articles for the *Guardian*.'

'I've been to one of those gift shops. The wind chimes are lovely.'

'It's better than trawling round Halifax asking people about car parking and litter.'

'Can you get me one of those pink fluffy mirrors?'

Two roads were diverging in a yellow wood and, to my parents' dismay, I took a third track even Frost never spotted into a wholesale trinket warehouse just off the Cambridge ring road. The bogey of cult hadn't killed off my credulity. I'd received a bulletin from beyond the range of the *Guardian* weekend supplement, about a Path to Enlightenment which had been walked by millions of people down the ages. The universe wasn't just an extended version of a visit to a shopping centre, or to be understood by repeated examination of long-winded Platonic discourses about the nature of reality. It was to be understood by transforming yourself into a Buddha.

The warehouse was staffed by men and women from ten or so communities dotted around the east side of Cambridge. For my trial period I was allocated a room in a terraced house with eight energetic guys in their late twenties and thirties, from Ireland, New Zealand, Scotland and the USA. In the mornings we meditated in the spare bedroom, ate breakfast together, and then headed off to the warehouse in twos and threes. One of them joked that they needed someone 'normal' like me in the community. I wasn't sure if I fancied being normal or if it was true. However, the Buddhist scene did support a varied supply of oddballs, that was clear.

A typical day opened and closed with a short ritual around a stupa on the warehouse floor to put the work in the context of Buddhist values. The aim of business, aside from making money, was to provide a place where Buddhist practice, friendship and community could become full time. The rub-a-long of a working day is more real, more mucky and therefore potentially more transformative of the whole of our selves, not just the spiritual bits we display on a retreat. I wanted my little glimpses of understanding to become part of my actual life, not end up as something that happened once and then got forgotten as the business of 'real' life takes over. Anyway, I thought I did.

Then we got going, one team unloading the huge containers of decorative soapstone, wood carvings, incense burners and other carefully sourced items from around the globe that might appeal to someone on a middle-to-low income. My team combed up and down eight to ten aisles with our trolleys, picking and packing orders into boxes. A third team cellophane-wrapped the boxes onto pallets, bound for gifts shops across the nation. Every now and then we stopped for peanut butter sandwiches, meditation or some group study of an aspect of Buddhist teaching, the 'Dharma' as I now called it. We were transforming our minds and shipping stuff out.

I had misgivings. Most days passed in happy activity and budding friendships, yet the whole arrangement made me feel a bit sick and lonely underneath. I was fired up by the idea of full time Buddhist life with other Buddhists, really going for it, and this unlikely warehouse was what was available, but I missed Kate like crazy. And it didn't pay well. Although the business sometimes made more than a million pounds annual profit from its retail shops and wholesale purchasers, the proceeds were used to support various Buddhist activities across the world. Employees were all paid the same, which is to say no-one was officially paid anything. We called it 'support'. Rent was covered, and food, plus £30 a week to spend on Buddhist essentials such as cinema and croissants.

'It sounds like a commune,' Mum said on the phone.

'It's not a commune, it's a community! Property is not collectively owned.'

'But how can you afford a new pair of shoes on the money you're getting?' she asked.

'We all get the same, including the managing director. Then if anyone needs shoes or glasses they get extra for shoes or glasses.'

'Everyone needs shoes,' said Mum, not entirely put at ease by my explanation.

'The idea is you give what you can and take only what you need. There is a notional shoe allowance, but I guess someone might need more shoes for some legitimate reason.'

It did sound a bit like a commune.

'What about if you want to go on holiday with Kate?' Mum persisted.

There was no four-star spa allowance. However, there was a retreat and travel allowance which I discovered could be diverted. Company cars were bookable for trips out.

Nothing was fixed, that had been part of the revelation of LSD and meditation, but I was gutted my idyllic life in Sheffield had unfixed so soon. We had no mobile phones, so sometimes a whole day went by without communication. I sent Kate many carefully scribed long letters, and occasionally got back a bit of scribble on a scrap of telephone pad. When we met in Manchester or Oxford, she wasn't exactly as I'd imagined while slogging up and down the aisles looking for rainbow pencil cases and frog key-rings. That Kate was a kind of sex angel of warmth, comfort and confirmation. Kate-world signified something different to warehouse-world. I was attracted to both, but now neither were satisfactory. The retreat vibes had evaporated. If Kate was doubtful or moody, I felt doubtful and moody back. By the time things improved it was time to part again.

After two months of picking and packing I was rescued from this dilemma by another postcard from Maitreyabandhu. A community was starting up at the London Buddhist Centre and did I want to join? Kate was moving to London to work on a fashion magazine, so yes, I definitely did – at least then my two worlds would be in the same town. Despite the warehouse not working out I still thought that I must join a co-operative business if I was serious about the Dharma. There were several run by the London Buddhist Centre so I took a trial at the health food store, which was run by six or seven committed Buddhists. After a few hours my heart was sinking through the linoleum. I didn't want to spend my life mindfully marshalling soya sauce and labelling jars of yeast extract. What would Adam think? What part of my brain regulated the need for tribal affiliation and a sense of higher purpose, such that it would explain this? *No seriously, Dave, dried apricots, that's cool.*

When I admitted to an Order member that I didn't want to work in his shop he said: 'Never mind, you don't have to work here, do you?' I was so relieved to hear this that I almost cried. I had too much unspent ambition to appreciate the subtle benefits of a livelihood in organic produce. Maybe journalism would do after all? As I had a law degree I thought it made sense to call up a news agency at the Old Bailey, the country's Central Criminal court. A week that started with a trial in eco-washing products and red-bush tea ended with a grievous bodily harm trial. I wrote the story up pretty badly but they told me to come back.

9

FREEDOM WITHIN

Before the towers of Tower Hamlets stacked up, the top turret of the red-brick fire station had been ideal for smoke spotting. Firemen were billeted along the corridors on the upper four floors that now made up the Buddhist community quarters. When an alarm was raised horses dragged fire engines from the ground floor, where meditation classes now took place. Eventually the fire station burned down, providing a parable about the danger of assuming that all the trouble lies elsewhere.

The renovated old fire station was now the heart of a Buddhist village, which *Time Out* liked to call 'an oasis of calm'. Triple glazing cut out noise from the traffic junction outside. Visitors could sit by a fountain under a large lotus mural, in a courtyard draped in flowering plants, or take their pick from the Buddhist-run yoga studio, health food store and one of two vegetarian cafes. More than seventy Buddhists lived together either in the building itself or in local residential communities.

My community occupied the two upper floors. There were ten of us, all men. The furniture was shabby and the corridors institutional. The communal kitchen and living room were mostly clean and functional, with a couple of giant fern-like plants gathering dust in big pots. Grandpa used to like the Zen saying about how all we really do is eat, shit, piss and make love, and that's one way of describing life in the community too, apart from swapping the making love with meditation. For unless I was being duped, the community was not a den of homosexual vice as described by the *Guardian*, nor a nerve centre operating suicidal cells across the globe. Two community members were gay, though the most apparent thing about having gay men in the community was that it tended to lead to better soft furnishings.

We were not monks. Most of us had partners or wanted a partner, though a few were happy enough without one, for now. Kate seemed okay with the arrangement, I thought. I saw her at weekends mostly, at her place. My room mate was a loud, large man with a south London-cum-Cockney accent that carried well across a noisy pub. Our room faced south with a distant view of Canary Wharf. We had a tallboy and a clothes rail, a chest of drawers and a desk, and beds in opposite corners. *Principles of Land Law* and *Administrative Cases in the European Union* gave some gravitas to my bit of bookshelf, law books balancing out the spiritual stuff as before spiritual books had balanced out the law.

Some guys wanted their own space, but I enjoyed the sharing, particularly chatting across the room before going to sleep. We'd lie in our corners chewing over our doubts about this strange thing that had thrown us together. He had an ex-wife and grown-up children. He was losing touch with his friends from the pub circuit and the terraces of West Ham football stadium.

'I got into the habit of driving my camper van to the pub so I could sleep in the car park and go straight to work in the morning.'

'Your friends sound like a collection of minor criminals.'

'They're as good as gold. This Buddhism malarkey though . . . It's taken all the fun out of it,' he sighed.

'Out of what?'

'You know, ten pints and a decent bar-room brawl.'

'Really?'

'Maybe not, I dunno,' he said. 'Loving kindness makes it all so difficult.'

Despite doubts about where he belonged, he studied Buddhism earnestly. I, too, was reluctantly drifting from former friends, not quite sure if it was a good idea, but for my roommate the cultural shift was bigger, from working class, anti-police, family gang-type culture to a tofu mountain of universal well-wishers. Sometimes a passion equal to the West Ham terraces got behind his love for Buddhism, and he could speak with the authority of life experience about how states of mind really do lead to suffering.

Next along was a science teacher who started coming to the Buddhist Centre after a spontaneous visionary experience on Mile End Road. Further along, two Order members shared a room, a Tai Chi practitioner who used to work for a cigarette manufacturer and a clinical psychologist who played the saxophone. They had given up their careers to work in a retail branch of the Buddhist gift shop business in whose central warehouse I had briefly worked. The room opposite was occupied by a yoga instructor with light green eyes and a thin edge of beard running down his pronounced jaw line. Before morning meditation he'd already racked up an hour of yoga. He gave me tips and I toiled away on a yoga mat twice a week, surrounded by blocks and padding to balance out my short arm. Sometimes it felt good, other times I ended up in a lather of straps and discontent.

The yoga guy shared with a Greek man with a lot of body hair, a back like a rug. He also worked in the gift shop. Whatever inter-personal dynamics were going on in the community he went in like a heat-seeking missile.

'Can I just ask, do you think you're a friendly person?' he'd say, kinking his joined-up eyebrow.

A guilty worry came over me. Had he heard something I'd said about him to someone else?

'I think so . . . fairly,' I said, hesitantly. He stood so close I could feel his body heat. His skin smelled almost sweet.

'I think so too. It's just I wondered, when you said you didn't want to go to the cinema, was that because you didn't want to see that film or was it that you didn't want to go with me?'

'It was the film,' I replied. 'I saw *Titanic* when it came out.'

'Oh. I thought that maybe you were avoiding me because I like to ask awkward questions.'

I was. He did. He seemed to relish honing in on what I, an English person, was really thinking.

'Er . . . you do stand rather close,' I said.

Surely he would now say something he didn't like about me.

'That's good to know,' he said, with a big grin, opening out his eyebrow. 'How about if I stand this far away . . . is that better?'

Every day we all ate together, or a meal was saved for us if we were late back. We put £15 a week in the food kitty and cooked our signature dishes, of varying culinary standards, on a two-weekly rotation or so. Other jobs were split up: the fruit and veg order, the Sainsbury's run, cleaning, guest management. On Thursday evenings everyone made a special effort to be together for the community evening, during which, for the first few months, we told each other our life stories, from birth onwards.

Owen was two years older than me, a blond-haired Kiwi with a blunt manner, big forearms and fingers unsuited to untangling wind-chimes at the gift shop. He could be doleful, but when he smiled big dimples appeared on his cheeks and his blue eyes lit up. He told us about his early adulthood smoking this and that, working in fast-food outlets, writing poetry. He'd wandered through Ireland, sometimes sleeping rough. Doomed to loneliness, he said he was, until in Manchester he found a Buddhist centre.

When it was my turn, I dealt with the stump part of my life story in thirty seconds, mentioning a bit of bullying, but maintaining it gave me no residual difficulty other than when I wanted to play the piano. I'd had a happy childhood, certainly compared to some of the stories that were told. But as the youngest in the community I felt I lacked a proper back story. I wanted more torrid love affairs like Owen had had, or a dazzling career. I would have preferred to have arrived at the Buddhist community by walking off the top of some definite worldly success, like when Leonard Cohen gave up song writing and moved into a Zen monastery.

The anchor of communal life was morning meditation. As with apples, the generally agreed minimum prescription was one a day, though four or five appearances in the shrine room per week was respectable. As many as made it out of bed sat together for an hour at 7am downstairs in the main shrine room. On community nights there was sometimes an evening 'sit' too. Our mats were arranged in a horseshoe shape with the shrine at the open end. The yoga guy looked like the real thing, the Greek man very still, eyebrow soft and relaxed, the Tai Chi practitioner quivering as energy released up his spine. Owen would start us off with a mournful poem like those by the Japanese hermit Ryokan who was always yearning for company while leaves fell outside his hut.

Sitting in silence with these men, a trickle of sweat running down my back from the risen heat of the six floors below, I felt free to be myself. With no women in the community we weren't competing for their attention the way guys do. Even when meditating it's possible to flirt or to try to meditate in a more sexy way – or you can keep your eyes open enough to get a look at the woman in front. With these men I didn't live in fear of making a politically incorrect blunder.

Despite the voluntary constraints and mutual expectations of communal living, it was a relief. I could stop pretending I had a plan about life. I didn't need to worry about careers or feel oppressed by lack of purpose. Community living was its own purpose, a means and an end, and the closeness of sharing was freedom from loneliness. Rather than a small ideal about how to live a good life such as society readily supplies, Buddhism has a grand and all-encompassing vision of transformation towards human enlightenment or Awakening. I wasn't sure what this big vision meant specifically, for me. Enlightenment obviously. But what's that? Was I required to give up on romance, family, career and saving up for a country house? Community life certainly wasn't aimed at or centred round achieving those things. Was there nothing left for me but a slow march towards becoming the popular image of a homogenous and bald-headed Buddhist? Not that there were any of those in the community.

Ultimately Buddhist communities of any kind are supposed to be a crucible for change, not just a good way to share organic veg. They are a place where a whole different cosmology is seeded and grown into. That's the missing piece. Sitting together in our horseshoe shape up at the loft shrine, listening to muffled car horn noises filter in through the roof tiles, this life felt as natural as dew settling on a lawn. Even in the middle of London, mental speediness could give way to a sense of space. I was discovering things about myself and learning how to relate to other men. Our togetherness, day after day, felt almost timeless; a full moon and a forest clearing and we could have been a brotherhood of the Buddha's disciples 2,500 years ago.

I went on retreats more regularly. Arriving back, I might stroll through the wonderfully non-retreat like markets at Brick Lane, enjoying the hustle of traders touting dodgy antiques, vinyl and vintage trousers, looking out for that elusive thing promised by so much stuff, finding a bagel and a faint feeling of disappointment. Then I'd go over to Kate's. She wasn't usually burning for a blow-by-blow account of twenty-eight meditation sessions, nor did she marvel at my limpid state of mind. She'd been having her own life while I was on retreat. She was a punchy magazine writer with a circle of artistic friends. My clarity of mind came down a peg or two after a glass of wine. Kate never said she was against me living in an all-male community, but nor did she say she was for it. The whole Buddhism thing didn't interest her and I wasn't bothered by that so long as it didn't mean we would split up. I loved waking up in a nice wide bed instead of at the community, and skipping meditation. We hung out or went to exhibitions. I embarrassed her once with a childish outburst against an installation, a film of a dog barking on a TV screen inside a pram.

When the immediate effects of a retreat had gone, community living kept me in touch with a perceptible change in how I thought about life. Some people in the wider Buddhist community suggested that the men living in all-male communities secretly had big problems relating to women, that they were *puer eternal* who were avoiding life's problems. We needed to get properly down into the psychological muck of relationships rather than keep our sexual partners at arm's-length. I thought that had a grain of truth. However, I knew what it was actually like in my community. There was no hatred of women, no homosexual conspiracy and no plot to overthrow the government. There was a closeness of living and a communal spirit. It seemed a good way to be.

10

MOON METAPHORS

It's easy to lose friends when you become 'religious'. To see a friend plunge into the River of Faith is just awful. We've spent so long as a species hauling ourselves up onto the banks of reasonable humanism and so long patiently waiting for scientific experts to reveal to us the outer and inner workings of the universe, only for some fools to commit voluntary madness by jumping back into a mode of consciousness dominated by myth and superstition. Off they go down the river with never a backward glance, looking so happy. I felt I had an answer to this charge, should any friend be willing to listen: the truth is beyond words. The words of the Bible, or Buddhism, and modern science are alike in one respect: they cannot literally be the truth.

'Words . . . are not things,' Grandpa wrote in the 1963 edition of *One and All*, the *Adult School Journal*. He was at the height of his love for all things Eastern. 'A word is not even the same as the perceptual image of a thing, still less can it be identified with the thing-in-itself . . . when we pause to think about it, this seems obvious . . . but too often in the heat of wrangling, the subtle distinction between "knowing about" and "knowing" is entirely lost to sight.'

Adam: 'How can you possibly believe in the Buddha? Just tell me in plain language please!'

Me: 'I don't *believe* in the Buddha, not like that. And I can't tell you in *plain* language. All language is metaphorical to one degree or another, isn't it?'

Adam: 'You're always trying to mesmerise me with metaphors.'

Me: 'Why not? They're important. Black holes – that's a metaphor. The taste of a tomato is beyond *plain* language. We can only point and say what the tomato tastes *like*.'

Adam: 'Metaphors create lovely feelings, but all the evidence is that everything we feel is the result of physical events within the confines of our skull.'

Me: 'Sure, something happens in the brain. Buddhism has no argument with scientific descriptions of genes and quarks. But it's a crazy reduction to shoehorn conscious, living, actual experience into a description of brain chemistry.'

Adam: 'You talk about actual experience, but what is *actual* experience?'

Me: 'It's um . . . mind . . . consciousness . . . what happens . . . Okay, let's not go into this again, for God's sake.'

Adam: 'The mind, whatever it is or is not, is in the brain, it's all in the brain! Nothing more – puff and it's out. And all this talk about 'awareness' and 'opening the heart' – it's motherhood and apple pie, if you ask me.'

Me: 'Yeah, I know it sounds airy fairy, but once you understand metaphor and myth, bang goes centuries of Christian literalism. The Truth isn't Christian or Buddhist. The goal of Buddhism isn't coming up with a perfect description of Reality. In Zen they say all the teachings are like a finger pointing at the moon. The aim of Dharma practice is to see the moon rather than believe in the finger.'

Adam: 'Moon talk! Mere trickery and self-delusion.'

Me: 'It's a metaphor! We are a society of wagging fingers who have forgotten the moon. That is the liberation which the Buddha said was the sole purpose of all his teaching.'

Even though I reckoned I could answer his hard-nosed materialism, the more haunting question for me was – so what? Was I any nearer to really 'seeing' the transcendent 'moon' just because I'd intellectually understood that no concept can be the reality to which it is pointing? Maybe I was a little bit nearer. If I'm honest, I felt I was. In fact, at times I felt so pleased with myself it was as if I'd personally come up with the Middle Way of the Buddhas.

Dressing up Buddhist

Divisive issues in community living aren't usually doctrinal. Whether it was acceptable to name-tag personal food in the fridge was more keenly debated than whether and in what sense a Buddha exists after his or her death; or doesn't exist; or both exists and doesn't exist; or neither exists nor does not exist. Once a week practical matters could be brought up at 'points'. Points were decided by consensus, the most cumbersome form of government known to man. Usually a kind of harmony won through and we agreed not to set aside a personal cheese stash and to be a bit more mindful about Julian's yoghurt.

One evening Rhydian, a bulky Welshman, raised a new point:

'I would like to wear a dress,' he said, sitting in a full-length red dress, looking for all the world like Alison Steadman in *Abigail's Party*.

This was new territory for points. We had to feel our way forward.

'I don't know, Rhyd. I've nothing against it . . .' someone said.

'Me neither,' someone added. 'Though isn't it a bit weird that we exclude women from the community and then start dressing up as them?'

'I don't want to wear one every day,' Rhydian replied, flicking his hair out of his eyes and fiddling with a bracelet.

'How often then . . . just so we have an idea?'

'Twice a week?' Rhydian said nervously.

'It's not safe for you to walk around the East End wearing a dress,' someone else chipped in.

'Actually,' Rhydian said, 'there's quite a lot of drag in the East End. There's a whole history.'

'Can we stick to the point please?'

'What the hell difference does it make if Rhyd wears a dress? It's a free country.'

'It's a free country, but we're in a men's community.'

'Okay, does anyone actually object to Rhyd wearing a dress twice a week?'

'I don't like the perfume.'

'Can I just clarify that, do you mean you don't like Rhyd's perfume or perfume in the community per se?'

'Both.'

Owen and I sometimes went for breakfast at the local cafe over whose formica tables every major development in the history of Western Buddhism has been debated. It must have the largest Buddhist clientele of any greasy spoon in the Western world. As for the world, I wasn't sure where it was any more. It shifted about a lot. Not long ago I'd been worried about leaving college and entering the *real world*. Adam said living in the community was *shutting myself off from the world*. Owen said the Old Bailey was *in the world*, whereas his gift shop, apparently, was not so much. The greasy spoon was certainly in the world. Its unadulterated worldliness was part of the attraction for any local Buddhist who had lost interest in buckwheat salad. Owen sat opposite me in his fisherman's pullover, sleeves rolled up, leafing through the menu, a sticky booklet which contained traces of most of the food on offer. A huge biker at an adjacent table was wolfing down a full roast.

'Geez, that stuff about Rhyd's dress cracked me up,' he said. 'I don't care if he dresses up as Lady Bracknell.'

'Me neither, but not when I invite a friend round.'

'Nor at the shop. Can you imagine?'

'How's it going up there?' I asked, without being very interested.

'We were studying one of Bhante's lectures at the team meeting yesterday – you know the one where he talks about the need to be useless sometimes, how all our work should come out of a sense of beauty, for its own sake. We're far too utilitarian about everything.'

'Bhante' was what we called Sangharakshita. Bhante means 'teacher' and is a traditional way of addressing a revered elder. The waitress brought us the four-egg cheese omelette and chips, on plates the size of an ornamental pond.

'And after the study, you carry on selling crap.'

'You've missed the point, mate,' Owen said, frowning. 'We can practise the Dharma all day. You should give up that court stuff. Murder and rape isn't doing your mental states any good.'

'True, though from what I hear it isn't always love, peace and harmony between you shop guys.'

'Yeah, but the shop is an alchemist's vessel. We experience whatever comes up between us and get into better communication. We're not working in any old gift shop. Sometimes I'm re-dressing the shop window display or feeling resentful about having to do the dusting, and suddenly I see my mind going on and on creating suffering. That's what spiritual practice is. Anyway, at least it's harmless fair trade crap.'

'It just doesn't sound like much fun to me, bubble wrapping your way to Enlightenment.'

'Why are you always on about having fun?'

Down the pub with non-Buddhist friends I was much more positive about Buddhism. I tried to convey my meditation experiences, half-expecting they'd sign up for the next retreat. Their minds seemed roughly like mine, so why wouldn't they? No need to believe in anything silly or religious in order to meditate. But my earnest revelations were just another fleeting pub topic. Instead of instilling a desire to meditate or rousing anyone's mind, I usually felt I'd cheapened the whole thing by mentioning it at all.

Honest opinions about what I was doing did surface sometimes, usually after a few drinks.

'Woo-ooo Dave, yoooo've been brainwashed!'

'Sweetie, I wash other parts of my body so why not my brain?'

'Love you Dave.'

Several rounds later . . .

'Dave, mate, I really respect what you're doing.'

'Thanks, man.'

'We're going on to a club, you coming?'

Was I ready to forego hedonism, mindfully noting a desire to get completely off my head but returning dutifully to the community so I could get up to meditate at 6.30am? That seemed unsatisfactory.

If I had a drink someone would inevitably point out:

'Does it fit with your Buddhism?'

'Not especially, no.'

'You can do whatever you like in Buddhism, right?'

'It doesn't quite work like that. There's an ethical precept not to take intoxicants, which is what this is, obviously, but a precept isn't a *should* exactly, unless you have taken a vow or you're a monk or something. Buddhist tradition simply says it matters what we do and our actions have consequences. Of course in a broader sense one is free to do whatever one likes.'

I gave people more information than they really wanted.

'I just want a pint.' That's what I should have said.

So that my interests weren't totally ignored I brought Buddhism up whenever there was a gap, and sometimes when there wasn't. I enjoyed being good old Dave, a right enough sort of bloke who chats about higher verities. I was afraid of drifting away from college friends. Whatever it was that had opened up for me had not opened up for them, as far as I could tell. They seemed optimistic about how their lives would pan out. I was more doubtful. I saw folly in blindly pursuing an ambitious career, but I wasn't sure if I wanted to live with the consequences of not doing it myself.

Keeping worship quiet

Adam, at least, was interested enough in what I was doing to argue with me. One evening he came over for dinner. It was strange seeing him in the community in his suit. He was on the civil service fast-track. His sticky-up hair was all trimmed down and his spacious nasal cavities, until then faintly comic, now seemed to indicate high office was ahead. I showed him up the stairwell past window sills lined with cacti and dusty little Buddhas, to the place where we left our shoes, nervous how he would judge his surrounds. I'd just returned from my first fortnight-long retreat. Other community members had put welcome-back cards and bars of fair-trade chocolate on my bed. Would Adam find that a bit girly? It was a single bed. Adam inhabited the grown-up world of double beds and impending matrimony. In the lounge there was a photo of Sangharakshita in a tweedy jacket. Could easily be a dodgy guru, cashing in behind the scenes. Fingers crossed Rhydian would not appear at dinner in a dress.

I wanted Adam to understand my new lifestyle was all quite reasonable despite the religious paraphernalia in the community. Thank God he wouldn't be there to see us perform a puja. Look, mate, I've been hiding it, but I'm gay. That would have been easier to say than: Look mate, I've been hiding it, but I've been worshipping the Buddha.

Grandpa's Buddhas were kept in a glass case on the upstairs landing at the Cheam house. There was no ritual to greet them each day. Pausing to tie a shoelace or straighten a tie, one might have wondered at how these curios once held a meaning for someone, somewhere. Their power had tapered down, like objects in a museum. The Buddhas on the community shrine were still in active service. Tara, an archetypal Bodhisattva figure, was usually the centrepiece. The myth goes that she was born from Avalokiteshvara, the personification of Compassion. Avalokiteshvara had solemnly vowed to lead all beings to the freedom of enlightenment and should he ever waiver, doubt or shirk from this task may his head split open. After aeons of saving thousands of beings, one day he looked up, so to speak, and realised this was but a drop in the vast ocean of beings. He fell into despair and doubt and his head duly shattered, only to be reassembled as eleven heads. His body acquired a thousand arms, each with a gift or skill to help achieve the vow. So deeply did he feel the suffering of unenlightened beings that he wept a lake of tears on which Tara, the very essence of compassion, then miraculously appeared seated on a pale blue lotus. Green Tara usually takes the form of a sixteen year old girl with full breasts and a shapely narrow waist, dressed in fine silks and sashes. Far more appealing than the blobby Buddha that otherwise sat on our shrine.

Our evening pujas – stylised poetry and hymns of praise from Indo-Tibetan Buddhism directed at figures like Tara – they all made me shift uneasily on my cushion. I knew the figures symbolised, externally, qualities which we could cultivate inwardly. Their meaning and power lies in what they evoke or represent. The statue of Tara was not Tara, that was clear; though it didn't do to manhandle her statue, as though the physical thing was unimportant. Despite our sophisticated symbolic understanding, I

sometimes wondered if the other guys really believed
that Tara literally exists, in the way that a teacup exists.
Grandpa would have argued a teacup doesn't literally
exist as a teacup either, but all that ontology was too
sophisticated. Our pujas were addressed directly to Tara.
But what was that?

Adam's presence at the community dinner table made
me aware of how split I was about all this. For him I wanted
to be Dave the sensible bloke, not Dave the guy who chants
to Tara. After food was served someone chimed a singing
bowl and we sat silently for two minutes, a practice known
as the mindfulness of salivation. As we ate, the community
were behaving well, chatting sensibly enough.

'So there are no women allowed in?' Adam asked.

'None,' Owen said, smiling nervously.

'I guess if you were really ill or dying they could visit,' I
said, to soften the stark reality of the rule.

'How does Kate feel about it?' Adam asked.

'She's fine. There isn't much to see up here anyway,' I
said, motioning to the saggy green sofa, armchairs and
bare yellow walls.

'It's not about excluding women,' said Owen. 'It helps us
relate differently to each other. Men act differently when
women are around and if they aren't here we can't blame
them or shift all our stuff onto them.'

'There are women's communities down the road,' I
added.

'Sex is natural enough though, surely, why would anyone
need to block it out?' Adam said.

'No-one here has to be celibate,' I replied, hoping to
squash that whole topic as soon as possible.

'Kate has been good for you, I reckon,' Adam said, turning to me.

'Are we more manly when we're with women, or are we more like moody little boys?' Owen went on.

For Adam, Buddhist practices, meditation and community rules about girlfriends visiting were as bizarre as my moonly metaphors.

The romantic myth had been beaten into me from my first fairytale on and, deep down, it was still my true religion. Like any good Romeo I was up for a Juliet. Half-doing romantic love sounded rubbish. The Buddhist myth was the heroic quest for human Enlightenment but it was a latecomer to my mythic landscape and had a lot of pushing back to do against Prince Charming and various damsels in distress. I needed to be a successful Romeo who could also keep up a regular meditation practice, which is a tall order.

I hoped, without any real evidence, that these competing myths could be reconciled somewhere up the road. An Order member once told me I didn't need to solve every conundrum in life straight away. Some problems can be put on the back burner, he said. They'll come around. I hadn't had enough sex and romance or done enough meditation to opt for one myth or the other, as if that was possible anyway. If I hit eighty-five and was suffering from too much sex I might reconsider the issue.

I guess my parents were hoping for a more conventional romantic move on my part and that my Buddhist phase might soften into a life path more easily explainable to the neighbours. They weren't opposed to my lifestyle choices, but it's an English trait not to be direct. English people use indirect means. For example, my parents would ask after my non-Buddhist friends or the Buddhist friends who had children and houses and not enquire after the others. I went along with this and highlighted the more acceptable friends. I did my best to translate my lifestyle into terms acceptable and understandable to them.

At the Old Rectory in Norfolk where they now lived, Dad's plough shares and potato dibbers looked more in place. Mum had a bold scheme for the garden, setting out flower beds, rose arbours and a vegetable garden. Grandpa too had been an obsessive garden plotter. He designed a winding path for the Cheam garden, under a huge old damson tree and round to the pond. Henry, the family tortoise of indeterminate age, would amble along it in his chipped shell, then veer off into the privet for reasons of his own. He normally wound up wedged in the compost heap, which was a dangerous location should Grandpa be test firing his old army revolver. Mum designed a similar ambulatory at the Old Rectory, with path edging tiles inherited from her father's garden. She was forced to inherit the revolver too as they were too scared to hand it in. Dad twisted the barrel and put it up a chimney breast along with the ammunition.

Sometimes sitting in the garden we discussed Buddhism and spiritual matters directly. If pressed, Mum usually ended up declaring she was a pagan.

'I don't know why anyone would need Buddhism. I just love my garden, that's all I need.'

'Great, Mum, good for you.'

'I can chill down in the garden.'

'It's chill *out*.'

Sangharakshita said one of the most important tasks

for a Dharma practitioner, particularly a Westerner, is to embody the emotional equivalence of their intellectual understanding. Westerners, he observed, often have intellects that have decisively outrun their emotions. Buddhist theory ends up sounding hollow unless it is really touching us deeply. Many people would do better, he believed, to bring up this aspect of their lives, forming friendships and relating more deeply to others, for example by moving into a Buddhist community, than to study any more philosophy about the emptiness of inherent existence.

Pujas in particular, he taught, help to refine our emotional energies, our inspiration and sense of devotion. Maybe I felt uneasy about them because they pointed to the split in my energies? I had a choice: to open up all this and reach some new level of understanding, or run away. Usually I did neither, I just sat it out. Yet even then the puja ceremonies had an effect on me. Even if the chanting was out of tune and the Buddha figure cheaply made, it didn't matter. By saying the words along with everyone else and not dismissing the whole thing out of hand, by the conclusion of the final mantras my sense of what life is was subtly amplified. The possibility of transcendental compassion within a world of suffering had entered the room.

Grandpa's knot of anxiety tightened as he aged. He had no spiritual community, no real friends, and no teacher to help him widen out his circle of concern. He was stuck at the top of his own spiritual system. He'd grown up in a materialist culture which had little to offer on bigger questions about life. Whatever his meditative breakthroughs they did not break through enough.

He too understood the dangers of mere intellect. His philosophical analysis of reality was a huge effort on the part of his intellect to go beyond itself, and yet it was ironically a massive overvaluation of how well the intellect alone can achieve that task. He was trapped by his character and his habits in a cycle of domestic pettiness. Mum had to suffer his way of manipulating domestic affairs to get what he wanted.

I didn't suffer my grandfather like Mum did so I'm free to sit back and sympathise, remember his funny, irreverent side and take him in as a whole. I relate to his predicament. The moon easily slips behind the clouds and becomes merely an idea of the moon. An opening to a higher state of consciousness can recede into memory. I choose to believe, against my mother's imagined doubtful looks, that he did glimpse the metaphorical moon, even if his actions were incongruent with compassionate action, which the Buddha said flows naturally from a deepening awareness of how things are. I wonder now, looking back, if he might have benefited from a puja.

He ain't heavy, he's my Buddha

Contrary to what I told Adam, things weren't so easy between Kate and me. If I said I didn't want to go out drinking she'd say something like 'Why don't we leave it this weekend then?' in a flippant tone, as if it was a matter of indifference to her whether I went out to the cinema with the Greek guy or her. One morning after she'd been out drinking with her colleagues, I went round. She was still tipsy with her messy red hair falling over her face in a winning manner. One of her front teeth was cracked in half, her lip red and swollen. Someone from editorial had pushed her over and she'd landed face down on the kerbstone.

'He just shoved me, I think, it's all a bit of a blur.'

'What a bastard. Did he take responsibility?'

'Yeah, I showed him. He was pissed. I don't think you've met him.'

She seemed to find the whole thing funny.

I wasn't trying to convert Kate to Buddhism, but at least it would have given us more in common to talk about. When I hired a room at a local lido for a meditation course, two minutes' walk from her house, she was happy enough to give meditation a go. I made some flyers to give out at Brixton Tube station. So as to be inclusive they read: 'If you can breathe, you can meditate.'

'Cows can breathe,' someone said.

'Yes, but they can't read,' I replied.

We gathered mats and cushions for sixty from the Buddhist Centre and drove across town. Maitreyabandhu, with oblong spectacles and his broad clownish smile, set about arranging his most transportable Buddha on a makeshift shrine, while singing *He ain't heavy, he's my Boo-ddha*. He could captivate a room full of strangers straight off the street with his stories and squiggly flip chart drawings of the various states of mind we'd be likely to encounter while meditating. He led the meditation with a woollen shawl drawn around his shoulders for warmth, his long face serious and quiet. Superficially it looks easy to lead meditation. You just chime the bowl-shaped bell to mark off the stages of practice and say a few words. Maitreyabandhu did it with elegance and care, instructing in a spare, poetic style. I wanted to be like him.

During the tea break Kate chatted to Maitreyabandhu and they seemed to be hitting it off. She enjoyed the classes and for a few weeks we could talk about mindfulness of breathing and hindrances to meditation. However, she had no big urge to meditate. Her career was taking shape. That was fine with me. So what that I lived in a Buddhist community?

The first time we split up, my misery pulled us back together. I loved her, I said. Surely love can transcend small matters such as where we live? I was still me and she was still she. But no fairy tale characters from the mythic past could dispel a nebulous feeling that things were not okay.

On the morning before the last night of the meditation course I left a note on her pillow for when she got back from work, telling her she was free. She obviously wanted to move on but was finding it hard to end it. Self respect got the better of me.

She came to the class. At the very end, Maitreyabandhu started up a chant in Pali in his reedy and slightly cracked voice, which meant *May all beings be well and happy*. Everyone circled the shrine chanting, before filing back into the Brixton night. Kate got her coat and shoes and we walked together around the empty lido in a blur of tears. The ritual had made the end the end. I went back in to help pack up cushions and soak up general commiserations from Maitreyabandhu and the others.

The next morning I lay in bed staring at the walls, grief stricken. I was marooned in the community forever with a weird collection of likeable blokes and my conflicting selves. No soft skin to curl up with. I took up smoking with Owen on the roof terrace. We were of one mind on the woes of romantic love.

A few weeks later, I saw a dress in the Buddhist charity shop and thought how much Kate would like it. Suddenly it was all obvious. The editorial colleague! The way she spoke about him. He cared enough about her to get drunk with her. Guys don't idly shove women over, smashing their teeth on the pavement. It was a sign of affection. They were together! She had deserted me for him. And why not? If I'd been a proper Romeo I'd have gone round and knocked the bastard's tooth out. I know which hand would have done the job nicely.

11

MY GURU READS
THE DAILY TELEGRAPH

On one of his visits to London, Sangharakshita –
Bhante – accepted an invitation to dinner at our
community. It would definitely be him this time. We'd
asked him to name our community. I didn't think Bhante
was Enlightened or a Buddha. I did believe he was a lot
further up the road than I was, further than Bob Dylan
even, further than anyone I knew, so I was excited. We all
were.

My working day at this time was a murder trial drama at
the Old Bailey, oddly sandwiched by peaceful mornings of
meditation and the evening sanctuary of the community.
Wherever I was, though, I had to bow a lot, a lot more than
I ever expected. The day Bhante visited was no exception.
It began, as every other day did, with Owen bringing a cup
of tea into my room at 6.35am. Every other day I took tea
to him. The theory was that although we might choose to
lie in on our own account, we would be forced to get up
if we knew the other was expecting tea.

'Morning, mate,' he said, 'it's happened again.'
'What's happened again?' I said, rolling over in bed.
'Morning, mate. Tea's on the desk.'
I squinted at my clock and watched Owen's lumbering

form leave. Getting up at 6.43am gave me just enough time to pull on slack trousers and any old top, sploosh my face in the communal bathroom, perform rudimentary stretching exercises while gulping tea and then gather my meditation accoutrements. At 6.58am I crashed down four flights of ex-fire station stairs, regretting there was no fireman's pole to slide down.

Bow number one happened at 7am just after stepping into the shrine room, which housed a big golden Buddha towards whom all bows were aimed. Once everyone had gathered, someone led the formal salute of the shrine, which ended with bow number two. One doesn't really talk to another chap about the other chap's bow. It's kind of personal. Owen came in trailing a blanket and did his bow, hinging down to forty-five degrees with his chin thrust out, looking forwards at the shrine. The yoga guy did a long, slow bow, his chin nearly touching his knee, sneaking in the opportunity to loosen off his hamstrings. Rhydian, not in his dress, curtailed his effort to little more than a nod. Hands are supposed to be pressed together at the level of the heart, a more pleasing gesture if you have two hands.

I didn't like it too much but it was hard not to go along with everyone else, so I started nodding. It's only a bow, I told myself. I was prepared to bow in church out of politeness. This was a formality, like taking off shoes in a mosque, not meaning much to me. In the Buddhist Centre though, I expected things to mean things. The lower my nods, the more vulnerable I felt.

This morning, though, let's say, I enjoyed the sense of directed brotherhood brought about by the communal bow and sat down on my stool. Flexible brethren sat on a single cushion. One or two managed with a tiny square object which disappeared completely under their buttocks, no thicker than you'd need to re-balance a wobbly table; plonk down and they're done. Casting off into my meditation I often drifted back into a dream image which has withstood thirty minutes of waking life. So as not to nod off entirely I would open my eyes and watch the floor, feeling the air flow in and out of my body.

Thoughts pile up like shingle. I pick at one, review another, replay a third as if puzzling out some enormous issue I can't quite heave into view. I make more effort to observe the actual feeling of my calves, my palms, the indistinct sense of my back being there. It all feels okay, if a bit nothingy. My attention reverts to a fantasy, gainsaying someone or sketching out a future life where I'm widely recognised for my wisdom and compassion. About 7.35am a moment of spaciousness arises. In the stillness and flow of body and breath an image appears – a wide lake on a windless day. Then a fish appears, then lots of fish and I wonder which species of fish and before long I'm scuba diving in Thailand, 9000 miles from the shrine room. I gently place attention back in my body. My awareness is more pliant and a feeling of wholeness arises, though not to the mind-blowing degree experienced on retreat a year earlier.

The final bell at 8am is always a relief, as if my mind secretly prefers chittering away to peacefulness. But so as not to appear too keen to dash for the door, I mindfully gather up my meditation gear, perform bow number three, then tiptoe past those whose meditations are sailing into a second hour.

Upstairs, breakfasts were being prepared. Someone once suggested, as an experiment, eating another community member's breakfast. If he likes cornflakes and toast with marmalade, rather than muesli in warm soy milk followed by rye bread and tahini, you just have to go with it. Being prepared to act beyond personal preferences is an important aspect of community living and Buddhism. Thankfully this suggestion was considered too extreme.

After breakfast I put a suit on and headed to the Tube.

It was going to be murder today.

The bell rang in the basement of the Old Bailey. The jury were coming back on a trial I'd been following for two weeks. The defendant was a blond athletic-looking Australian guy, twenty-eight, in London on his gap year. He'd been working as a barman in a pub and become friendly with the landlady, even staying over with her family at Christmas. A few weeks after he left his employment at the pub, on a night when he knew the safe was full of takings, the prosecution alleged he snuck back. Unfortunately the landlady woke up and cornered him.

Notebook in hand, I pushed through the court's swing door and gave a bow to the Bench, to Justice incarnate in the form of the judge. This was definitely more of a nod bow, with hands held respectfully together just below the navel. Anyone entering the well of the court must bow. I squashed next to a reporter from the Press Association. Behind us sat the most hard-bitten hack in the office, an old guy with watery eyes and bifocals, who had a regular by-line with the *News of the Screws*. He composed his stories in six or seven words with Zen-like economy using a blunt pencil in the margin of the daily court listing. 'Little battler', he called the landlady, borrowing a phrase from the prosecution QC.

They tussled, the Aussie's balaclava was pulled off and he then hit her with a rolling pin and stabbed her in the neck. There was a DNA match on the rolling pin and balaclava. They were lovers, he claimed. He'd gone there for amorous purposes and found her already dead. The defence pointed the finger at another boyfriend who was prowling the vicinity in a jealous state of mind on the night of the murder.

The jury came in. The room was compressed with the tension. Three hours earlier I'd been wrapped in a blanket enjoying the peaceful vision of a lake; now my breath was squeezed and shallow and my fingers were going numb. The defendant was brought up from the cells. He was a few yards away from me, ashen and impassive, looking ordinary like most murderers. I looked down at my shoes, feeling guilty for being there. Ushers ushered bits of paper. QCs pretended to be busy with post-it notes. Journalists scanned the gallery for family, victim's relatives, titbits.

The shuffling settled, the foreman stood up and the usual formula began:

'. . . on the charge of murder do you find the defendant guilty or not guilty?'

'Guilty.'

The tension broke, the room exhaled.

'Rot in hell,' someone shouted from the gallery. There's more belief in heaven and hell than you'd think and the courtroom brings it out. A curse from the depths. I scribbled away with adrenaline pumping, elbow to elbow with the other hacks as the judge restored order and moved straight to a sentence of life imprisonment.

'I'm running with "showed no emotion",' said the guy from the *Standard* as we bowed and left the court.

'They'll have him on watch down in the cells,' the *Screws* man said, brushing past.

'Suicide?' I asked.

'Of course. Callous bastard. I'm off.'

I saw many killers at the Old Bailey. Armed robbers had the most threatening vibe. When an arms dealer went down I understood why people use the expression *throw away the key*. Easy to talk about compassion. Sometimes I felt sick with the reality of it. Evil is evil. Suffering is suffering. Justice is a real thing and it needs to be done. Newspapers call some of them 'monsters', especially the rapists. The Buddha practised compassion in all circumstances, it is said. The courtroom gave me more imagination for how profound and difficult that must be. The Aussie guy was not in the monster category. His traits were states I knew: greed, shame, fear, stupidity. He didn't seem fundamentally different from me. The landlady had unmasked him, he'd killed her and now he was unmasked in front of everyone. It troubled me that he'd left the pub with £2,500 and spent it. I couldn't relate to that.

Whatever larger light Dostoyevsky might have shone on this pathetic act, I had 800 words and fifteen minutes, not 800 pages and three years in a dacha. I had to get the story out before anyone else, my little hand pecking at the left side of the keyboard as fast as it could. The nationals would pick this up, and the Aussie press. It wasn't a grubby little stabbing in Peckham. He'd be in his mid-forties before parole was considered. I winged it over to the editor who checked it, tweaked it and banged it out. At 4.30pm, after at least four more bows in the afternoon court session, I headed back to the community.

My first scoop

When Bhante came into the community dining room, spot on time, we all stood up and I felt an urge to bow which I held in check. The embarrassing reflex came instinctively, not like bowing to a Buddha statue or the judiciary just because everyone else does. He was a medium-sized man, a little portly, wearing a grey jumper. There was nothing that unusual: a rather large straight nose and thin lips on which played the trace of a smile. None of the beads and mysticism implied by the term guru, which was a term he didn't like. He said gurus who made claims to Enlightenment tended to suck in the most credulous.

Bhante was on a diet regulating his carbs-to-protein ratio, which basically meant having more tofu. He was ushered to a chair. I squeezed in next to him, keeping my elbows in when reaching for the condiments – engevita, tahini, soy sauce – watching Bhante out of the corner of my eye. His movements were minimal and stately. He chewed slowly. He didn't do much with his facial expression – no laughs or reassuring smiles and glances. We ate in silence, holding back our usual ping pong of banter.

Before dessert Bhante asked how things were going at the gift shop and had anyone been to see anything interesting lately? One by one my community fellows disclosed previously undisclosed tastes for opera, Schopenhauer's philosophy, and some remarkable insights gleaned at the latest Caravaggio retrospective. No-one mentioned how we'd recently wheeled out the communal telly to watch the

FA Cup. In reply, Bhante, unhurried and steady of speech, touched on Plato, Renaissance literature, modern and ancient poetry, painting and current affairs. We were in the company of a truly great conversationalist. It was wasted on us – we were never going to read the commentaries on Thucydides to which he directed our attention. Buddhism was hardly mentioned.

Dessert was a tofu cheesecake made by someone's mum.

Although Bhante looked ordinary, he clearly wasn't. The Buddha described a true monk as someone mindful enough to be aware of what his hands and feet are doing all the time. Bhante didn't flap about like most people. He was bizarre, in a neat and normal way, but I didn't agree with the guy who insisted afterwards that Bhante had seen through to his innermost being. Bhante had enquired what the guy did for living, that was all.

'And what do *you* do for a living?' he asked me.

'I'm a . . . journalist,' I said, thinking nervously about the *Guardian* article.

'We had better watch what we say, huh,' he said, smiling, his big eyes flashing with warmth and humour. 'Huh' was a verbal tick, a slightly inflected upbeat to end a sentence; not quite enough, when written in print, to merit an exclamation mark. His accent, like a lot else about him, was hard to locate – a school teacherly diction, but softer, more musical, with emphasis on odd parts of the sentence. I could imagine him reading *Little Red Riding Hood* and doing the scary bits really well.

'David got his first scoop today, Bhante,' someone mentioned.

'And what, may we ask, was the *scoop*?' Bhante asked.

I explained how the day before I'd been at an inquest about a Harrow schoolboy who got drunk on his father's tequila and fell out of the window to his death five storeys below. There were no other journalists in court, so my copy was taken up by the *Daily Telegraph*.

'Oh yes, I read that,' Bhante said.

'You read the *Daily Telegraph*?' I asked, astounded.

'I have to say I did wonder why it was that his parents hadn't gone to the trouble of getting a more secure drinks cabinet, huh.'

He was spot on. The sub-editor had cut out the coroner's remark about the parents not putting a lock on the drinks cabinet, given that their son had raided it before. How did Bhante find time to wade through the *DT*, let alone remember a story which got a few column inches on page 8? I thought he was supposed to spend the day meditating and running a worldwide Buddhist movement, whatever that entails. I'd totally trumped the other guys and their operatic tastes. While I'd been sitting on the Tube that morning reading Bhante, he had been sitting at home reading me. I polished off my lemon cake trying not to look smug.

Before he left he named our community Navasamaya, which meant 'new bond'. We dedicated our efforts to the happiness of all beings with a short ceremony. I can't remember if it involved any more bowing but it probably did. Afterwards, as Bhante stood by the window posing for a photograph, I noticed a strange white light emanating from the crown of his head. I blinked in disbelief at what I was seeing. He moved slightly to reveal the aircraft warning light flashing on top of Canary Wharf.

12

FUNNY TEETH

Nanna stood at the kitchen window rolling up bits of lard for Robby the Robin, who was hopping impatiently on the ledge. She was in her eighties, hunched from osteoporosis, with red, papery forefingers bent sideways at the last knuckle and hair done up with auburn tints. She was pleased I was pursuing Buddhism. 'First the Mahayana, then Zen, then finally . . . the Tao.' This was the correct order in which to pursue Eastern ideas, Nanna once told me. Grandpa must have said it. She put the kettle on while I joined Uncle Howard, who was reading Krishnamurti at the breakfast table under a philosophical sweep of wiry hair.

Nanna came through with the teapot.

'Is that Sangharak-sheeta still about?'

I was startled. I'd never mentioned this name to anyone in my family in case they looked him up and found the *Guardian* article.

'Sangharakshita?' I said.

'Yes, I remember him,' Nanna said. 'He had funny teeth.'

Uncle Howard looked up from his book.

'Oh yes, Sangharak-sheeta, how is he? Been meaning to ask.'

'You've heard of Sangharakshita?'

'Oh yes, he came round when I was a boy,' Howard said.

'To *this* house?'

'They were dreadful,' Nanna said.

'What were?'

'His teeth. All yellow, with awful, horrid gaps.'

'It's true, his teeth were bad,' Howard said.

Sangharakshita had spoken at the Cheam Eastern Philosophy Group, which met upstairs. Forty years ago he had brushed past the breakfast table in his robes. Mum, Nanna, Howard – they had all met him long before I did. Grandpa must have met him at the Buddhist Society. The visit had been a 'coup' for the group, Howard said, as he was the senior Buddhist of the day in the UK.

Nanna led the way to Mum's old bedroom in the attic in search of a record of the event. Grandpa never threw anything away. In an eaves cupboard was a box of handwritten notes and old papers, including a dusty, typeset journal from 1978. On the front was a picture of the Old Fire Station, celebrating the day it re-opened as the London Buddhist Centre. In my mother's old bedroom, I'd found a picture of my current bedroom window. Nanna showed me an article by an Order member about communication exercises where Grandpa had underlined bits and added notes in the margin.

'I've done these,' I said, recalling the weird gazing exercise with Maitreyabandhu, still in disbelief about all these revelations.

'Grandpa used to like them,' Howard said. 'He'd make us look down a cardboard tube at each other. All you could see was a disembodied eye peering back at you. It was an existential encounter between I and Thou.'

Existential encounters between I and Thou were exactly the sort of thing that set Dad off with his hooting laugh. Having to look after me had given my parents an excuse to stop attending the group.

There were more newsletters and news clippings in the box, one about Sangharakshita officiating at the first Buddhist ordination of a woman in the UK. Grandpa had corrected the journalist's Sanskrit with a biro. Nanna eventually found the record of the group's meetings, which spanned fifteen years. Mum had written the entries in her best calligraphy. It was a potpourri: Taoism, Vedanta, Zen, then a quick romp through the Upanishads.

At the entry for Easter 1965 there it was: a photo of Bhante in his monk's robe, grinning in my grandparents' front garden. Thin and bespectacled, he gave the overall impression of a happy librarian in sandals. He was flanked by two lay followers from the Hampstead Vihara, Ruth Walshe and her husband Maurice, a great translator of Pali Canon (including no doubt many texts on loving kindness) who in a few short years would be openly loathing Sangharakshita.

Mum had drawn the outline of a meditator in ink and written: *Visit of the Venerable Sthavira Sangharakshita. Subject: Anatman.*

Sangharakshita's account of his journeys in India and the Himalayas, his meetings with Bhutanese royalty, Sikkimese maharajas, the Dalai Lama and Pandit Nehru had always seemed a bit like a myth to me, but his visit to the Cheam house was truly unbelievable. My mother met Sangharakshita before I was born. She had never told me, but why would she? It meant nothing to her. Yet I was born into a family where I was very likely to hear about Buddhist teachings and I pondered the meaning of that, wondering if it was karma or poppycock.

For Mum, Sangharakshita was another Eastern intrusion into her life, which did nothing to break the fundamental boredom. She and Howard weren't allowed to go upstairs to the Meetings Room to hear the talk. Sangharak-sheeta – Nanna always said it like that – spoke about Anatman, the doctrine of No Self. Vishnu, the old Indian man who used to bring them sweets, was there too. Grandpa had asked him to oppose Sangharakshita with the Hindu position of Self or Atman. From the cold hallway downstairs they could hear Vishnu shouting. His arms flailed about when he argued about profound topics. Sangharakshita was giving as good as he got, Howard recalled.

'I'm not sure who won,' he said.

Nanna didn't know either.

'Don't they have dentists in India?' she asked.

Nanna had spent marginally more time in the presence of my Buddhist teacher than I had, and all she remembered were his teeth. Self or No Self, it seemed they had had a fine afternoon of Hinduism versus Buddhism, followed by handshakes and a photo on the front lawn. Grandpa never met him again, as far as I know.

Buddhism is a lousy career choice

Sangharakshita went to many such meetings around this time and reports on occasion being driven to tears of frustration by the narrowly intellectual approach he was met with. It was hard to convey the spirit of Buddhism, or the inner meaning of mantras, to the tea-and-biscuits folk who met in the living room in places like Cheam. Eventually

Sangharakshita's teeth were rescued by Western dentistry and he started a new Buddhist order and movement in the Summer of Love. The Order grew. Punk rock happened, rubbish strikes, unemployment, Maggie Thatcher. Every year men and women went on a long retreat in Spain or Italy, returning as Order members with funny Middle Earth-sounding names. The names were part of it. Aragorn son of Arathorn wouldn't have got through the Paths of the Dead with a name like Kevin.

One of the re-named was Ratnaghosha, who grew up in poor rural Ireland in the nineteen-fifties, with hand-me-down clothes from his seven siblings. His job was to thin the beet, weed the potato drills and fetch wood with the donkey. He was shy and liked to read quietly at the back of the church. On Good Friday, at three o'clock, the sky seemed to actually darken, he said. In those times, finding out what Protestants believed was as hard as finding out about sex, but there was less incentive. He'd assumed his was a miserable Catholic childhood, he told me, until the fourth time he told his life story at the community, when he started to recognise it was much happier than he'd realised. He was now Chair of the London Buddhist Centre, with a boyish quiff, a beard and blue-green eyes. To me he was as wise as Gandalf, but closer in size to a hobbit. One morning after meditation he asked if I would like to be the fundraiser for a new retreat centre.

Career ambition, to the Buddhists I knew, was viewed like a heavy cold: if one waited patiently enough, it too would pass. But to me, being a fundraiser sounded more pivotal and important than working in essential oils at the gift shop. I said I'd think about it, knowing at once that I'd say yes.

I'd heard enough macabre stories for a lifetime. I'd recently written up the tale of a south London pizza shop owner who tried to cover over the evidence of an after-hours knife attack he 'launched' on a rival pizza shop franchisee by pouring tomato paste over the floor and hoping the cleaner would mop it all up with the blood. The next part of his plan was to bundle the body into a wheelie bin and push it down the high street to his hatchback. The defendant then cut it up like pepperoni and spent an utterly shocking fortnight trying to dispose of bits of the body at various locations in the north of England. An arm was found in a bag in the woods, part of the head by a tennis court.

After the verdict I followed the old reporter from the *News of the Screws* as he plodded, heavy-shouldered, into the lift back to the newsroom. He was a master of the seedy story. I told him enthusiastically about the retreats we could run with a bigger retreat centre and how I could work with my friends if I stopped working at the Old Bailey. He took off his glasses and gave me a soft, rueful look:

'You made a good decision. Best off out of a bad business.'

Even though I retained a veneer of journalistic neutrality when musing over the value of what normal people were doing with their lives, nothing seemed half as significant or exciting as the Order. Free from the need to uphold any cultural or religious form of practice from the Buddhist East, the Order was searching for an authentic and new Buddhist culture amid the spiritual and artistic heritage of the West. I swapped the Old Bailey for the Old Fire Station.

Without Kate to visit, the Buddhist Centre was becoming my whole world. The morning commute was four flights

down to the basement where the coal used to be kept. It
was an office, cushion store, workshop and general hovel, all
in one. The fire escape was behind a cupboard, up a metal
ladder and through a locked iron grill. Houdini would have
struggled to get out if the photocopier had caught fire. There
were six of us on the Centre team. As well as fundraising,
I did book-keeping and one morning a week on reception.

Jnanavaca, pronounced with a soft *gnana* as in gnocchi,
followed by *varcher*, was the Treasurer. His name meant He
Who Speaks the Truth. Born in Kenya, of Indian descent,
he was a slender man with wide soft ears, as big as the wings
of a small bat. After studying physics at Oxford, Jnanavaca
worked in management at Marks & Spencer, then quit to
move into a community with Maitreyabandhu. I loved his
talks about how the world view emerging from physics
coincides with the Buddha's world view. I was head down
at my desk composing an email about a fundraising walk
for the new retreat centre when a rubber band whizzed
past my ear. I looked up. Jnanavaca at the desk opposite
was gazing innocently at spreadsheets, over the remains
of an almond croissant. I went back to my email. Another
rubber band brushed past, followed by a rapid, high pitched
burst of laughter. It was a wondrous noise, as might issue
from a startled game bird.

'Someone has been spending too much on rubber bands,'
Jnanavaca said.

'I'm glad we've someone from M&S in charge of the
money,' I replied. 'It's a reassuring brand.'

'By the way, I've got the employment contracts sorted
out, you'll be pleased to hear. Yours is here if you want to
take a look . . . I've had to make up a job title, I'm afraid,'

he said, leafing through his in-tray and passing over my contract. New regulations required job descriptions and contract terms to be in writing.

'Office Boy?'

More rapid-fire laughter.

'What, you don't like it? I thought it might be good for you. We don't want your ego playing up too much do we?'

'And what are you down as, Chief Croissant Buyer?'

Order members like Jnanavaca, Maitreyabandhu and many others I knew believed in a loving and intense version of friendship. Whether I was on a retreat in Scotland, visiting the Birmingham Buddhist Centre or hanging out with a community of Order members on a remote Spanish mountain, this spirit of friendship was everywhere to varying degrees. On retreats it was common to pair off and go for long walks and intense discussions, like Romantic poets meeting in the Lake District. Even in the depths of the countryside, Jnanavaca had an adaptive instinct for where to find a decent coffee and cake.

Jnanavaca, Ratnaghosha and Maitreyabandhu were friends to dozens of people in the community, giving generously of their time and attention. The Buddhist Centre was alive with the friendliness generated by their friendliness. Bhante had been the exemplar, meeting streams of people for decades, writing thousands of letters, giving and receiving thousands of tokens of affection. He thought friends should really matter to each other. We were encouraged to rejoice in each other's good qualities and to speak well of each other behind each other's backs.

Bhante's view was that men often failed to develop emotionally open friendships with other men because they hadn't got over a latent fear of homosexuality. In the Sangha, gay and straight men became close friends, living together in communities and sometimes sharing rooms. On the physical level men could be tactile and affectionate with other men; usually nothing heavy or too awkward, just subtle things, indicating closeness and care. I preferred the heterosexual back-slapping type of camaraderie but stretching myself a little seemed all good and fine. In the past, though, Bhante and some Order members had discussed whether actual homosexual activity may be beneficial for friendships between men. I was glad this line of enquiry seemed to have been dropped.

Bhante still maintained there was an 'erotic charge' to friendship. I found that term a bit scary, but for sure I was strongly attracted to Jnanavaca. I went to him with my doubts and difficulties and he listened attentively. It wasn't like talking about my emotions to a girlfriend. In that instance there was usually a motive force towards sex. Jnanavaca offered a kind, open perspective. I did sometimes fear our closeness might imply sex in some way. There was a giddy feeling that the boundary between us would dissolve. Was this the 'erotic charge' of friendship? Probably. If an image of sex with a man came into my head I shut it out as soon as I could. It made me cringe, like I cringed at salad cream when I was a boy. How could anyone like that stuff?

Whatever the meaning of it all, in Jnanavaca's presence I lit up with happiness. As we walked around the local park he once said my life seemed mainly to have been lived in the 'god realm' – happy, un-complex and blessed with good parents.

'You seem to have a basic positivity from all this, but I wonder if your missing hand has been the factor which gave you just enough suffering to push you onto the spiritual path?'

'Maybe. I don't know,' I replied.

I was resistant to the idea that I was a Buddhist because of my missing hand.

'It's not the only factor, I'm just saying, but without it you might have been a lawyer by now.'

'Thank God for my missing hand.'

13

THE MIDDLE WAY

I spent the Christmas before the new Millennium at home. Christmas was a crunch point for Mum. She had a low opinion of anyone retreating from family at that time of year and made noises of disappointment and disapproval that were hard to bear if ever I mentioned going on the community winter retreat. I enjoyed the hullabaloo of presents and games, but there was something special about Christmas time on retreat, something about which I'm fairly sure Christ would have approved. I didn't tell my parents that with whatever consciousness was left for me after a long day of mince pies and stollen cake, I was brewing up a decision to start the next thousand years by requesting to join the Order.

Back in London, I had no New Millennium party invites. I banged on bedroom doors down the corridor looking for someone to head out with to see the fireworks, but most were still on retreat. Owen was lying on his mattress looking tousled and melancholic, with a Coleridge biography spread out on his chest.

'Nah, I'm knackered, I think I'll stay in,' he said.

'Come on, let's go down to Tower Bridge.'

'Mate, I'm knackered. Sales have been mad at the shop. You wouldn't believe the stuff we've shifted.'

'This isn't a boring end of the century party, you know,'
I said.

'I'm going to do a Tara puja later if you want to join me.'

'Oh Jesus! Tara can wait, can't she?'

'Nah, you go and enjoy yourself.'

Owen was impossible to budge, so I tagged along with
some people I knew vaguely. The fireworks looked better
on TV. None of this mattered greatly, because on the
second day of the Millennium I was going to Nepal. Retreat
allowance topped up with savings was just enough for a few
weeks trekking. I'd packed some posh calligraphy paper
and resolved by the end of the trip to write my request
for Ordination on it. The Himalayas, I hoped, would tower
over my doubts.

In Kathmandu I met up with a friend from college. Before
our trek we visited a palace where they kept a Buddhist
princess – a teenage girl who came out trussed up for tourists
every hour on the hour, like a cuckoo clock. I wasn't sure
that locking up a young girl was very Buddhist and didn't feel
too allured all round by the aroma of Nepalese Buddhism-
cum-Hinduism. But no matter, I wasn't becoming Tibetan,
Nepalese or Burmese and needn't associate with any fanciful
folklore. I was safe from all that, part of the rational Western
world where the ultimate explanatory theory runs that there
was once a Big Bang and everyone tells their kids Santa
comes down the chimney to drink sherry. On the wall of
the princess's palace I spotted a mythologically perfect post
box in which to drop off my letter requesting ordination,
should I find the courage to write it.

I was allowing my little hand to be more on public view
than back home. In England if I notice, say, a woman

watching me use my stump to open a train door, I feel exposed to the thoughts I imagine she might be having. Disability is a social signifier that seems to trump whatever place one occupies in the British class system, and not usually in a good way. Conversely, I didn't give a stuff what a Nepali person thought, as the Nepalis are outside of my class consciousness and they don't have the power to demote me. In the middle of a busy street an elderly man took hold of my stump and turned it over to inspect both sides, like he'd found an interesting stone on the beach.

'I'm very sorry,' he said.

'Thanks,' I said, taken aback by the sincerity of his commiseration.

No-one had ever said that before.

As we picked our way along narrow, dark alleys, I kept to the travellers' mantras about avoiding uncooked food and not looking at beggars in case they follow. Due to leprosy there were lots of curtailed limbs on view and I soon discovered mine had talismanic properties. Seeing a Westerner with a disability made some beggars quite jolly. I became a person and not just a money pot. The leper who squatted outside our hostel held out his two stumps each time I passed for a low down hi-five. It felt unsporting not to oblige him merely for fear of catching leprosy. Maybe he thought I was a fellow leper. The physical similarity between us only highlighted the ways in which my life was unimaginably different to that of a limbless, outcast street beggar.

I was reminded of my childhood football hero, Glenn Hoddle, who had recently suggested that all disabled people were alike in suffering the consequences of karma from a former lifetime. Most commentators considered this an offensive and stupid view – stupid to believe in former lifetimes and even stupider to believe you could be penalised for crimes carried out in a different strip. I once saw Glenn playing an exhibition match against Sutton United. The way he caught high balls and flicked them across the pitch was like magic. Why, though, did anyone expect metaphysical clarity from a midfielder?

I guess the board of the FA came down hard on Glenn because they were aware that taking the doctrine of karma as a total explanation of why things happen to us leads to fatalism and social apathy. Why should we adapt football stadiums for wheelchair users if they brought it all on themselves? Glenn was sacked as England manager, but he wouldn't have been treated so roughly by the Nepali FA. All over the East a similar view about karma pops up, not just among Hindus but among Buddhists too. Mainstream Buddhism, though, is more nuanced. The law of karma describes how our actions (karma) are experienced in terms of inner and outer effects (vipaka). Karma is not action viewed externally. It refers to the state of mind out of which an action arises and which gives the action its character. States of mind include the whole flow of more or less conscious plans, schemes, attitudes and ideas with which we bicycle through life and which motivate our behaviour. The inner effect of our violent or meanly motivated actions is always eventually felt by us as unhappiness or some kind of pain. *Scrooge* is the teaching on karma we get as children. Scrooge was not a happy sort, even if he got a bit of pleasure from his meanness. His actions affected how people treated him, the kind of world he lived in and probably his physical health too if Dickens had gone into his ulcers. Then he changed his ways. . . we all know the story.

However, if Scrooge had been hit by pigeon poo, it wouldn't be easy to say it was to do with his miserliness. That's the magical thinking of a child. Wisely reflecting on how pigeons have to shit when pigeons have to shit, leads to a happier frame of mind. Maybe the superstition that being struck by bird droppings is 'good luck' guards us from taking it as a personal insult from the universe. It's a short cut if we don't have time to think it all through, and arrive at a balanced position that recognises both the existence of an inherently ethical structure to human experience, and non-ethical laws applicable to being hit with bird poo.

It's more likely that my disability resulted from a blocked blood vessel in the first trimester than because I was a bit light-fingered last time round. Most of the time I didn't consider karma much. If anyone it was Grandpa, not Scrooge, who gave me a proper lesson on karma: seeming clever and appearing to know stuff, while over the years underlying mental states funnel one into a kind of emotional trap. I registered that as a possibility for me.

Some Buddhists muddy the waters by saying that our karma causes us to be born in the first place, so *whatever* happens from then on can, in a wider sense, be laid at our door. Born into a world with birds, we are subject to their offerings. The subtle teaching here is: whatever happens to you, however it happens, try to look after the way you respond. Raging against pigeons will only create more suffering. Karma is a doctrine that gets more mysterious the more we allow the universe to be mysterious. Ultimately the Buddha pointed to an immeasurable freedom, beyond mere happiness, that arises when we have decisively seen through the tightly held delusion that we are a fixed self in a really existent and fixed external world. Then we can laugh at what lands on us because there's nothing left to defend.

First there is a mountain

Our trek took us up the steep gorge of the Kali Gandhaki river and around the Annapurna mountain range. The sand-filled wind rarely let up, blowing through glass-less window frames into rooms with no electric light. Occasionally we passed a grit-covered villager selling souvenirs. I stood aside feeling embarrassed while my companion, a film maker quite advanced into the alpha spectrum, drove home deals to save me 50p on a yak's wool blanket.

At a rundown temple my strengths came to the fore and I told him everything I knew about Tsongkhapa and the Yellow Hats, and the yogi poet Milarepa. A boy monk, coughing, filthy as a chimney sweep, pointed us to blackened wall hangings of gurus and their assembled lineages, all the while wiping his runny nose on the sleeve of his robe. There were Wheels of Life depicting the various heavens and hells and middling states into which one could be born again and again.

Behind the temple, high up the side of the valley, was a steep graveyard. As we wandered around the piles of stones marking each grave I felt the quiet but uneasy smugness about being alive that I often get in graveyards. Death didn't look too promising, even though Tibetan and Nepalese Buddhists conceive it as an opportunity to make spiritual progress. My ideas about it hadn't moved on much from when I was eight years old and looking out of my bedroom window into the garden at my fallen bicycle and Sandy the dog chewing on his branch: death imagined as a blank hole where once there was stuff, or an endlessly long period of boredom.

Oddly enough, in my kind of nihilism I'm still in the picture somewhere, having an experience of nothing. If I make a more thorough effort to completely blot myself out, then being dead is potentially not so dreadful an experience because it's not actually an experience. All consciousness stops, therefore all experience stops. The expanse of time after my death need not bother me any more than the dinosaur period, which I can calmly survey without a trace of concern that I was, apparently, equally dead back then. There will be no endless desert of time and space to trudge across, there will be Nothing.

Each morning I'd meditate as the sun emerged in streaks of pink and orange on the snowy ridges above. In London meditation was a good way of dealing with the fizzy hangover from over-exposure to entertainment, news and advertising. There was none of that here. My thoughts circled back to me in the middle of my seemingly separate little world. When we were out walking, the bliss of fatigue made me happy and carefree.

On narrow planked ropeways we criss-crossed over gorges and soon we were up on the Tibetan plateau, surrounded by the hugeness of rock and earth and clean horizon lines. On the level stretches of moonlike landscape I dropped behind my friend and thought about what I was doing. Entering the Order wasn't just about enjoying new facilities. It was a doorway into a living myth. Doorways into myths don't open up too often and I felt that I had to cast aside doubt and stride through.

My doubt about ordination was that although the Buddhist community seemed like a place where I was unlikely to make a total mess of my life, I worried it lacked something. The lives of committed practitioners scared me. They lived in communities for ten or twenty years, went on retreats three or four times a year, had little wealth and usually no children. I concluded that for reasons of artistic freedom Bob Dylan would advise me not to join a Buddhist Order. Though when he was born again as a Christian he did claim a person either has faith or unbelief – 'and there ain't no neutral ground'. We can sit on the fence about life but it makes no difference; our actions are continually drifting us towards a heaven or a hell of our own making.

Requesting to join the Order would be sticking two fingers up at my nihilism. However, I'd spent so long kneeling at that shrine, lapping up its promise of complete obliteration and utter meaninglessness, that Nothing-after-death seemed like a scientific fact, as plain as the barren escarpments between which we walked. Nihilism is also easier than thinking through complicated Buddhist ideas; one stroke and you're done with the whole thing. You can put your metaphysical feet up. The Buddha called nihilism an extreme view, a mere belief. No-one ever experiences Nothing. We imagine Nothing-after-death and then call it a fact. The Buddha also said that imagining an ultimate Something (e.g. God or Self) existing forever outside (or behind or within) the world of particular things, like knives and forks and people, is an extreme view too. Our demand that things either be existent or non-existent is more than a philosophical error; it's an ingrained wrong way of perceiving reality.

To be a Buddhist was to try to walk the Middle Way between existence and non-existence. It sounded pretty cool put like that. Buddhist meditation was supposed to loosen up our inherited metaphysical certainties, particularly about ourselves. Dharma practice changes consciousness so much that even basic beliefs, that most people would not consider a belief, or consider at all, come into question. Such as, is there an inside and an outside to experience? Is awareness (mind) essentially different to or separable from what one is aware of (world)?

Our path to the top of the Annapurna circuit was dotted with stupas here and there, conical white monuments shaped a bit like wine bottles. I explained to my friend how they symbolise the elements that come together to constitute a life and then dissolve. The traditional Buddhist view, roughly speaking, is that consciousness – which we misunderstand while we are alive – carries on, a bit like how a patient wakes up after the operation with no sense that time has passed. Only the patient now has no body, which is so bewildering for most 'people' that they soon take new birth in a situation which has some connection and correlation with their strongest habits of mind. For the Buddhists in Nepal the fact of death is made less meaningless by belief in the onward journey. Prayers are offered for a good passage to the next life.

Bhante was aware that rebirth was a tough one for some Westerners, even committed Buddhists, and that a delicate line needed to be taken. It can be hard for us to conceive of life, spiritual or otherwise, as having any kind of good, post-death outcome. Like Prospero said, our little lives are rounded by a sleep. As the Christian ways of connecting our little story to the bigger story of God's creation got weaker and weaker, it was replaced by a materialist story, which for all its wonders, demotes us to a collection of amino acids, driven blindly on by evolutionary forces. When we die we leave not a rack behind. We have no easy or consoling way of feeling part of something greater than ourselves. Bhante said Order members didn't have to believe in an idea like rebirth in a literal way, but neither should they reject it out of hand. Once when an Order member asked what happens when a person dies, Bhante opted for pragmatism: 'You'll soon find out.'

To me, the doctrine of rebirth wasn't that comforting even if I believed it. After all, rebirth didn't mean that I *personally* would be reborn, hopefully in slightly better packaging next time. Buddhists often say a person is a flux, a stream of psycho-physical energy, or some such soulless sounding phrase. The Buddha himself taught that a person has no ultimate existence and, despite our firm conviction otherwise, cannot finally be found anywhere. To say 'I was born in 1974' is conventionally true but ultimately not how it is. 'I' had no concept of 'I' until about 1978 and I've shed my body many times since then. Some people report remembering previous lives, but could it make any ultimate sense to say that they actually *were* that person? We are like Trig's favourite old broom in *Only Fools and Horses*, the one that over the years had been given fourteen new handles and seventeen new heads. The trouble for me with all this type of thinking is that once I deconstruct the notion of a person, nihilism swishes back in. If there's no ultimately existing person, then surely there must be Nothing. Yet according to Buddhism, there's 'no person' right now and all this is not Nothing, is it? Transcending dualities is steep work.

To stick up for Glenn Hoddle, I wouldn't need to take his statement personally because even if my disability was because of something done in a previous life, that person wasn't really *me* as I conceive myself now. It was some other rascal. I'm not personally identified with past historic patches of the flow of events. Should someone claim I was ugly in a previous life it wouldn't bother me that much, unless their intention was to point out that nothing has changed. In the end I guess Glenn had to go. The inter-relation between the karmic doctrine of taking personal responsibility for the state of one's being and the doctrine of the ultimate emptiness of personhood was probably too much for the Football Association to factor in. Great sages from the East have fallen at the same fence.

Thankfully Bhante said it was enough to set out with the feeling of 'provisionally' being a Buddhist, rather than having to sort out the metaphysics of the cosmos first. I could ask for ordination even though my car still veered towards the blank Nothing end of the spectrum if ever I took my hands off the wheel. But it was important, Bhante also said, to have some provisional sense of faith in the *possibility* of transcending subject-object consciousness and to develop an imagination for the archetypal Buddha figures, which embody the desirable qualities that flow from Awakening. However nascent or vague this confidence or faith, for a Buddhist the most important thing was then to orient one's life to the Three Jewels: to the Buddha, to his Dharma and to the Sangha. This act, Bhante asserted, formally known as Going For Refuge, unites all schools of Buddhism throughout the ages. According to him, it can take place on progressively deeper levels:

> One – Cultural Going For Refuge – doing merely what your Buddhist culture does.
> Two – Provisional Going For Refuge – definitely interested, toe in the water.
> Three – Effective Going For Refuge – a mature, psychological commitment.
> Four – Real Going For Refuge – direct understanding of how things are.
> Five – Absolute Going For Refuge – what the Universe is up to, generally.

Bhante ordained a person when he thought they had made an effective commitment to orient their lives to the Three Jewels. Ordination was not about adopting a particular lifestyle, like being a monk or a hermit. Provisional feelings of sympathy for Buddhism had resolved into a practical and heartfelt determination to bring these ideals to life as much as possible, in harmony with teachers and friends. If this commitment was carried out sincerely and for long enough, then Bhante said it was within the grasp of all Order members to penetrate the inner meaning of the teachings to some degree or other – that is, Real Going For Refuge.

The Buddha called his teachings a raft, a way to cross the river, rather than a dogma to cling to for its own sake. The other shore is wisdom, and wisdom alone frees a person from the whole fearful structure of being a being heading for death. I found the idea that Buddhism was a raft pleasing, but when I asked the surrounding mountains for their view about joining the Order as a raft, they said my life was so short it hardly mattered what I did. Rebirth is nonsense, they went on, religion merely consolation for the impoverished and dusty lives people endure up here. I often get that sort of response when I try speak-to-nature exercises; nature turns out to be a misery guts.

On the goat-less track

At the end of the trek I hadn't decided anything. I didn't need religion as much as I needed the *Rough Guide*. My friend flew home, leaving me a final day on my own, so I took a bus to the weekly livestock slaughter at a shrine twenty miles south of Kathmandhu. The *Rough Guide* said it was good. The bus was crammed with worshippers, goats and traumatised roosters sliding around in the hold. At each turn down the steep valley the outside wheel appeared to be airborne.

The shrine of Black Kali was down in a shaded area of the valley. As a non-Hindu I wasn't allowed in the temple precinct, though as it was roofless proceedings could be viewed from above. The mood was jolly enough, combining open-air abattoir with family picnic. When families got to the front they threw rice at a carved stone image of Kali, slipped the butcher a few rupees, then gave over their unfortunate creature. Blood washed the temple floor and carcasses were delivered into a surrounding industry of stripping, cutting and boiling. Stall holders piled up guts and little mounds of eyeballs, or testicles. I didn't like it much, but nothing was wasted and it was probably better to have it out in the open than the secret abattoir hell realms that I'd never even seen back home, to which the UK *Rough Guide* does not direct tourists.

As I walked up a goat track and away from the temple, I was, however, quite glad to put some distance between me and the carnage. At a food stall halfway up the valley my appetite returned. Suddenly I knew this was the moment to write the letter. The picnic with Black Kali the Destroyer had given me a jolt: all my thinking was delaying me from doing what I had already decided to do. It was now or never in terms of my journey to the East. I ordered potato pancakes, laid out my special piece of paper and dug out my bundle of biros.

Children crowded round, giggling at the bearded one-handed white man in shades. Children can always be relied on for honest feedback about my hand. They make noises of disgust or stand stock still and order me to open my fingers. When I tell them I can't they look back and forth between me and the stump, computing the possibility that I'm tricking. The bolder ones touch it to see if the fingers are curled up in some clever way. They repeat this several times until doubt is banished. One kid told me I had a pig's trotter. Meanwhile parents hover nervously in the background, unsure of the protocol.

Letter done, I dished out remaining biros and walked on up the goat-less goat track, out of the shaded valley and into bright sunlight and fields full of yellow rice flowers. Paths laced through the paddies towards a hill which from afar seemed to be completely covered with giant cobwebs. In fact they were thousands of prayer flags strung from tree to tree. This was Padmasambhava Hill, a place where in history or legend Padmasambhava once stayed in a cave on his journey to bring the Buddha's teaching to the barbarian lands of Tibet. The cave was little more than a crevice. I gave in to a hawker who was keen to roll out some flags for me, adding one more weave to the spider's web.

At the foot of the hill was the small village of Pharping. There was a collection of new Tibetan-style temples belonging to one of Bhante's teachers, an imposing and very old man called Chatrul Sangye Dorje, a 'highly revered' Dzogchen practitioner. I had no idea what Dzogchen was, but it sounded likely he could see right through me and possibly strike me dead. To my relief, he was away in India. The largest temple was lined with hundreds, maybe thousands, of identically sized Buddha figures and a puja was in progress, led by a child lama. I took a seat. I wasn't sure about child lamas, but Buddhism was a good choice. The colour, warmth and light contrasted well with the cold valley of slaughter below.

Back in Kathmandu I went to the princess's residence to post my letter, then up to my hotel roof garden for pizza, chips and a beer. I watched monkeys skitter over the rooftops as the sun went down feeling very happy indeed with the whole journey. At midnight I woke in a sweat, clutching my bowels. I immediately knew it was the potato pancake. After a few hours in the bathroom, I belted up tight and hauled my luggage and a uselessly purchased huge Nepalese board game called Carrom into a taxi. On the plane I tried to look casual about my continual visits to the rear. On the Piccadilly line I just about held on, turning the delicious progress of colonic squeezing into a meditation practice: stay with the present sensation and don't shit your pants. A few weeks later someone from the public health department came to the Buddhist Centre to tell me, and everyone else, I had a highly infectious type of dysentery called shigella.

When I wrote to Bhante giving him the whole story of the mountains, the request for ordination and the shits, he wrote back with bone-dry humour that sometimes when we make a move on the spiritual plane there is a corresponding movement on the physical one.

14

CATS AND DOGS

My mother trained me to believe that any institution on Earth would be lucky to have me, so I assumed it would only be two or three years before I was accepted into the Order, slightly quicker than average. Jnanavaca and Ratnaghosha were my key friends and mentors on the nursery slopes of Buddhist practice. I needed to go on a series of study retreats and enter a process which would lead to ordination, though not as a monk, so renouncing sex wasn't required. A year had passed since splitting up with Kate. Ratnaghosha kept suggesting a girlfriend would be a good idea and I needed no convincing.

'You should be able to click your fingers and hey presto,' Ratnaghosha said.

I couldn't. Buddhist parties were too low on sexual polarisation and booze.

A friend's girlfriend, who ran a casting agency, gave me a more realistic appraisal than Ratnaghosha:

'You seem proud to earn less than £10k per year and, I mean, it's just not attractive is it, having to ask every time you want a new pair of socks?'

'Not all women think that way,' I protested.

'Take it from me, honey, you're not showing off your assets. Birkenstocks are not that cool.'

After a couple of years in the community I was friends with dozens of people and felt connected by near degree to hundreds more. Bhante said the Order was a network of friendships. The holy grail of Buddhism was not an individual possession, but more like the flow of communication from one friend to another. He believed it was possible for any human being to be friends with any other human being. I asked Ratnaghosha and Jnanavaca if they would take part in a 'kalyana mitrata' ceremony to mark our friendship and they agreed.

Kalyana mitrata means something like 'beautiful, auspicious friendship'. Forty or so people gathered to witness the ceremony in the shrine room. Jnanavaca, in a bright purple shirt, was trying to be solemn and serious, though he kept breaking out into his startling rapid-fire laughter. Ratnaghosha, with trim white beard and grey rollneck, was beaming as usual. They both wore a kesa, a white strip of silk around the neck, worn by Order members when they taught a class or took part in a ritual. The celebrant, a senior Order member, gave me some admonitions:

'This bond is for life, whatever that brings. Genuine friendship on the spiritual path is a rare thing and must not be given up lightly. Although this ceremony casts you as the junior partner, in reality things are more fluid. You may have to look out for them as much as they look out for you!'

Jnanavaca and I sat at the front on cushions. Ratnaghosha had dodgy knees so he sat behind on a chair.

'What these men are doing is more important than marriage,' the celebrant said.

I glanced at him nervously and people laughed. That sounded shocking.

'Do you mind me saying that?' he said with a smile.

I didn't mind. I didn't entirely believe it, but I had enough feeling for what he meant. I loved these men and felt fortunate to have met them. Life, spiritual or otherwise, would be pointless without good companions. Most of my worries were naturally appeased when I was with friends. These two, I felt, would be friends until death. Their death, I assumed. Instead of rings on fingers, we tied red cotton threads around each other's wrists, to be worn until they frayed.

Can my mother come for tea?

In early spring Bhante came round for dinner again. It was mostly the same folk in the community. One had left to join the Sannyasins – a proper cult that lot, we all agreed. Owen and Bhante had become quite chummy. Owen had visited Bhante in Birmingham a couple of times and they studied together and went for walks. No sexual overtones could I detect. Owen seemed very pleased with himself. Naturally it was Owen, not me, tasked with collecting Bhante and bringing him upstairs when food was ready.

I sat opposite Bhante, who was wearing a crimson fleece and grey flannel trousers. When he wasn't smiling I was struck again by the almost intimidating neutrality of his expression. The skin of his forehead, eyes and cheeks seemed to have relaxed away from the bone. After the main course I took the opportunity to get Bhante's backing over an argument I'd been putting to the community for some weeks. I thought my mother should be able to come round for tea. Some of the guys were okay with this, others not, for what I considered feeble reasons.

'We've been talking about opening the community to mothers, Bhante. Just a visit, for a cup of tea. I was wondering what you think,' I said.

Bhante was a sensible man who would respond to a case well put. With him on side I could dispense with the views of any community member who disagreed with me.

'Oh, I see, huh . . . so would you like your mother to visit?' he said, turning his neutral gaze on me and interlocking his neat, smallish fingers.

'Yes. I'd like to show her the place where I'm living, seeing as she looked after me for twenty years.'

'If you want your mother to see the place I suppose you could always make her a video, huh?' Bhante said, smiling at me now.

I had expected him to agree with me instantly.

The guys were listening hard.

'Umm, it's more about her actually coming in and seeing the place herself and having tea,' I said. I was shy about making such an obvious point.

'Of course. Then I suppose there are always sisters and aunties . . .' Bhante said.

In the law courts this is known as the floodgates argument. A judge often stops a claim by saying that if this one claimant is allowed, the Bench will be inundated with an impractical number of similar claims. I had that one covered.

'No, Bhante, my proposal would be to keep it strictly to mothers, and once only. So that's a maximum of ten visits.'

I was being generous here. One or two community members were glad not to have the option of inviting their mothers and wouldn't do so, while some mothers were no longer alive.

'Well, it's not up to me, of course, and you as a community must decide,' Bhante said.

I looked at Owen. He raised his eyebrows as if to say, 'Mate, you're screwed.' Bhante's answer would be interpreted as a 'No', so I had to press on.

'Some other communities have invited their mothers in, and no-one has actually died as a result,' I said.

'If it *were* up to me,' Bhante said, 'I'd keep the tradition as it is. It is quite a special place and there are not many men's communities like this.'

The tradition of closed single-sex communities dated back to the first communities at the Buddhist Centre in the late 1970s. That didn't impress me. A stupid rule is a stupid rule. My last card was what lawyers call the *sui generis* exception, a totally unique instance on the particular facts and not capable of creating a binding precedent.

'What about a single visit for my mother only, without setting a precedent for anyone else's mother? That's just one visit only. I'm sure we can all cope,' I said, glancing around.

'Sometimes,' Bhante said, softly, 'young men just want to get their own way.'

During dessert I simmered with ill-will, unable to look at Bhante. My gambit had failed and the conversation moved on. Not only had he not backed me up, he'd handed the other side a trump card. Now and forever more, if I wanted anything they would recall that I was the *young man who wanted things his own way.* Owen came to my room after walking Bhante back to his apartment. I was lying on my bed feeling wretched and greatly regretting bringing the matter up.

'Bhante said I should check to see if you are alright. And he sends his best wishes,' he said.

Our teacher was a dinner guest, and I had tried to use him to resolve a dispute. And I had lost. I also had a guilty secret which I didn't share with Owen or anyone: not only had Mum never expressed the slightest wish to visit the community but, truth be told, I wasn't that interested in actually inviting her, either. It was more a point of principle.

The silent teachings
Eventually I found a girlfriend, with a little help from an older Order member, a Jewish lady from New York, who was in the habit of looking for matches in the Buddhist village. She said things like: 'You don't want to go near her, honey, she's a bit kooky, take it from me.' At a fundraising soirée at the vegetarian cafe she elbowed me into the path of a pretty young Australian student, about 5 foot 2, long dark hair, also independent-minded and sincerely Buddhist. The ache of new romance reduced my quibbles about community rules to irrelevance. Every other weekend I drove to her university campus in the Buddhist Centre car if it was available, or a friend lent us his flat in London. I had regained the best of both worlds. When the closeness with my girlfriend got a bit cloying I could retreat to a community of men to dry out and regain my submerged sense of self. Then at the weekend I could go off and happily drown it again.

Later that year I decided to visit Bhante on my own. I wanted to see what he was like one-to-one, and what I was like, and also to apologise for getting angry with him. Nowadays he was living in the granny flat annex of a big detached house on a suburban street in Birmingham. A few senior Order members lived in the main house. The Order had grown to about one and a half thousand members, in places as far flung as Finland, India, New Zealand and Venezuela. Bhante wanted his senior disciples to work out the structures necessary to keep the movement going when he was no longer leading things.

At the appointed hour his secretary left me in the hallway, saying to knock and go through. In my mythology, this was no mere granny flat annex, this was the epicentre of Buddhism in the West. I knocked, heart thumping. Bhante appeared, smiling and pulling a coat over his mottled grey cardigan. He suggested we go straight out for a walk. En route to the local park I was hyper alert crossing roads for fear that our precious seventy-five-year-old teacher might get hit by a car. That must not happen, certainly not on my watch. Bhante cut through lines of traffic with decisive vigour and the greater danger was mine. As we neared the park I put to him my only planned question:

'I never liked Christian monasticism, but is Buddhism any different? Isn't the life of a celibate monk a bit bloodless and cerebral? Wouldn't it be better to have children than live a kind of passionless life in a Buddhist community?'

'Ah, well, you will work all that out, no doubt,' he said, glancing at me, then taking a gap in the traffic over towards the park gate.

That was the end of that discussion.

As we rounded a pond en route to the cafeteria I told him I'd read all his memoirs.

'I find it amazing everything you have done in your life,' I said.

I was starting to feel a bit insubstantial, like a puppy flapping around the ankles of a St Bernard.

'But you have done a great deal also with all your studies and travels, and of course your work for the retreat centre,' he replied.

We stopped at the park cafeteria for tea and cake, sitting in plastic seats with our plastic trays. I hadn't imagined us meeting over the clatter of crockery and spiralling din of mothers and babies. He said it was busier than normal.

'Do you have a favourite poem?' he asked.

'Poem in October' by Dylan Thomas came to mind, but I thought it was too unserious and romantic. I went for 'Dover Beach' by Matthew Arnold, at once regretting my choice of a poem that leaves the reader on a bleak, faithless shore watching the meaningless shingle slop back and forth.

Bhante said he liked it too.

'By the way, I'm sorry for getting angry when you came to dinner,' I said unburdening myself as soon as seemed polite.

'I quite understand,' he said, smiling warmly. 'It can be difficult living in a community because one doesn't always get what one wants, huh. For example, I would quite like a cat, but the community here doesn't allow cats.'

We discussed the merits of cats over dogs for some time. If I'd wanted a special mantra, or advice about how to live my life I'd have been disappointed. All I gleaned was that I'm more of a dog-type, while he's definitely a cat-type. By the time we got back to his flat and said goodbyes we'd spent ninety minutes together. On the train back to London I felt joyful, as if his steady, unruffled way of being had got into me. Back in town I met my ideal Buddhist girlfriend at a cheap hotel. That day, divided between guru and girlfriend, was pretty perfect.

Later that year Bhante formally handed on the headship of the Order at a special day convened at Aston University in Birmingham. The Order, he said, was mature enough for him to step back from day-to-day duties and see how everyone got on. As he came into the main campus hall to make his handover speech there was a spontaneous outburst of no-clapping. The five or six hundred people gathered stood up in silence while Bhante took his seat. Though he was an old man, in boring old man's clothes, I felt his whole life's journey in that short walk to the podium, from the plains of India and the Himalayas, his dusty robes trailing behind him. Clapping just wasn't enough. I was spellbound. Despite the frailty of his age, he had great momentum, like an ocean liner. For over fifty years, unhurriedly, with devotion and one-pointedness, he had been making an inspired attempt to establish the Dharma in the West.

There's a similar instance of reverential silence in the life of Zen master Shunryu Suzuki, a shaven-headed Japanese monk with a kindly face, sensuous lips and dark glittering eyes. Known as Suzuki Roshi, he founded the Zen Centre in San Francisco and wrote the famous *Zen Mind, Beginners Mind*. Although physically small, Suzuki was said to be able to move impossibly huge boulders when doing landscaping work at the Zen Mountain retreat centre in the hills outside town. Suzuki said his American students were often more sincere in their efforts to understand Zen than students in Japan.

One evening, at the very end of his life, they gathered in the meditation hall, waiting to see their teacher, perhaps for the last time. In the last few months, as his health failed, Roshi had made plans to hand on the headship of his lineage. A hush fell as the old man, bent small with age and illness, appeared at the temple door. With great effort he started an unaccompanied dodder towards the shrine. And then suddenly, in the middle of the hall, he stopped. His students held their breath, hoping he wasn't about to keel over. The Roshi looked up at the shrine, then firmly hit his staff on the temple floor. Three times the bang echoed across the hall.

Whatever fancy Zen teachings pour from a teacher, no teaching is more inspiring than the teacher themselves. Grandpa said Eastern religion couldn't be properly understood by a Westerner. Immersed only in his books, he missed out on the direct wordless teachings that flow from one person to another in mysterious ways, like an echo across a meditation hall.

Bhante knew that handing on a new religious order is tricky. Many die out or dwindle and split following the death of their founder. Suzuki's successor, an American, resigned amid accusations in the usual areas of power, sex and money. Leading a spiritual community is not easy whoever you are and whatever skills you have. If you want your failings and weaknesses exposed in public, plenty of blame and the weight of other people's projections, apply within.

Bhante said it was a great burden for a single person to lead a spiritual community, so he'd decided to hand the baton to four men and four women equally and collectively. He didn't bang any staffs and his talk was simple. He stepped down from the rostrum and left the hall as we stood in silence.

15

AFTER THE ECSTASY, THE LAUNDRY BASKET

Potash Farm was a mock Tudor farmhouse with a six-acre paddock, fringed by gently swaying lines of poplar and rolling Suffolk fields. The farmer, a hale old man in a checked shirt, came out to greet us. Ratnaghosha was in his grey-green jacket, looking neither smart nor scruffy, his clothes as even-minded as he himself.

The farmer asked if we could identify the tree on his front lawn.

'*Gingko biloba,*' said Ratnaghosha.

First strike, the Buddhists.

'How long would you be here?' the farmer asked.

He wasn't going to sell his farm to yuppies who sold it on after a year.

'At least fifty years,' Ratnaghosha said with confidence.

We made appreciative noises about the roof drainage system he'd installed on his barns. Barns big enough for future expansion of a retreat centre, Ratnaghosha said to me. The farmer was a conscientious type. He went to the local library, we were later told, to read up on Buddhism, to see if we were suitable to be let loose on his farm. Thankfully we were. Ratnaghosha sold futures in retreat time to another Buddhist Centre and negotiated a bank loan. Fundraised monies and proceeds from the sale of our current smaller retreat venue were enough. After getting planning permission for change of use, the purchase was completed and a team of volunteers set to work. A builder in the Sangha extended the sewage capacity to cope with thirty-five simultaneous ablutions. A garage became the men's accommodation block, leaving the women the run of the main house.

Jnanavaca and I discussed the prospects for my ordination while knocking down the remains of an old pig pen to make way for a solitary hut. He was a sight, wielding a sledgehammer, goggles around his bat ears, arms all akimbo. I'd had some positive feedback, but I latched onto the negative stuff. Facts about my inner life were being named. Someone at work said I was 'a bit of a golden boy' and I could be more open to what needed doing rather than merely what I wanted to do. Jnanavaca said I could be more aware of my moods and not let them run the show. Strong angry reactions affect other people, apparently.

I'd got angry about money. Our 'support package' was the same for everyone, covering basic living costs plus a small allowance. I asked for extra money to socialise and do stuff I wanted to do, like pay for hotels with my girlfriend. I received more extras than anyone on the team, a concession to my being younger and 'needing' a bit more. I had no car, no pot of savings, no spare flat. I felt weak asking for things and angry if turned down. After a discussion about a trip to France with my choir I was so cross I went upstairs and tried to smash the community washing basket to pieces.

'Hardly seems fair, does it?' Jnanavaca said.

'I know, I just want an extra couple of hundred quid . . . '

'I meant for the basket.'

'It just bounced!'

Another time I tried to karate chop my desk in two. The Centre couldn't run if we were paid regular wages. I understood that our work was an act of generosity for which we were supported according to simple needs, but that didn't help. Jnanavaca said people usually value themselves and their work according to how much they get paid and so uncoupling that equation isn't easy. Wanting more money was understandable at my age and I could always find a better paid job. I thought he was saying I wasn't good enough for the spiritual life at the Buddhist Centre, even though he assured me he wasn't saying that.

I wondered if my bursts of anger were displaced feelings about my missing hand, stored up feelings of impotency and invalidity at the hundred clumsy ways I have to do things. Or perhaps it was rage at missing out on the everyday beauty of having two hands working together: gripping a baseball bat or dropping an apple from one hand into the other or sweeping up a child onto your shoulders. Our hands are in continual communication with the world even when our lips are closed.

Or maybe I just wanted more money.

Sometimes I wondered if I'd got something wrong because after two years living and working at the Buddhist Centre I was more grumpy and more prone to feeling miserable. Ratnaghosha reminded me that the Order wasn't a polite meditation society and said it was good to be able to listen to what other people had to say about me. Owen gave me the benefit of his views at the greasy spoon.

'Mate, I don't think you've got any ideals,' he said, with a nervous smile, rolling up his sleeves.

'You always want to sort me out. Maybe you should focus on your own omelette.'

'It doesn't feel like you want to be here,' he persisted.

'I know what my ideals are. I want to live a good life. I fear dying without having done what I need to do, whatever it is. What else is there? I do want to be here,' I said, feebly.

Owen didn't buy it.

Yet I did want to be there. A good part of me loved it.

The *Evening Standard* ran a little inset feature on me about how I had 'the calmest job in London'. They portrayed me as one of those peaceful, placid, wouldn't-hurt-a-fly Buddhists who smile all day. I went along with it to get publicity for the retreat centre. Oh, how the harried *Standard* reader, stuck in a Tube tunnel, must envy such a person . . . And yet, they surely also reflect, how dreadfully dull such a person must be. I didn't mention the laundry basket.

Over coffee, Maitreyabandhu looked at me quizzically, head slightly cocked. I knew feedback was on its way.

'I wonder if maybe you're much more emotional than you realise.'

'Isn't everyone?'

'Yes, I suppose we are primarily emotional. Sometimes, though, it's as if your articulateness is a defence against deeper communication.'

Several friends had pointed out how I got stuck arguing about who was right and who was wrong, and it all felt a bit harsh. My reasoning driven by the kind of negativity that wants to get everyone else down to the same level. Owen said my style in our study group was a bit combative.

'Like his isn't!' I complained to Maitreyabandhu.

I felt deflated and strangely hopeful after getting feedback. I was being taken seriously. But emerging from the chrysalis of spiritual practice was not the butterfly of my dreams, but more of a depressed moth. I didn't help that my girlfriend flew back to Australia. I refused to move there or even visit because I was on a quest for ordination and I needed holiday time for retreats. Anyway, I didn't want a girlfriend on the other side of the world. For all my sureness, when we parted at Heathrow, I cried a lot more than she did.

Living in a Sangha was a lot tougher than I expected. Ratnaghosha said I seemed to be working at the Centre and living in the community 'despite myself'. Feedback came from working and living cheek by jowl with others and because I'd asked for ordination. I needed to demonstrate my heart was in it. I said I wanted to be ordained, but if anyone had actually tried to ordain me I would have run a mile. No wonder Grandpa meditated in his study with only his little family to get under his skin and no honest friends to say it as they saw it. Wise figures were kept safely on his bookshelf. More than once I'd dreamt I was beside Grandpa's grave. There was an awful smell and the ground started to churn up. In rising panic I'd tamp it down with my foot but still the body cracked up through the soil, breaking through the planks in the coffin lid. It was horrific.

As a well-known Buddhist teacher in the US had warned in his book, which I'd never bothered to read because the title boiled it down so nicely: *After the Ecstasy, the Laundry*.

I had started meditating and it had gone very well, and so I expected things to continue in that vein. But then the laundry, and the laundry basket.

Potash Farm was a building site for nine months. Each morning Ratnaghosha did his meditation on a chintzy sofa the farmer left behind and by 6.30am was layering on paint in an outbuilding or heaving rubble around. In the evenings when the youngsters turned in exhausted, Ratnaghosha carried on, even tempered and energetic, his grey-white beard covered in brick dust. As a young man he had moved to London from Ireland, a gauche country boy with a single pair of shoes, who tried hard to match his brothers Guinness for Guinness in Kentish Town. 'Too quiet, too serious or too drunk,' he said of himself. He was never bothered about not having much money.

'What will you do when you get older,' I asked?

'If no-one looks after me I might just become a tramp.' he said. 'Or die.'

'You're only saying that because people love you and you know they'll look after you.'

'No, not really. Nothing is for certain. Well, I don't mind people looking after me, of course. I thought about being a tramp earlier in my life.'

Aged twenty, Ratnaghosha – not yet Ratnaghosha – left his job as an accountant on the strength of a single dream and set out on a journey to be a saint, but not a Christian one. He hiked around England with a book on techniques of self-flagellation by St Francis of Sale. He eventually threw the book over a hedge in Devon, splashed out on a second pair of trousers and walked all the way to the north of Scotland. Life couldn't just be about accumulating wealth, but he had no other concrete plan, so he bought a touring bicycle and pedalled alone around Europe, working in warehouses, paint stores and on farms. After a couple of years cycling and scraping by, he joined a Berlin commune of exiled Polish musicians and dope-smoking troubadours, pouring his idealism into producing a radical politics and art magazine.

Some afternoons he sat in the quiet of a local Buddhist temple, reading like he used to in church, not speaking to anyone. One day a monk asked him what his meditation practice was and explained Buddhist ethics. Ratnaghosha knew on the spot that he was a Buddhist, and he never looked back from that moment. I felt a confidence and natural ease around him despite my various conflicts and doubts, all of which he assured me he'd been through himself.

'We need to be bigger, not better,' he said, enigmatically.

Money was tight, so we built the shrine room from straw bales and called it ecological. Five of us spent a week covering the straw in a limey concrete. We imprinted our lime-blistered hands, plus one stump, in the final patch of setting concrete. On the outside it looked like a messily iced cake; inside, a cave. Ratnaghosha named the farmhouse with a new non-agricultural mythology: Vajrasana, the Diamond Seat on which all Buddhas attain Liberation. The first retreat started the same day the last toilet was plumbed in.

16

ON SOLITARY

Bhante said it was vital, every now and then, to free yourself from the immediate influence of both society and the Buddhist community. We might look like well-adjusted citizens or pleasant Buddhists, but who are we when our community is reduced to one? A single week *on solitary* was for novices and I'd done two of them. Three weeks sounded impossibly brave. A few Order members had done six months or more on solitary, a marathon I wasn't ready to train for. Two weeks in a cottage, far from the madding crowd of Buddhists, seemed a respectable stint in the wilds of my own mind.

Grandpa lauded the benefits of solitary meditation. 'Approached positively,' he writes in his book, 'my loneliness takes on the uniquely regenerative quality of aloneness.' And where did he do his solitary meditations? The Buddha sent his disciples out alone to face down their terror in the jungle. Grandpa went to his dressing room with Nanna on hand for tea and biscuits.

I struggled up a hill in mid-Wales to a stone cottage dug in just under the brow, weighed down by my estimation of a fortnight's supply of kidney beans, soya milk, Green & Blacks chocolate and other essentials. Halfway up, my nearest, and only, neighbour came out of her cottage to explain that there was an armed criminal on the loose. 'The police say he's tall with red 'air,' she said in a thick accent.

'He was last seen over that way, but don't you worry, it was over two miles away.'

I gazed across the indicated terrain. There was nothing there, not even a sheep shed, only my cottage.

I lumbered on to the cottage. It had one good-size room with an armchair and floor space to roll out a yoga mat, plus a separate shower area and a sleeping platform up above. I checked the cupboards for dry food supplies, then sat down in the evening sun with a cup of red-bush tea to the prospect of silence and space and nothing. Before bed I selected defensive weaponry from the kitchen drawer in case of the madman. Where else could he go but here?

At 6am I was startled from sleep by footsteps on the roof. I sat up, thinking what to do. The clip clopping went on. Only a red-haired madman would walk on the roof! Then it dawned on me that the cottage had an easily approachable front door and there was no real reason to be on the roof, even if you were mad. I went outside to see the last of a line of sheep crossing the roof on the part of the cottage which was deeply dug into the hill.

After porridge I jammed on my hiking boots. The sun was up and the day full of promise as I set out along a lane. It reminded me of the lane we used to walk down near Grandad's farm, which was referred to simply as The Lane. Without looking up, Grandma knew who was behind the wheel of every tractor heading down The Lane. 'Barry's running late,' she'd say, peeling the spuds as another one rattled past the window. Spiritual or agricultural, a common purpose with others makes a difference to life. By now the farm had mechanised and village life was already more a thing of nostalgia. There was no boxcar derby like the one Dad won as a boy, and people no longer carried out all the major functions of their life at the cricket club. The village was geriatric – even Young Ernie was sixty-five. He played skittles in the club with his father Big Ern, who made a pot of money from selling land for drag-racing. I was coming up to thirty and hadn't made a dime.

On his thirtieth birthday, Dylan Thomas set out walking, noticing the roadside bushes 'brimming with whistling blackbirds' and the sun 'summery on the hill's shoulder'. I looked for lapwings in the fields but there were none. The openness of the fields blew in a feeling of loneliness which I'd forgotten about. Probably the sort of feeling that solitary retreats are supposed to help a person face up to. I focussed back on the things rather than the spaces between things: hedgerows, sparrows, cows and sheep giving me long munching glances. Noticing things existing outside my head was a relief. I took a footpath downhill through a grassy field to a hedge and over a neglected stile.

Odd to be out walking on my own. I felt guilty for having nothing better to do. How would I explain myself if I ran into the farmer? I climbed over another slippery, rotten stile. Farmers hate walkers, I thought . . . he probably has spies . . . if we meet it will end in mortal combat. A rook on a field gate gave me a beady look. Half a mile further on the path was blocked by a broken tractor, its huge rusting wheels grown around with nettles and brambles. I tried to get round this way then that, then backtracked to the cottage, rehearsing a letter to the relevant farming minister:

Dear Sir . . . I was on a solitary retreat in Wales recently and was outraged that the circular walk from my cottage appeared to have been deliberately obscured by a rusting tractor . . .

Back at the hut I still had twelve hours before bedtime. The amount of space ahead felt physically shocking. Busy people say they wish for exactly this, but they should try it. I thought about chopping wood like Thoreau at Walden Pond, but there wasn't an axe, or a woodpile. Maybe I should do more meditation, or try a drawing? I'd better wash up breakfast first. Second thoughts, I'll save the washing up for later. What shall I have for lunch? I know, I'll read. I took refuge in *A Suitable Boy* for a couple of hours. Lunch didn't meet my expectations. I hurried in preparing it, hurried in eating it, and felt sorry when it was over. In the afternoon I had a nap to duck under a patch of restlessness, then got up and sat down to meditate.

My plan was to meditate three times a day. One friend decided not to meditate at all on his solitary but just to *let things unfold*. If I *let things unfold* I tended to unfold into a funk of unhappiness. Regular meditation helps me stay grounded in my lonesomeness. Another friend boasted about doing six hours of meditation per day whenever he went off on his own. That was too much for me and anyway I needed a lot of time to find out which Boy would be Suitable. I was glad I'd thrown a 1300 page novel in my rucksack.

On the third afternoon I sat down to meditate opposite a shrine that the previous solitary retreatant had decorated with wildflowers. As I lit a stick of incense a familiar voice piped up with remarks about superstition and scented candles and twee little Buddhas.

I'm just pretending to be a Buddhist. I'm only on this solitary retreat because I've heard it's a good idea. Retreats are for people who can't cope. Successful people don't need to meditate in damp huts. They work hard and enjoy a glass of wine in the evening. They go on proper holidays. I am not successful, ergo, here I am . . .

It seemed like infallible logic, as insurmountable as the rusting tractor. Yet I couldn't give up and go home after three measly days. I was stuck in a hut stupidly confirming how pointless it was for another eleven days. The overbearing farmer in my head, who sounded rather like me, suggested I wasn't my own man. Coming up to thirty, no wife, no family, no prospects. I carried on sitting, feeling sapped of strength.

I opened my eyes.

The Buddha on the shrine was bronze, with one hand in his lap, and the other reaching down. This gesture recalls the mythical moment when Mara, a personification of all the forces that resist human awakening, confronts Siddhartha like a grumpy Welsh farmer, telling him he has no right of way. Siddhartha, unmoved by the farmer's bluster, simply touches the ground, at which point the Earth goddess springs up to bear witness to the rightfulness of Siddhartha's claim to the supreme knowledge of a Buddha. Mara slinks off in fear, and his farm and the whole fabric of the universe begin to tremble at the Buddha's conquest.

Gingerly I reached my hand down towards the meditation mat, just to see.

'A cheap trick,' said Mara. 'What else you got?'

What's it all about, David?

That evening I sat out on the verandah drinking hot chocolate, wrapped in a shawl, watching the sun through its final setting. Darkness removed the need to think about what to do next. I loosened the reins and let my thoughts bubble up, expand and knit with memory.

Grandma had ground to a halt the day after Grandad was cremated. Her limbs stopped working. After a brush with cancer in his early sixties Grandad had quit smoking. He kept an unfinished silver pack of Benson & Hedges in the glove compartment of his Datsun Cherry, a car he drove as slowly as if he was still pulling a hay baler. He substituted cigarettes with a tin of polo mints all broken up into little pieces, which my sister and I nibbled on the way to the fairground rides at Wicksteed Park.

I felt warmth flood into me recalling the enfoldment of childhood.

When cancer came back in his late seventies, Grandad died after a protracted period of dependency and grateful grumpiness. For several weeks after the funeral, either from relief or grief, Grandma was in a state of semi-paralysis. It was tough for her but she didn't make a fuss. She'd had a lifetime of not making a fuss about things. She'd had eleven siblings, so maybe fussing didn't work. She was a practical and loving woman, who wore brown plaid skirts almost every time I saw her. Not fussing was her philosophy. One weekend I went to visit her in her last bungalow. Her limbs had slowly started working again, but she never got back to full crumble-making power after Grandad's death. She now found life a 'bother'. It was a bother getting over to my parents and a bother getting back. Birthdays were a bother, the garden was a bother, everything was a bother.

'Hallo David my dear, how are you?' she said, taking both my arms and looking at me. 'Such lovely hair, so handsome.' I was never a bother and I always had lovely hair.

'We've finished the new retreat centre I was telling you about, Grandma.'

'But what about the Armenian babies?' she said, getting out some side-plates.

'It's in Suffolk, Grandma. What about them?'

'Who's going to look after them?'

Over fruit cake I reflected on her critique. The Buddha's motivation was to bring an end to all existential human suffering, but the babies in that morning's *Daily Telegraph* needed feeding right now. People are being tortured while we do the shopping, children are dying of starvation while we cook dinner. Along with Grandma they were unlikely to appreciate any doctrinal points I might make about the true nature of suffering.

Our last meeting was at a hospice. Grandma was in the final stages of lung cancer. She was all ribs. Gone too was the soft fatness of her story-telling arms.

'What's it all about, David?' she asked.

I didn't know what to say.

'It's not right this thing . . . It's awful . . . I'm sorry,' she said.

Struggling to breathe, Grandma asked what I was doing with my life. I said a few hopeful things. Inwardly I called on the Buddhas or any higher power to help me know what to do. I tried to stay present to what was happening despite the churning emotion. Suddenly Grandma was struggling to prop herself up on her elbows.

'I love you all,' she said. The words burst out of her under force. 'Have a happy life, David.'

'Thank you Grandma . . . thank you . . . for everything.'

I held her hand, bleary with tears. She gave a long out breath and settled back down. The next morning she died.

My retreat settled down after the bout of heavy doubt. I can't say what changed exactly. Doubt is a mental state and they always change, the way the weather always changes. My harsh self-criticisms didn't seem quite so true. The panicky urge to fill time subsided. On walks I stood by open fields without restless expectation of a nature moment. On the verandah I slackened and sat content for nothing much to happen. *A Suitable Boy* was in a world within my world; at the last she chose wisely, and I shared her happiness like it was my own.

On my final afternoon walk I found a sheep lying on the path. For some reason it was unable to run away. I walked downhill to the nearest farmhouse. The farmer greeted me warmly and invited me indoors to greet his tiny wife. We drove back up in his truck. Gently turning the sheep over he pointed to the maggots embedded in her flank, eating her alive. He said it was good thing I had called by when I did as she could still be treated. After lifting the sheep into the truck, he drove off.

It was only when I'd left the cottage and got to the train station that I noticed just how changed I was. I felt more permeable to the world, more gathered up and responsive. At the station store I chose a sad looking egg sandwich and glanced at the tragedies and scandals in large print. The woman at the checkout was a little taut, not unfriendly, with way too much make-up. I met her eye and we smiled as she passed me the change. On the platform a father leaned down to tie his daughter's shoelace. The guard hadn't tucked his shirt in and his stomach overhung his belt. I was present in that train station as well as passing through. I felt sad that I couldn't tell anyone about what happens if you get off the train and spend two weeks alone.

17

IT MAKES SENSE AT EVERY LEVEL, EXCEPT THE ONE ON WHICH I LIVE

Mahananda was a good-looking man in his mid-fifties with a bald head and thick beard. Part of his charm was that he wasn't a very good Buddhist. When life in the community got a bit much he'd sometimes sit in his car and smoke a spliff. I ended up sharing a room with him when I moved downstairs to the other community in the same building, fourteen more men all practising and living together. I used to joke that in fact there *were* women in the community but we had been so badly brainwashed that we couldn't actually see them.

The odd tipple and occasional spliff aside, by the time I got to know him Mahananda had eroded many of his worst habits, apart from playing the accordion, which he still did wonderfully badly. Mahananda meant Great Bliss, and he was indeed a big, gregarious man, though easily made nervous by anything transactional, almost to the point of tears. He'd pile up bank letters under his bed for weeks then open them in a flurry of paper knives and high drama. He had a bottle of Goldwasser under his bed, 'in case things deteriorate', he said. His mother was an Austrian born Jew. Before being captured and sent to Auschwitz in 1942 she had lived with her husband on false Aryan papers in

Krakow, Poland. After liberation, with all her family dead, she arrived shoeless in England by boat. That first day she met a lawyer at the Polish embassy and soon they married.

And so Mahananda was born, not yet Mahananda. Another Polish friend living in a nearby community was planning to start a Buddhist centre in Krakow, the old Polish capital, so one spring Mahananda and I went with him to reconnoitre venues before a visit with Bhante himself. Mahananda took us on a side trip to Auschwitz. We sat in long grass beside the ruins of the gas chambers which his mother, due to her skills in language and typing, had escaped. In an empty shower block was a wall of photographs of men and women posing happily with family and friends, unaware of what was to come.

Later in the year we went to Krakow again, this time with Bhante. After his lecture at the Jagellonian University, we all sat out at a cafe in Krakow's main square across from the amber market and the gothic tower. A trumpeter trumpets a curtailed herald out of a turret every quarter of an hour to re-enact the moment his medieval predecessor was killed by an arrow in mid-trumpet.

The waiter took orders. It was a deep blue, warm, early summer day – ideal conditions for a cool, crisp Polish beer. Mahananda and I had had one at the same spot the day before. But now Bhante was with us, which made me conscious of a dilemma. There were eight of us, seven guys and one female Polish Order member. One by one we ordered our green teas and orange juices, apart from the female Order member, who ordered a glass of lager. When it arrived Bhante smiled and said: 'The only man among us, huh.'

Communal living opened up avenues for friendships I would never have had. It's banal to say I enjoyed it, but I did, mostly. It was supposed to culminate with people agreeing I could be ordained. The meaning of my life was becoming caught up in the need for this validation.

At work I was refused another of my requests for extra funds on top of my allowances. Jnanavaca held the purse strings, so I was spiky and unpleasant to him. He reminded me I was free to not work in this way, to go out and earn more money and try other things. It was alright to be miserable, but I couldn't be ordained unless I was willing to take more responsibility for how I affected other people and how that impacted on work. We used to go for lunchtime walks, having frank and uplifting discussions. Now I went on my own to stare at the stupid ducks. Instead of a shinier version of me, an angry, depressed creature was emerging in a quagmire of self-doubt.

One time, when Jnanavaca was saying this sort of thing again, I felt a pain in my chest, like a spike digging in. I felt what seemed like every pain that had accumulated in my body suddenly shooting through my chest like a hot arrow. I don't know how this related to my disability and early traumas of rejection, but at that moment it was too much to bear. It was too painful, and it was now high time for self-defence. My openness to Jnanavaca and Maitreyabandhu shut down. They'll never ordain me. I'm invalid, that's what they're saying. Sod them.

Someone in my new community had more tangible problems. He was dying of a brain tumour. He was a northerner, overweight, good humoured and straight talking. Prior to becoming a Buddhist, he'd been a drug smuggler. By a miracle, as he called it, he'd escaped both jail and dying of overdose. Before he was allowed to join the Order he had to take responsibility for his past by clearing his many financial debts. When his illness was in its final phases, he moved out of the community to be with his partner and adopted daughter, who had been allowed in the community to be with him. Ratnaghosha went to see him at his home. There were times when he was angry and in denial about his condition, but in his last weeks Ratnaghosha reported an increasing aura of joy and equanimity. It was like being with a saint, he said. In dying he was the best he had ever been, angelic almost. The only thing that got him down was not having enough money to bequeath for his daughter's education. Ratnaghosha quickly raised the money by asking around the wider community and was able to give it to him before he died.

On the day of his funeral the courtyard gates were opened for the hearse to back in. For a few hours before the service mourners were invited to come in and sit around the body, which lay in the open casket in the shrine room. I was in the basement counting cash deposits for the upcoming Winter Retreat. Jnanavaca sat opposite looking at accounts on his computer. I had headphones on to cut out communication and I ignored his gaze. I was not open to any more feedback. I wasn't good enough to join their precious Order. Who do they think they are anyway? I totted up the cheques and over three thousand pounds cash into a large envelope ready to take to the bank, then went upstairs to have a cup of tea and look at the body.

When I came back to the basement I opened the safe, but the cash wasn't there. I looked on my desk, down the side, underneath, then in the bin, then in everyone else's bins. Then everyone else looked in their bins and in everyone else's bins. After a few rounds of this, we concluded the money had been stolen, that I had left the envelope on my desk and someone, taking advantage of the comings and goings for the funeral, had come and gone with it.

The next couple of weeks Jnanavaca and I reached a stalemate. He tried to instigate a new system for the banking.

'You mustn't wear headphones when counting the money,' he said.

'That doesn't make any difference,' I said.

'Yes, but I'm saying you mustn't.'

'And I'm saying it doesn't make any difference.'

Whatever the explanation, it was my fault. I stalked out of the Centre and refused to talk about it.

Then I stalked back in again.

I still had to organise room allocations for the winter retreat and send out confirmations. The day before the retreat we loaded up a van with meditation mats and cushions for 120 bottoms and headed off to the school in Oxfordshire, the same place where I had done my second retreat. On the first day as retreatants arrived I checked them in and pointed the way to their dormitory. Despite my difficulties I was glad to be on retreat. I sat at the check-in desk in full professional retreat gear: birkenstocks, baggy trousers, fleece. That was the first impression Joanna had of me. Not much of an impression, she would later say.

Joanna was a petite Polish lawyer with a sharp nose, clear blue eyes and dyed blonde hair growing out at the root. She smiled at me in the dinner queue so I sat next to her. I tried

my few Polish words. When they ran out, I mentioned the
case no law student ever forgets. Donoghue v Stephenson
(1932). It's not a great mealtime topic, but. . .

Mrs Donoghue buys a bottle of ginger ale which turns
out to be harbouring a decomposing snail. The snail slides
out as she pours the last dregs into her glass and down her
throat it goes. After a bad night she wants to sue someone,
however the cafe owner is too poor to make it worth her
while. So, for the first time ever, the court allows a tortious
action against Stevenson & Co, the manufacturer, for
negligent ginger ale production, even though they weren't
in a contractual relationship with the woman who drank
the snail. On the facts, Stevenson & Co were found to have
been negligent because the bottles were made from dark
brown glass which meant they couldn't be seen into for a
quick snail check. Therefore the onus was on them to make
sure no mollusc of any kind had slithered in.

Joanna didn't seem put off by the snail story or by how I
used my stump to push peas onto my fork. She had arrived
in the UK nine years earlier from her hometown in north-
east Poland, working as a waitress and a nanny while sitting
A-levels and then completing a law degree. Her short skirts,
waist-length blonde hair and a passion for human rights
made her popular around the Inns of Court. But just as she
was on the verge of becoming a barrister, her boyfriend
died of cancer and grief undid her plans. Being a lawyer
no longer had any meaning. Nothing had any meaning. In
the depths of despair she came across a small book about
awareness of the breath by the Vietnamese monk Thich
Nhat Hanh. In it, she said, she found a reason to be alive.
She knew she could bear the pain because every Monday

evening at the Buddhist Centre she could sit and watch her breath.

After the retreat I breached data storage policy and emailed her. We started dating, or, according to her account, meeting. I played the long game, which is the kind of game I play when I can't play a shorter game. The longer game is the better one, though it offers wider openings for self-doubt. After our dates/meetings I went back to the community with a Buddhist psychotherapist parrot on my shoulder:

'You're becoming pretty attached here. This could end in suffering.'

'I think you might be projecting your anima figure.'

'Freud called love the psychosis of ordinary people.'

'Who's a pretty boy then?'

The pipe of disappointment

In the summer of 2003 I stopped working at the Buddhist Centre and went camping with some friends in woods, beaches, stone circles and at various festivals in Devon and Cornwall. For three months we lived outdoors, some nights just lying on mats without a tent. Wherever we stopped, we set up a dome for meditation classes. People came in, except at an anarchist camp where everyone preferred the 'class war' lessons in the dome next door.

The summer culminated at the Buddhafield festival, a free-spirited, five-day event with sweat lodges, poetry slams, meditation and fire rituals. There was a naked woman on a shire horse. In fact, nothing you'd find in the Pali Canon, but also no drugs or alcohol. I went to Buddhafield every year and felt totally out of place among the circusy folk right up to the moment about halfway through when I felt completely at home, circumambulating an old oak tree or something. I was feeling quite happy when I entered one of the teepees in the camping field:

'Gay Apollonian bullshit if you ask me,' said a strapping man, an Order member with a deep voice. He was smoking a roll-up and seemed like the big chief. He got up and minced across the teepee while the others laughed.

'Be fair, they aren't *all* gay,' said another Order member, again to laughter.

It was a bad time for the Order. Bhante's ethical credentials were under the microscope again, this time not in the *Guardian* but in the Order's own journal, which contained a long and critical letter from one of his former lovers. It was less sensationalist than the *Guardian* article and therefore more credible. The issue was not lack of consent, or secrecy, or sex per se, but the possible harmful consequences of sexual relationships between a spiritual teacher and a young disciple. Bhante himself had spoken about the dangers of students 'projecting' too much onto spiritual teachers, making them into guru figures, but some people were saying he hadn't always exercised enough caution in relation to his own sex life. This man alleged that Bhante had abused his position, leaving him confused and hurt when Bhante casually moved on.

All this unleashed a new wave of doubt and unhappiness in the Order. Several people who'd had a sexual relationship with Bhante said they were happy to have done so. Some Order members were sorry for this man, but thought he'd done what he did because he wanted the attention from Bhante. It hurts when we don't get what we want, but best to take responsibility and get over it. For others that wasn't a good enough response. This man had been hurt and he wasn't the only one.

I wondered how Bhante had not seen the likelihood of a mess. How could he have done what he did without ignoring some of the feelings and forces at play? I couldn't believe he ever had malicious intent. I had to sort it out in my mind. How can someone be spiritually advanced and yet do this?

For the natives in the teepee the matter was decided and Bhante had come crashing down to earth. The big chief guy characterised the Order as full of naive idealists who thought they were right about everything and who lived in fear of feminine forces and the Dionysian-side of life. Buddhafield, with its naked saunas and bare-breasted rituals, was a great place for a Dionysian to hang out. Buddhafield was, in fact, run by Order members and they themselves were Order members, two points overlooked in the powwow. Anyway, there was a good deal of satisfaction that sex, good old sex, was bringing people down a peg or two.

I gathered up my poncho and left the teepee. It was dispiriting to hear Order members call other Order members 'the mafia', and I wondered why they were still in the Order. I realised I would have to be a guide unto myself in deciding what I thought. I looked up at the stars in the night sky and as usual they had nothing to say.

The pipe of disappointment was being passed around the Order and totem poles of betrayal were going up everywhere. I too spoke unfavourably of just about everyone higher up the pecking Order, except Ratnaghosha.

Not outright hostility, just weasel words to bring them down a bit in the eyes of others. I hadn't been abused and didn't feel abused, but I still felt the urge to smash things up a bit, to stick one to all that gay Apollonian idealistic bullshit. Yeah.

Some Order members demanded confession, apology, explanation, recantation, but Bhante was too ill to comment, which gave rise to more speculation. Later he asked everyone to remember that he'd grown up in an era when homosexuality was illegal, which might be one reason why he was reticent to speak about his sex life. A lot of Order members were waiting for things to settle down, finding it distasteful to discuss their teacher's sex life in public. You wouldn't do that to a friend, and you'd think twice about doing it to an enemy.

Ratnaghosha, even tempered as ever, bright and happy, wasn't much interested in the discussion. He was living alone in a hut in Suffolk for a year and didn't seem wobbled by fractious debates. He listened to my rants without opposing my point of view. I'd feel like a bull who'd charged at a gate only to find it was already open. I'd end up halfway into the next field not knowing where to go next. He was in touch with the something, let's call it the Dharma, and was always open to exploring how things are, which sometimes is that things collapse.

I wasn't exchanging postcards with Jnanavaca and Maitreyabandhu any more. I was still feeling angry and rejected. But it seemed cowardly to dismiss them in my mind. Did I have to take a sledgehammer to my feelings for them and Bhante and the Order and walk away? Was that what authenticity required? If I didn't, was that just a sign that I was still in the clutches of a sinister group, unable to admit the true scale of Bhante's devilish sexual exploits and his misogynistic family-hating cult? With his soft Irish accent Ratnaghosha said mysterious things like how I'd be happier once I'd softened into things.

Softening was a hard thing to do, he added.

Owen withdrew his ordination request. Things had turned sour during a retreat. Owen said the retreat leader was being authoritarian and telling him what to do and he wasn't having it any more. Back at the community he was on the warpath and I got short shrift when I asked what was up. I assumed he wasn't being serious and it would blow over. But Owen was serious. Soon he'd left the community and circulated a report on why: it was a cult.

Traditionally, cults are to do with suicide, guns or men with a hundred and fifty wives. They have hard borders to separate the saved from the damned, and members show unconditional acceptance of whatever the leader says. Was I just too psychologically unsophisticated to see I was in a cult? We had no guns. Apparently I couldn't even join, though someone said this was just a clever variation on the cult theme. Would it all end in a Waco-like stand-off with police outside a shrine room?: *Be careful, they've got grown men in there trying to develop universal loving kindness. Drop the beads and come out with your hands up!*

One year I baked a friend a cake to celebrate her fortieth birthday. She'd lived through the horror of the war years in the former Yugoslavia. Now she lived in a Buddhist community with a dozen peaceable women. We took her on a road trip around the UK with a few friends. Then one day she was gone, without a word. Was it my cake? We later heard via someone else that she'd burnt her Buddhist books and escaped the 'cult'. She'd joined a church instead. She didn't return our calls, and anyway it's not productive trying to contact someone who thinks you're in a cult. You are walking into their trap.

The London School of Economics has a department which monitors new religious movements to keep the population safe. I asked them what they had on Bhante and his Order and Movement. Their appraisal was distant sounding, like if a sociologist called your family a *typical nuclear unit*, but I could recognise what they wrote as a description of the organisation I was involved with. There was no reference to cults. The person I spoke to said the only common factors in the various uses of the word 'cult' were that it tended to refer to a religious group with under a million members and which one doesn't personally like.

The young man reported in the *Guardian* article, the law student who killed himself, felt he couldn't leave the community for fear of being a spiritual failure. Did anyone actually say that to him? Maybe they did, but maybe it was his naïveté loading up a tiny Buddhist centre with more meaning than it could stand. Or maybe I'm projecting my projections onto his projections. Sometimes feelings and memories can be so painful that the source of the pain has to be externalised. 'It's a cult,' they think. Suddenly it all makes sense. Now they know what to get away from. The weird thing is that then *they* appear brainwashed. They trawl through anti-cult websites and develop a cult-like absolute certainty and disdain for anyone who doesn't share their point of view. They go to a psychologist, who confirms their worst fears. Friendships come to an end. Maybe our friend wanted to get in touch, just like I wanted to get in touch with Maitreyabandhu and Jnanavaca, but we were part of her past, and her past was all bad in the bad cult. If she met with us her new story might run into difficulty because nothing is that simple. Thankfully Owen's angst wasn't as strong. He wanted to explain what was wrong with the Order, so we stayed in touch.

Selling cigarettes on the Edgware Road

I carried on living at the London community for another year. It was hard to consider leaving. In the last eight years good friendships and connections had built up. But a Buddhist community derives its purpose and direction from the Awakening of the Buddha. I needed some confidence and clarity about what that meant to me. I wondered what I should do. An older Order member once joked that if he ever left the Order and gave up his spiritual aspirations he'd quite like to set up as a tobacconist on the Edgware Road.

'Soften into things . . . be bigger not better,' Ratnaghosha re-recommended. He didn't seem worried whatever I did, which gave me some confidence. When I repeated my doubts to a senior Order member, who was ordained at nineteen years old and was now almost fifty, he said maybe I needed to let myself 'think the unthinkable'. He thought I could follow my instincts and not worry about speeding to ordination. I could entertain ideas that scared me. Could I drop ordination, drop the whole thing, go do something else entirely? There was no shame in it, he said. It was indeed unthinkable, so I started thinking about it right away.

Towards the end of my summer outdoors we camped near the stone circle at Avebury. I lay on my roll-mat with a copy of my CV, keeping an eye on the cows nearby. I hated CVs and the thought of going back into ordinary work institutions. I asked Joanna for help. Her flat backed onto the Edgware Road. She was helpful, friendly, hard to read. She was in the process of changing the focus of her life from barrister to Buddhist, and had applied to do an MA in Sheffield. Boldly, selflessly, I offered to show her around my old stomping ground. We stayed with my old Tibetan Buddhist friend. I eventually summoned the boldness to kiss her. Shortly after our host's dog, Deefer, came into our bedroom.

'Deefer Dog,' I said.

'Deefer?' she said.

'Dee-fer Dog,' I said. 'Dee for Dog.'

If laughter is important for a long relationship we were off to a good start.

Back in London I found work at a medical charity. Every chance, I was up to Sheffield, bolting out of the community to the National Express depot. Mahananda lent me his car so I could get there quicker. Soon we decided to live together, though not on the Edgware Road. Joanna didn't mind where. If I led the way, she would follow. By some miracle, unstructured wanderings with a confused Buddhist suited her fine.

On my final community night, Mahananda organised a party. I dressed up in high heels, Joanna's black skirt, bra and a long blonde wig. I wanted to get her into the community, in spirit at least. The guys were admiring my efforts when Mahananda came traipsing down the stairs dressed exactly like me. Two Joannas came face to face in the lounge. His wig was even longer than mine and got tangled up in the keys of his accordion during a Yiddish song of farewell. The evening ended with a leaving ceremony, a ritual where I asked each member of the community in turn to forgive me for any harm I may have caused them. They forgave me and then asked me to forgive them in the same way.

The next morning Mahananda backed up a hired van and we loaded up my stuff next to Joanna's. I was sad to leave but happy to go. I'd never lived in a proper domestic arrangement and it seemed like a wonderfully exotic prospect. Jnanavaca came out into the street to say goodbye before we pulled away. He wished me well and said to stay in touch. Our cordiality was painful. I worried I was betraying something deep. Leaving a community without bitterness or rancour to trade cigarettes hand over fist on the Edgware Road is not as easy as it sounds.

Soon we were rolling along the M4 towards Bristol with Mahananda amusing Joanna with the baby-speak Polish he'd learnt as a boy. At the flat we signed the contract and handed the landlord a deposit. Mahananda looked pensive. I assumed the administration was making him anxious but when the landlord had gone he blurted out: 'They're jumping off the carpet! Fleas! Look at my calves!' Flea extermination was not how I'd pictured my first night living with a woman. We dropped our stuff at a local Buddhist community and went to a B&B. Mahananda setting off back to London with the van felt like the final moment: I was no longer living in the community and a new life could begin.

18

PROSTHETICS

My new life began in a canteen office of the University of the West of England, with two jovial women who supervised me entering food data. They brought me up to speed on reality television. The old Chinese man in San Francisco had warned me I had a long way to go. My job was to balance the reported count of bananas, muffins and assorted confectionary in the various food outlets across the campus against the quantities and pack sizes indicated on the combined delivery chits. A bit of a comedown from the quest for Enlightenment.

I sent a letter withdrawing my ordination request. It felt like the right thing to do. I was starting again, setting the counter back to zero. I had planned to do an MA in Buddhism at Bristol University. The professor in charge of Buddhist studies was a kind, avuncular man with a large cross hanging around his neck. After two decades as a Buddhist scholar he'd become a Catholic. When my MA grant was rejected I realised I didn't care. I remembered Grandpa in his coffin on the desk of his study, all the spines of his book neatly arranged by subject and author behind the glass and mahogany bookcases. You can't think your way to Enlightenment.

The MA was just an idea to get me out of doing anything as tedious as counting vegetable deliveries and Snack-A-Jacks. One afternoon I spent a whole hour looking for a missing seven pence worth of carrot – not even a real carrot, just carrot on an invoice. The careers of college friends were blooming. I felt humiliated and sick at the thought of drifting through admin roles for the next thirty years. While driving home, the will to live suddenly broke forth. I made the first career resolve of my life. It was truly unthinkable.

'I'm going to become a solicitor,' I told Joanna.

'That'll keep you busy. Are you sure your law degree is still valid?'

'Valid?'

'They run out after seven years.'

'Run out? Fucking hell!'

I hit the kitchen wall hard with my stump and sat in a state of misery while Joanna looked up the Law Society rules. Exceptional permission to proceed to qualification was possible up to ten years after graduation. I'd graduated nine years ago. After an exchange of letters, someone at the Law Society, who obviously wasn't too assiduous, agreed with me that I'd stayed 'very much in touch' with legal developments during my years at the Buddhist Centre, and granted me permission to apply for a solicitor's training contract.

Now we had to infuse my life with commercial dynamism for the CV.

'What shall we do with the Snack-A-Jack counting?' I said.

'Temporary financial administrative support,' Joanna said.

'What about last summer. Temporary tramping? Temporary Druidism?'

Squeezing my backstory into a CV made me wildly angry. Why on earth shouldn't a person spend some time camping around old wells and standing stones on Dartmoor? Why shouldn't one spend a little time invoking the ancient and neglected guardian spirits who dwell in such places, asking them with rituals to revive themselves and rescue the British people and their landscapes from the grip of a severe imaginative impoverishment? I grabbed the CV as it came out of the printer and tore off a strip with my teeth.

Joanna was in stitches.

My CV bluffing and general bullshit powers slowly grew. In a few months I had interviews at law firms lined up and a place to study at the College of Law in London. I handed in my last grocery data sheets, ate a final ravioli and spotted dick in the campus canteen, and we moved back to London, to a flat just off the Edgware Road, working at more data entry, this time at the General Medical Council.

With interviews approaching we went shopping on Oxford Street in search of a suit. Joanna held my stump loosely as we walked along. I found it frustrating not to be able to grip her hand. She was in boots and a Barbour jacket, all the blonde now grown out of her hair. My baggy Buddhist clothing had been purged and I now wore tight jeans and a Ralph Lauren shirt.

'Why don't you just get one?' she said. 'You could put your name down and see what happens. They're probably free.'

'Prosthetics are for people who want to hide,' I said.

'Never mind people.'

'Maybe I should get a hook?'

At Moss Bros as the suit salesman pressed my shoulders to check the fit, the stump retracted deep up the jacket sleeve like a nervous snail. Joanna told the tailor to move all the fake buttons on the cuff higher up.

I'd never understood the appeal of a hook, apart from pulling a toboggan or scratching one's nose, perhaps. One reads about bionic hands in the papers and how they're coming on leaps and bounds. To me they just look like a slightly flashier version of the same old robotic thing that can swivel and grip a polystyrene cup. No doubt real transplanted hands will be commonplace one day, but I'm not sure I'd want my stump cut off and replaced with someone else's hand. I like my stump. It is not, nor has it ever been, a 'missing hand'. I never shed tears of grief about losing a hand because I never lost one. If my stump was taken away, on the other hand, I'm sure I would mourn it. Parents of limb-deficient children face difficult choices. Some are offered a medical procedure which transplants healthy toes onto their child's stump to act as pincers. I'm glad no-one messed with my toes as I'm very pleased with my feet.

I never considered having a prosthetic limb. I don't recall a doctor ever suggesting I get a prosthesis and I'm sure I would have resisted the idea. In my mind there was something shameful about them. Admitting an urge to have a fake limb would have meant acknowledging that, uncovered, it was a problem. As a child I didn't want a problem, therefore I didn't want a fake limb.

Joanna had no problem with the stump. To her it was unique, funny and bizarre and she'd grown quite fond of it, as some people can be fond of an ugly little dog. She gave it a name which translated from Polish as 'little arm'. I wasn't so well received in her family. Her father assumed I was incapable of work and warned his daughter that sticking with me would be misery. I'd never been exposed to straightforward prejudice before. I was very angry, although it was quite bracing, almost refreshing of him to be so blunt. The British are generally way too sensitive about saying the wrong thing. They feel suddenly worried after saying 'Can I give you a hand with that?' As a place to live though I prefer sensitive Britain.

Joanna's frankness and the approaching interviews made me think again about prosthetics. Perhaps the urge to cover it up was honest and healthy. Future clients might feel more at ease if I covered it up. I would feel more at ease if they felt more at ease. What's wrong with that? Is it okay to concede to the social reality that prosthetics really do help?

I decided to give it a go. The camouflage expert at the Prosthetics & Camouflage Unit in Chelmsford was a perfectionist. I was expecting something that looked as if it'd fallen off a tailor's dummy. He produced a mirror image of my right hand when it was resting at my side and filled up with blood. For six weeks I went back and forth to the Unit, for drawing on veins, skin pigmentation, even hairs, and then finally he was ready to relinquish his work of art. It was moulded in a close fit to my stump and held on by suction. It will get a bit sweaty inside, he warned, but talcum powder sorts that out. It looked superbly real. It would fool everyone apart from the camouflage man, who was still anxious that my knuckles were too red as

I walked out of the door and into the Essex sunshine, looking symmetrical for the first time ever.

The next week was my first training contract interview, at a large law firm in Holborn. After checking in at reception, I went to the bathroom to straighten myself out. The prosthetic was thicker than my sleeve, so I had to take it off in order to remove my overcoat. It came off with a sucking pop noise, flicking talc down the front of my jacket and tie. I put the hand on the edge of the basin and was starting to wipe off the talc when someone came in. I grabbed the hand and went into a cubicle, knocking more talc onto my trousers, as if I'd been snorting cocaine. Panic set in. I thought about putting it in my briefcase. What if I needed to open the briefcase to get out my CV? There'd be a severed hand on display. I could ask the receptionist to look after it? No no. I put it back on, used spit and loo paper to tidy up, folded the coat over my arm and arrived at the interview in a lather.

The next interview went better, but I felt extremely self-conscious about the pink lump of silicon attached to my wrist, much more so than about my stump. The interviewer asked if I was interested in becoming a partner. I blathered and avoided the question. Joanna reminded me that heart-searching honesty wasn't required at a job interview.

Are you *interested*?, he'd asked.

Yes, I was *interested*, I should have said.

My beautiful new hand was useless. I couldn't feel through it. I couldn't do buttons up. I couldn't push or pull a door. It was no good for scratching my nose, typing or carrying a bag. Hollow out a garden gnome and strap it over the end of your arm if you want to find out how a prosthetic feels. I started wondering if I was a hundred percent sure I wanted to pass for a boringly normal two-handed guy in a Jasper Conran jacket. Does part of me actually like the extra attention that comes with looking a bit different? The careful labour of the camouflage man was shoved into the back of my sock drawer, along with an assortment of left-hand gloves which for some entrenched psychological reason I can't bring myself to throw away.

Over the course of a dozen interviews I was quizzed about everything from meditation to money-laundering regulations and how I might estimate the number of lost golf balls in England. The founder of one firm asked why should he employ someone who liked 'navel gazing' on retreat when he was running a commercial operation? I argued back and we hit it off, however in the next round I failed to impress the panel who asked what I'd do if I became prime minister. Number of hands made no difference.

The breakthrough came on the day a young whale swam up the Thames through the Barrier and past the London Eye. Joanna and I stood in the crowd gathered on Battersea Bridge experiencing the communal jollity that breaks out in England when something actually happens. The whale was a messenger from the wild regions of the Earth. We were being reminded of the wider universe which gets rudely forgotten in daily life. On tip toes we could just make him out, surrounded by a team of London whale experts having their moment. Everyone was rooting for him to get back to the open sea, to escape the smallness of city life, to reach a place big enough for whale thoughts and sonar.

In my pocket was a letter inviting me to take up a training contract. I was flushed with the victory. By the fourteenth interview I had become a straight-talking pro, capable of brazening out all the Buddhist stuff. I was a commercial bulldog in disguise. Underneath all these changes though another resolve was clarifying. Before I began my solicitors' qualifying course I wrote a letter re-requesting ordination. It was more prosaic and less dramatic than the one posted in the letter box of the Princess's palace in Kathmandu. Joanna and I moved just round the corner from the London Buddhist Centre and she started working at the Centre's vegetarian cafe.

Forty children, thirty-nine hands

On the Central Line coming home from the College of Law I saw a smartly dressed guy with half a forearm missing. He held the handrail with his good arm and cradled the *Metro* in the crook of his elbow, trapping his bag between his legs. I didn't want him to acknowledge our common bond so I put my stump into a pocket. Making micro adjustments to the position of my stump was my way of managing this background reality. My attitude towards all this hadn't changed much over the years. There'd been no moment of satori, no breakthrough to a major new level of understanding. I'm sure the one-armed banker noticed me without appearing to, the same way I noticed him the second he stepped in. I tucked my stump under the book I was reading.

My discomfort on seeing the banker made me think. My whole life I had managed to avoid one-handed people, not hearing about their experience or sharing mine. Why was I afraid of acknowledging what we had in common? I was worried by something. In the summer break before my training contract started, I got in touch with REACH, a charity for upper-limb-deficient children and volunteered on an outdoor activity week. At a training weekend in the Welsh mountains I was one of six adult volunteers, each with cut-down arms or little buds for fingers. It was like discovering a new set of instantly close friends. As we walked over the barren hills I had a feeling of almost joyful tenderness towards them all. We ended up in a pub. One guy boasted he could hammer in a nail with one hand. I wanted him to demonstrate on the dart board because although I can manage this, I get very intense and grumpy about it and lose three nails on the floor for every one that goes in. I caught myself thinking that my disability wasn't very substantial compared to some of theirs, a bit lightweight.

As other people came into the pub it complicated things. I felt an urge to get away from the freaks and blend in with the two-handed pub goers on the tables opposite, who were pretending not to be fascinated by the sight of a bloke with a total of three fingers carrying a round of drinks and the woman counting out change on the bar with her stump. It made me squirm. I was being made to really see what I looked like to everyone else. I imagined we were like the oddball extras in the bar scene at the trading outpost in *Star Wars*.

The activity week itself was held at a centre on the Cornish coast. Parents dropped off their children and soon we all were present. In total there were fewer hands than people. At breakfast, I saw myself when I saw a girl clasping the jam jar to her chest to get some purchase on the lid. That's how I cover myself in jam. The outside of a Marmite jar has always got Marmite on it, but I clutch it to my chest anyway and do it myself. I could prepare food more slowly and thoughtfully, but I hate conceding the time. And it's worth staining my shirt rather than let a smug ten-digit bastard open things for me.

One morning a transcendentally beautiful eleven-year-old girl from the Hebrides sat opposite me. She had a red Alice band holding back long brown hair, glitter make-up around her eyes and two shortened forearms bent back at the elbow. Unlike some of the kids (and adults) she used no hiding techniques. Posing for photos she stood hips square on and beaming at the camera. With the same sort of arm on both sides she looked quite balanced. I watched her pick up her cutlery and make precise use of the few digits that came from the end of her arms to cut into a sausage.

'This is the same boring music they were playing yesterday,' she said.

The surfers who ran the centre had Jack Johnson on a twenty-four-hour loop. She looked at me looking at her.

'Could you pass the tomato sauce?' she said.

I put down my cutlery, passed her the sauce. Then I got up and went outside to look at the sea or else I'd have had to explain my tears. It was her shining beauty, not her lack of hands, that struck me. How I would have hated coming to this camp as a child and how I would have enjoyed it in the end. My unsolvable problem had weighed on me without the relief of sharing it with others. Every day we did a different outdoor pursuit. We could all take a look at each other and, with everything in plain view, genuinely forget about it, maybe for the first time. Funny arms were normal, thus ignorable.

I started seeing things like a parent for the first time. One girl cried because she couldn't do up her zip or her shoes or anything. Another girl insisted she could do it and demonstrated how. This difference may have come from parental attitudes. Up to then I'd assumed my birth was an occasion of nothing but joy; the sorrow of my first appearance hadn't occurred to me. I grew up like all happy children, feeling whole in myself, knowing nothing of the future, the potential difficulties, and other parental anxieties. Another young girl cried and cried when an older girl carelessly told her she would definitely be bullied in high school. It reminded me of when Bob Dylan was told someone had called up the auditorium to say that he was going to shoot Bob at the gig that night. Bob replied that he didn't mind being shot, but he didn't dig being told about it in advance.

Most painful to see was the muted anger in some of the boys. Life had imposed these odd-looking limbs on them and they were locked in a frustrated struggle against their situation, unable to join in the games. They hated being what they were. The girl with the Alice band had it worse than any of them objectively, yet she had it better. But as the week went on even the most unhappy boys softened up and joined in. A thin boy, brown as a berry as Grandma would have said, was in my group for canoeing and abseiling. He was missing his right hand – the more public facing hand and the harder one not to have. He was a clever boy who wanted to make that impression. Wherever we went he carried a science fiction book with him. I wondered if the book was a prop to deflect attention from his missing limb. One of my props is a watch and I feel naked without it. The boy wouldn't put down his book until the last possible moment.

'I was looking forward to the next chapter,' he said, smiling tensely and edging out over the cliff edge.

'Don't worry, these ropes could hold a Mini,' I said.

'Has anyone actually tried this with a Mini?' he replied, letting out the rope with his left hand and disappearing downwards, waving his stump and grimacing up. Maybe he was just a twelve-year-old boy who loved reading and who, like most teenagers, wasn't yet at home in his body. Maybe he'd end up on a meditation retreat one day. At the end of the week I was sorry to say goodbye to the bold girl and the bookish boy, in particular. I wished them well, feeling a wave of sad, hopeful love.

19

WE ARE WHERE WE ARE

'Fuck. Fuck.'

Dickinson smashed down his phone. This time it didn't break. He stood at his floating desk staring at his computer in a sullen fury. He was an old-fashioned lawyer with thick-rimmed glasses and trousers braced above the navel, who believed in the importance of law – unlike most lawyers, who believe in the importance of lawyers.

'Get what's her name in,' he said, referring to the West Indian pool secretary he'd recently described as *Fresh off the banana boat*. I liked working as a trainee under Dickinson, his charming brand of racism and irascibility aside.

The secretary came in.

'Listen both, I have egg literally dribbling down my face and streaming onto my shirt over this,' he said, miming the egg's journey. 'I'm sorry about the confusion yesterday. That was my fault, mea culpa, maxima culpa. But we are where we are . . .'

I enjoyed his way of dispensing with the past.

'. . . and where we are is now, and we need to re-do the Share Purchase Agreement, again.'

Our client in the Swiss pharmaceutical industry was keen to ensure the eventual extraction of even more money from the business they were taking over. After checking amendments to version seventeen of the contract I hurried off to make copies. The firm was spread over three floors of a building which stood on the site of a former mental hospital in the City of London. The corridors and rooms were triumphantly bland, designed as if only to channel electrons of legal data. The photocopier room had a token pot plant which must have survived by sucking vapour from captive trainees. A fresh-faced Mancunian from civil litigation was copying leases. I dreaded a rotation in his department as it was even busier than mine.

'I need to do these SPAs really fast. Can I get ahead of your next run?' I asked.

'Sure. I've got a tree's worth to go, but they can wait,' he said.

'Thanks. Was it late again last night?'

'Eleven,' he said, proudly.

'Why do you always stay so late?' I asked. He circulated a lot of joke emails in the evenings.

'It's dead busy in PFI. I'd kill to be leaving when you guys do.'

He seemed annoyed by the implication that it wasn't always strictly necessary to stay late. My ideal department had reasonable hours and a partner without a personality disorder. Trouble was, I'd already been in that department. Choosing a seat was sailing between the Scylla of one partner who threw files around when things weren't going her way and the Charybdis of the guy who had a habit of sacking people by text message. It was like Chile: teamwork, collegiate approach, open-door policy – then disappearance.

After the deal closed Dickinson took me out with the client to an old-fashioned City club with heavy napkins and wooden tea trolleys. The cutlery was made from big game. The client fixed up corporate buy-outs and spent most of his waking life taking planes from one meeting to the next. The Buddhist community had buffered me from contact with people who go to such exhausting lengths to secure property. He was in a buoyant mood as he detailed for us his current means of transport, aside from his two business cars and the two family 'run arounds'. 'I've just bought my dream motorbike. My wife has her sports car and now I have my bike. I'm going to ride it up to the boat at the weekend.' I liked having a thicker wallet and taking taxis to swish restaurants, but I could see why Jesus said it was so much easier for a camel to get through the eye of a needle, than for the rich man trying to get to heaven on about eight wrong modes of transport.

The real cost of a shoe allowance
Throughout the two years of my solicitor traineeship I tried to keep up a morning meditation practice. Joanna and I sat together facing a little shrine on the window sill, starting with either a chant she'd learned from a Buddhist monastery or one I knew. If I was feeling tetchy I set my stool up in the spare room. Keeping up the inspiration was harder without a dozen brothers and a dedicated shrine room. Some mornings settling my mind on the breath was like trying to get a wetsuit on a chimp.

When you live in a Buddhist community even if you have a bad day, the conditions around you tend to coax you back to awareness and harmonious connections with others.

Outside in the real world, the conditions of life are angled away from awareness and slide you down towards whatever poison takes your fancy. I picked up a Radio 4 addiction. In the community I'd missed out on a morning dose of John Humphrys' stinging replies to politicians intent on saying nothing. Soon I lacked the moral strength not to listen to Radio 4. Eating breakfast in a quiet kitchen was far too challenging.

The *Today* programme was a fix for morning anxiety, smothering my internal babble with a stream of external babble about what the Minister for Education had to say about the latest set of SATS or what someone else had to say about the Minister of Education. Over a slice of toast, a soothing feature on Iranian foreign policy, or a despatch on torture in the Congo followed by a Cabinet person saying how different they were to the Tories, by half a percentage point at least. At least once a week the debate about science and religion popped up.

'Why the hell don't they find out about Buddhism and get over all this crap about science and God?' I complained. 'We've been listening to this rubbish for the last four hundred years.'

Joanna moved to turn the radio off.

'No, leave it.'

One morning John Humphrys interviewed someone about their PhD on the potentially positive effects of birdsong.

'So tell us,' he said, 'should we be listening to birds more?'

On the bus to Liverpool Street the birdsong thing came back to my mind. Do we need a scientist to tell us it's good to listen to a blackbird? Will funding only be given to protect woodlands if someone with a PhD can demonstrate a positive neurological correlation in the pre-frontal cortex? Indignation about the state of the world plus a double latte buoyed me up enough to hit my desk running. For six months I was coordinating court injunctions against misbehaving tenants, an easy enough seat of manageable boredom and intense bursts of blame.

'You forgot to book counsel!' my line manager yelled at me.

It's okay to make a mistake, they said during the induction. Everyone makes mistakes once in a while.

'I've got the client in court and no fucking counsel!' she went on.

Most mistakes can be fixed, they assured us, just let your line manager know. The worst mistakes are the ones we try to hide.

'That case was settled last week,' I said.

'Why didn't you say something? The client will think I'm the idiot. Always put a case-closing letter in the fucking file.'

'It's . . . um, here,' I said, leafing through the file, enjoying being right but trying not to sound like I was enjoying it.

'Put it at the *top* of the fucking file where I can see it!'

She needed a blackbird CD.

I carried on retreating when I could. I spent a fortnight in Wales at a retreat centre in a collection of grey stone buildings on the side of a valley, just up from a freezing fast-flowing river. For a while life was set against something bigger and more real. Before meditations I stopped to watch the resident flycatcher darting around in loops back to his post and small birds flitting inside the bushes. Buzzards screeched above a sheep field. Back at my desk, as I checked through the umpteenth set of amendments to an intellectual property contract, the birdsong, the running river, the ungraspable living world was reduced to nothing much.

Sometimes my manager said she wished she could go on retreat.

'Your retreats sound really peaceful,' she said.

She thought karma meant calmer.

Lawyers experience the world as a place for which they are providing the supporting documentation. With a target for billable hours and existence resolved into six-minute chunks, there's usually not enough on the upside even to justify a stroll in the park at lunchtime, even though everyone bleats on about what a good idea it is. Capable employees usually fail to escape the gravitational pull towards the partnership, the high seat of dysfunction. Unless they're secretly enslaved to an evil power or supporting a starving family, it's fair to assume that being a lawyer is voluntary. Dreams of a different way of life lie dormant in the un-billable nether regions of a lawyer's mind.

One Zen teacher said incessant busy-ness is laziness masquerading as virtue, a mere excuse to avoid looking inwards. Leonard Cohen didn't join the Zen monastery because it was a cool thing to do. He was depressed. His life, he said, had a glamorous cover story, but inside he was shipwrecked.

Now I was independent of the Buddhist Centre, with my very own shoe allowance, I could move towards ordination at my own pace, which was turning out to be very slowly. No Buddhist text recommends sweating away at corporate deals or disguising a desire for a large salary under a thin veneer of professional values as a means to Awakening. Friends assumed I must be trying to 'reform the system from within'. I certainly wasn't.

During my third rotation my meditation practice finally went under. The partner, an alpha female, was grinding an obedient team of two-faced lawyers out of some reasonably pleasant individuals. The post-room manager called her The Penguin, and when she wasn't there he would waddle in with the post. I had no meditation strategy for dealing with a person like her. One morning she was late in and I caught myself wondering if she might have been hit by a bus.

Like any miserable lawyer I took my moods home. One bank holiday we went to the Durdle Door, one of England's finest geological features, for respite. I lumbered along the wet shingle beach in my hiking boots as Joanna skipped ahead in plimsolls and a body warmer, looking for fossils nearer to the cliffs.

'The Durdle Door is shit,' I called over.

The unimpeachable beauty of the scene increased my sense of misery.

'I wish we hadn't bothered coming. I need coffee and a piss,' I went on.

Joanna intensified her rock survey, moving upwind and out of earshot. I'd been complaining for two days.

'Shall we go back to the apartment then and drive to Lyme Regis for afternoon tea?' she said, wandering back to show me some pebbles.

'I don't care about Lyme Regis.'

'What do you care about then, exactly?'

I hadn't a clue.

We drove down to Lyme Regis to look at a local festival with candles. I took us via the scenic route with Joanna holding the map.

'If you hold it in the direction of travel it's much easier,' I said, glancing across.

'Just turn right next time you can and that'll be fine,' she replied.

'Is that right you mean right or right you mean left?' I said, familiar with her directional bravado.

'It's right I mean right!' she said.

We turned right.

'This looks wrong, we're heading inland, this is the opposite way,' I said, with rising irritation.

'Never mind, we'll get there.'

I looked across to the map on her lap.

'If you'd turned it around you'd have seen that.'

Her silence deepened and my fury built as we sped along a thin country lane. I felt like smashing the steering wheel to pieces.

'You've sent us the wrong way again and you don't even care!'

My little hand downed and upped the gears around corners like it was rally cross.

'We're going home. I can't stand this,' I announced.

We hit an A-Road with a signpost to Lyme Regis.

'Well, at least I've got us back on track!' I said.

This took things a bit too far and we both started giggling.

'Why are you such a god forsaken miserable sod?' she asked.

I had no answer. Lying on the grass later I felt relaxed for the first time in a while. Every Sunday afternoon I felt okay for about an hour and half, before being dragged down again by the thought of another week. We ate ice cream in the late afternoon sun and watched tourists wandering along the Cobb. I tried to work out why I'd got so bad-tempered, and why I'd reserved it all for our holiday.

'I know that wanting to be someone or somewhere I'm not is the cause of suffering,' I said, 'but sod all that Buddhist wisdom. It's obvious. I just can't do it. Look at me. After ten years of cultivating inner contentment I'm completely self obsessed.'

'Not *completely* self-obsessed,' Joanna said.

'I've been on dozens of retreats. I spent six years living in a Buddhist community and training for ordination. I worked for peanuts for the good of Buddhism. Now I can't even get out of bed to meditate. A decade of meditating on loving kindness and I feel a random hatred for anyone who gets in my way.'

She suggested I'd lost perspective, but I didn't want to break my flow.

'I've lost friends . . . I used to have friends but I bored them to death by going on about Buddhism. And now I've hardly got any Buddhist friends either, because I bored them to death with my doubts about Buddhism. Even the cult won't have me.'

Joanna listed a few good friends, Buddhist and non-Buddhist. Her facts irritated me.

'Maybe I should have become a lawyer when I left university. At least I'd have some decent money by now. I'm thirty-three, I hate my job, and I haven't even qualified.

I can't even quit and go off and have a spiritual Awakening. I've already done that and it didn't work.'

'It's soooo terrible, poor little you . . .' she said, playing an imaginary violin. Her mocking strategy was more effective than reasoning.

'Pooooor you. Dismal Jimmy at the Durdle Door,' she said.

'Where'd you learn "dismal Jimmy"?'

'From you.'

Most weeks I went to a class at the Buddhist Centre, setting out cushions at the start and making tea at the break. I was proficient at that by now. Sometimes I bumped into Jnanavaca.

'I want to undo the friendship ceremony we performed,' I said at one of our tense, cordial meetings.

'Can I ask why?' Jnanavaca said, frowning.

'It was premised on an error of expectation between us and not helpful.'

'Oh, well, I don't know if there is a way to undo it, not formally.'

'I think I'll feel more able to re-engage with the Buddhist Centre if we call it quits on that front.'

'Well, okay, let's just leave it then, there's no need to go into it.'

Jnanavaca thought Ratnaghosha was blind to my hardheartedness. Ratnaghosha thought Jnanavaca was taking things too personally. I wanted to be back in harmony with Jnanavaca and Maitreyabandhu. I pretended I was immune to anything they had to say, but deep down I knew there was something important in being able to bear with criticism. Whenever we met up, though, I felt inferior. Somehow *they* had slipped over the fence and into the green pastures of faith and abundant good qualities where I could never go. I was stuck on my little patch. Sometimes I thought them better than me, sometimes the same, sometimes that they lived in a Buddhist fantasyland. In the old days I'd have shared my thoughts and fears with Jnanavaca and opened up my interior world to his kind, astute perspectives. But I wasn't going to do that any more. I had Joanna to suffer all that.

The story about myself was dug in like a nasty splinter. There seemed no next chapter. I couldn't change. On one level, it was a conflict between the boy in the playground who had a problem he believed could never ever be solved, and the more optimistic boy who struggled to get on and succeed at things. On another level, it was conflict between the reasonable worldly life I'd grown up to expect and the spiritual life which ultimately has nothing to do with that. Through Sangharakshita's life and teachings, I'd had a glimpse of the Buddha's Dharma. I didn't ask for it. It caught me unawares. As the life-changing implications of the Dharma began to bite, I became more unhappy. Financial and emotional dependency made it hard to leave the Buddhist community. Worse was the sense of failing at the spiritual life by giving up the conditions which I had come to see as indispensable to progress. If a friend pointed out my good qualities I took it as a well-meant lie. Any criticism, however fair, played into my worst fears of being rotten to the core. This conflict in myself was played out as a battle with other people.

Jnanavaca and Maitreyabandhu were right not to support my ordination. I needed to integrate and resolve something in myself. Ordination was a pivotal moment.

It consisted of two ceremonies, one performed in private, one in public. If I ever got there, Ratnaghosha would officiate at the private ceremony with just me and him. A private preceptor's role is to witness that the ordinand is acting out of their own inspiration and will continue do so regardless of what anyone else thinks or does. The public ordination marks acceptance into the Order and a commitment to live the Dharma life in harmony with others, for the benefit of all beings.

The ordained person gets the title Dharmachari (m) or Dharmacharini (f), meaning Farer in the Way, and a new name. Bhante called this *the stage of spiritual death and spiritual rebirth*. Spiritual death refers to the movement towards giving up fixed self-view, not taking life so personally, and taking the implications of impermanence seriously. Spiritual rebirth refers to the beautiful qualities of heart and mind that flow from this dying and the movement towards realisation of non-duality. Ordination marked a connection with a reality beyond self-clinging, a bond symbolised by receiving a visualised meditation practice on an archetypal Buddha figure.

Ratnaghosha lived in Cambridge, where he was now manager of the Buddhist warehouse where I had briefly worked. At fifty-two he was full of spritely vigour beneath his bland outfits. He was happy to ordain me, but it wasn't only for him to say. As we wandered along the Backs I hammered up my stupider thoughts for his amusement.

'Be bigger, not better,' he said again.

He told me about his long solitary retreat and a history book he was reading. We went to see a painting he loved of the Virgin Mary at the Fitzwilliam. Buddhist tradition talks in terms of stages and steps, but in real life it's not so simple. Things come higgledy-piggledy and the slow drift of progress is more easily discerned in retrospect. Spiritual progress is 'glacial', as one Order member put it to me. Slowly we move beyond our self-story, laden as it often is with guilt, resentment, blame or envy.

Ratnaghosha said that the best was yet to come, that ordination was just the start of another journey. He wasn't blind to my shortcomings. Once, as we walked back to the Cambridge train station, he remarked how, since I started work at the law firm, I was swearing more.

'Actually I think you've become cruder in general,' he said, cheerfully.

'Well, Ratnaghosha,' I replied. 'We are where we are.'

20

BIG MIND

B y 2008 the Order had turned forty and was starting to wonder what it had done with its life. There were resignations. The early generations of Western Buddhists had been heroes to me. Led by the visionary Sangharakshita, they gave their lives to building centres, retreats and communities, conditions which would allow the Dharma to flourish in the West.

It wasn't just about meditation, or adding a sprinkling of mindfulness to what already existed. They wanted to bring a new society and a new type of consciousness into being. They were fired up by Bhante's vision and basked in the glow of its meaning and purpose. Whatever they said about it later with hindsight, at the time they experienced an uplifted imagination for life's potential, which the lawyer who had recently retired from my commercial property department had never known, unless he hid it exceptionally well. He was a good man, too gentle and even-minded to make the partnership, with hair on the rim of his ears long enough to comb. After twenty-five years at the firm he left with leaving drinks and no-one mentioned him again, except for his initials on files he hadn't managed to close down.

'Have you seen RDO.17.65?'

When you are fired up with vision you don't miss having a wine cellar and detached house in Tunbridge Wells. Working in a poorly paid cooperatives or sharing three to a room was no hardship. It was the good life and for some Order members it still was.

But for others, regrets were now surfacing about lives that had not been lived. There were accusations that group pressure had caused people to sideline families and children, or not have them in the first place. I'd always imagined I'd have children at some point in the future, but the urge hadn't yet become specific. Some friends had become fathers regardless of what they said about it. In the 'early days' most Order members didn't have children and spoke openly about not wanting any. It was a young community and there was no etiquette for ordinary life events like announcing an engagement or a baby on the way. Instead of a slap on the back and a celebratory drink you got an awkward silence and a sense that babies and spouses would make a mess of Buddhist practice.

Whichever way you spin it, Buddha and Jesus weren't family men. They didn't co-author *The Joy of Sex* either. That doesn't mean they hated families or were against sex. Bhante shared the orthodox Buddhist view that anyone, monk or lay, with or without family, can develop to the furthest extent on the Path. Some people find it reassuring to settle the question of whether they can become a Buddha *and* have a family. It's nice to know. Bhante said that for some men having children may be a necessary way of maturing. However, he said that some lifestyles, such as monasticism, are in general more conducive to spiritual growth than others, and additional family responsibilities were, in general, best not taken on by anyone wanting to lead a full-time spiritual life. And who wants a part-time spiritual life?

Others were critical of Bhante's attack on coupledom. He once called the 'neurotic couple' the 'enemy of the spiritual community'. Such couples were 'like two paper bags trying to get inside each other', he added for good measure. I understood this to be a colourful way of saying that relationships can devolve into a futile attempt to solve one's own sense of inner lack. They can, right?

Some people took such statements rather personally, as though Bhante had said: 'David, you and Joanna are a neurotic couple and an enemy of this community. You are like paper bags, one trying to climb inside the other.' Had he actually said that, I like to think I'd have told him to bugger off and mind his own business. Strip away the context for what we say and we are easily made to seem obnoxious. Was our interaction about my mum visiting the community evidence of Bhante's misogyny, or me trying, unsuccessfully, to back a dinner guest into a corner?

Perhaps naturally enough, a number of those pioneering Order members were wondering whether they had fallen prey to what a Buddhist psychologist called *spiritual bypassing*. This refers to the condition of a spiritual seeker who presumes that, whereas ordinary folk are beset by all sorts of mental and emotional difficulties, blind spots and shadowy aspects, as they bluster through life, he or she has the inside track and can proceed directly to universal love and compassion. This is the smug phase of spiritual practice. After a few glorious laps, life starts dropping hints that things might not work out as projected. A tendency to depression or loneliness returns. A friend with three kids starts to look happier than you. You feel flabbier in body and purpose. Then it gets worse: the government puts back the state pension age, your mother gets dementia and the inheritance leaks away in care-home fees. They don't even seem to need you at the Buddhist Centre any more.

Mid-life reveals the bitter truth that life doesn't really work. It's not hidden in Buddhist small print, it's the First Noble Truth of Suffering, or Dukkha – pain, loss, un-satisfaction, death. The Buddha was supremely happy, well beyond happy, but his take on the woes of ordinary life was radical and deep. This sorrowful world is on fire with greed, hatred and delusion, he said. The Way beyond sorrow is hard to find and hard to tread. In theory, as we understand the Noble Truth of Dukkha, we give up the endless game of making life better and gradually unbind from the causes of Dukkha. Then happiness naturally arises, along with a freedom of heart which, from the point of view of ordinary life is hard to imagine, because it goes beyond the problem of death.

Sounds good. Does it work, though? Some Order members were mired in a mid-life feeling of things having not worked out. Joining a Buddhist community and doing a bit, or a lot, of meditation hadn't saved them. They wished they hadn't done things they had done. They felt Bhante had led them up the garden path into childless communities and poorly paid cooperative businesses and now the bottom had dropped out of their belief in it all, leaving them with uncomfortable thoughts about the choices they had made. Had they been messing with deeper forces than they'd realised? I assumed I wouldn't get into that kind of mess, which was probably the same assumption they made.

Put another way, the Order's mid-life crisis was also a crisis about Insight. Insight refers to the decisive moment when a practitioner crosses an important threshold. Trying to give too precise a definition about when exactly that moment is, is where the trouble starts. To swap metaphors, with Insight one Enters the Stream. The current flowing towards Buddhahood is now irresistible. Okay, it's a metaphor, but it's metaphorical of something, so people reasonably wanted to know: has anyone Entered the Stream? For some, doubt about the Order's capacity to produce men and women who had Entered the Stream was confirmed by the fact that several senior Order members were going on retreats of up to three years with teachers from other schools of Buddhism, who taught under different systems of practice. They were then coming back with teachings and practices which clashed, or sat at odds with, some of Bhante's teachings, or seemed to, or might have done – hell knows, it was a tough debate to follow.

Gary, a friend from my first community, was an affable and overweight man with a nest-like beard. After five years in the Buddhist gift shop, he'd left the community and gone back into software design. One day a man, who wasn't an Order member, was invited to speak at the Buddhist Centre at the launch of his book about his Awakening. Gary and I went along. In the book he claimed he'd made substantial and real spiritual progress, telling the reader what this consisted of and how to achieve it. His confidence about Insight was infectious and for many people, including Gary and me, it keyed into the general question about whether anyone in the Order had attained it.

Did Ratnaghosha have Insight? How would I know that? Could I deduce it from his even temper, from his actions, or from what he said? He'd passed a lot of stress testing from me over the years, but surely there was more to it than that?

Did Bhante have Insight? Wonderful teacher of Buddhism though he was, did he lack a clinical finish inside the six-yard box? He could seem a bit intellectual and a bit preoccupied with art. He wasn't too picturesque either.

Did I have Insight? No. At least that was clear. Yet how did I know I didn't? Well, if I had Insight, then Insight was pretty disappointing and not worth worrying about.

Some years later this speaker wrote an open letter saying that Order members 'plateaued' out as good people but lacked Insight. Maybe he was right. As far as I know, no-one wrote back to assert their attainments. Traditional Buddhism advises caution about claiming attainments. Claiming direct knowledge which you don't have is cause for expulsion from the monastic order.

Enlightenment, whatever it is, is not 'you' or 'yours' to attain, so unless done with care, any talk about Insight and Entering the Stream can seem a bit fishy. Still, though no-one expected all Order members to have Insight, one or two would have been nice. Gary had grown sure that the whole Order lacked Insight. He didn't know the whole Order but he carried the weave across from the people he did know.

Gary didn't appear to have Insight either.

But that was about to change, as there were other teachers of Enlightenment in London, and before long Gary was going to see some of the more extreme. One appeared to re-assure Gary that he, Gary, was Already Enlightened. Not because of any efforts Gary had made, but because people are Already Enlightened if only they but knew it. We met at the greasy spoon to discuss spiritual developments.

'Sangharakshita's always on about developing into an ideal happy, healthy human being. But look at the guys in the community. It doesn't work, does it?' Gary said, rhetorically.

'I know what you mean, I guess,' I replied.

'All this personal development, it's nonsense.'

'Yeah, life's not easy.'

My hackles were rising. I'd heard this from him before.

'No need to get stuck in all that business about ethics either,' he said.

I was squeezing brown sauce onto my chips, and bracing against an onslaught of Instant Enlightenment.

Gary went on: 'There's no such thing as right and wrong. It's just convention. You have to get beyond that.'

I wanted to stab him with my fork to see if his theory held up.

'Gary, that guy you go to see talks bullshit,' I said, flinching with irritation.

'Come and listen if you like, then say it's bullshit,' Gary replied, fairly. 'There is no Path, and no amount of ethical do-goodery is going to get you there. You just have to wake up and smell the roses. We are already Awake, brother.'

'So you go to see this twat in order to be told that there's no need to go to see him because you are already Awake?'

'There is no Path. We are already Enlightened.' Gary repeated.

'I assume people only go to see this bloke once? I mean, once he's said that why hang around?'

'Buddhists can't see the Big Mind.'

'Oh, fuck off!'

I abandoned my plate and walked out. We had reached the end of rational appraisal. But then fully aware that this demonstrated my Small Mind was alive and kicking, I came back in and apologised.

My friend had been taken in by the We Are Already Enlightened school. I'd been to this type of talk. The speaker uses a phrase like 'Big Mind', contrasting it with 'Small Mind' a hundred and fifty times. It's a good idea and easy to get a flicker of what the speaker means, perhaps even a genuine sense of what liberation from ego-centred concerns might feel like.

Bushes are just Bushes, one thinks.

Why have I been making it all so complicated?

Just let go. . .

Big Mind. This. Is. It.

About ten seconds later Small Mind creeps back in like a commando and merges himself into the Thus Illumined Bushes proclaiming victory and telling everyone about Big Mind. I want to say, hey, give it up, you're just a tiny Little Mind dressed up in the Big Mind's clothes! Stop trying to fool me and come out with your hands up.

Bhante called all this kind of teaching antinomian, but hardly anyone understood what that meant.

'Have you read *The Power of Now?*' was a phrase I heard a lot at this time.

'Eckhart Tolle is amazing.'

Yup, he's great. He's onto something, I agree. I enjoy his writings and maybe he's Enlightened. It's not a question that keeps me up at night.

After hearing a lecture by someone who stresses Enlightenment and how simple and readily at hand it is, I agree and agree and agree, then file back onto the pavement essentially unchanged, apart from wondering if all those hours of meditation practice were actually unnecessary, or if I've just been subjected to an hour of anti-intellectual, pseudo-spiritual jujitsu. Anyway, I don't want my dualistic assumptions undermined all the bloody time. I like them. And is Enlightenment really so democratic and easy, or are we just feeling relieved that the concepts by which we struggle to understand the world have at last been made irreducibly simple? The 'heady' types can kid themselves they aren't heady any more because they have *direct experience*, whatever that means. They can abandon any meditation practice they secretly didn't want to do and, as a bonus, there's hours of fun ahead inflicting the same outpouring of soulless tedium on their friends until everyone has Big Mind.

Living the question

Some old sage, long ago, told his students that the path leading out of the sorrowful round of birth and death was so long and hard that it was better not to start, but that having started it was better not to stop. It's quite easy to stop practising the Dharma and end up just *thinking* about practising it. Thinking about it slots into the daily round of preoccupations as easily as throwing another shirt into the tumble-dryer.

I thought about the Dharma every day, even on days I didn't meditate, and even on days when thinking about it troubled and confused me. And I loved the Order. No single perspective or final truth emerged about the past, the present or the future. Many in the community acknowledged that they'd been 'too wilful' about meditation and life in general. I felt that too. I couldn't 'work with' my mind as I had previously. It wasn't playing ball any more. I needed a new approach. Others were feeling similarly and before long Pure Awareness retreats were popping up. Pure Awareness is an open style of meditation which embodies a more receptive attitude to whatever is experienced. Some people said that other practices were a waste of time compared to Pure Awareness and so arguments started up about that.

Owen and I hadn't been in touch for a while. When I ran into him at a Buddhafield festival it was like seeing an old army buddy – five years in the barracks bringing each other tea, meditating side by side, arguing, hiking about. He had a sleepy young daughter perched on his forearms, blonde and blue-eyed like him, with the same dimpled cheek.

'So you're back in the cult then?' I said.

'Yeah, listen, about that . . . er, hold on mate . . . she says she wants to go get her face painted as a Pawnee. Shall we grab a cup of chai later? That's about all they've got round here.'

Over spiced tea and energy balls he told me about his new life as a father and his higher studies in English. He apologised to me for some things he'd said and done around the time he left the community. It was great to see him. Maybe we could have a proper friendship in the future, one where we openly liked each other. Maybe we could go on retreats together again, and look forward to a rancorous old age, arguing about who was the most wise and eccentric. But that wasn't going to happen.

Towards the end of my third rotation at the law firm I went on a Pure Awareness retreat. Day after day I sat there, like one of those huge radar dishes in the deserts of Chile, patiently recording data from distant galaxies without judging or analysing. I don't think I woke up to my True Nature, but I enjoyed a feeling which I call being fairly-excited-by-an-intuition-that-this-might-be-going-somewhere. Maybe that's faith. One morning as I came out of the meditation hall I was given a note telling me to see the retreat leader. They had received news that the previous night Owen had been rushed to hospital with septicaemia. The GP hadn't picked it up and sent him home, where it had spiralled out of control. Owen was rushed to hospital with acute organ failure and died.

Before the evening puja I said a few words about Owen to the other retreatants. He was like a brother with whom I compared my life: better than him, worse than him, better again, then lately realising it wasn't so clear or so important. Now he was no longer breathing. What did that mean for this strange quest about which we had bonded, discussed, disagreed? If life is like a long question, Owen's answer was cut short. I felt bound to honour the question and carry on, out of duty to what Owen and I had shared. Back at work, my line manager, whom I so vilified, was genuinely sympathetic. Her daughter was a similar age to Owen's. For nearly three minutes a reflective mood undercut the carry-on in our department.

Owen's funeral was at the Manchester Buddhist Centre. The ceremony was a puja, whose words evoke a universal spiritual journey, the heroic archetype of going beyond self and other with an aspiration to deliver all beings from suffering into Awakening. It felt truer for being chanted over a dead body, I don't know why. The wicker coffin lay at the feet of the Buddha surrounded by flowers and candles. I wanted to look inside but the lid was closed. Like Joanna, Owen was thirty-five. I imagined her dying, me dying, and which way round would be worse.

After the ceremony we went to the crematorium. I took the left corner at the front of the casket. The other bearers were taller than me and it started listing my way as we went down the aisle towards the bier. It was so heavy, I was beginning to panic. Was his poetry collection in there with him? The platform onto which we had to hoist the coffin was too high and if the others went for it the whole thing would fall on me and Owen would roll out for the last laugh. An undertaker swept under my corner in the nick of time. As the body was committed, his partner started up an old native American chant about Walking in Beauty, which we sang in a round.

21

MAKING MERIT

At the Thai forest monastery in Hertfordshire where Joanna was doing her retreats, the monks and nuns had a complex routine of rules to remind them of practice and its purpose – rules for eating, sleeping, meditating, clothes, meeting people, travelling and more, all broken down into hundreds of minor rules. One, for example, resulted in it being okay to drink orange juice in the afternoon if someone offered it to you, but not if it was orange juice 'with bits'. Monastic rules can devolve into pettiness, but any life can devolve into pettiness. Starting the following year, Joanna was going to be the live-in retreat centre manager. Self-respect made it awkward, though not impossible, for me to complain about her wanting to immerse herself in the life of a Buddhist community. The thought of her becoming a nun made me feel sick.

My law firm had rules and observances too, written and unwritten, but none to support spiritual growth. Towards the end of my training contract Dickinson observed that I didn't seem interested in corporate transactions. To cut it as a lawyer, he said, I needed to think outside the box. Joanna and I were planning to get eight thousand miles outside the box, on a long train journey to Thailand. Our Polish

friend, my old community roommate Mahananda, wanted
to come with us. At sixty years old he was a striking man,
expanding steadily in girth, with a bald head and fulsome
beard. Following his mother's death he was sole heir and
landlord to the family's four-storey house in Primrose Hill.
We swept aside the pickled condiments on his kitchen table
to make way for *The Times Atlas of the World* and over the
next few months we arranged visas and tickets as far as
Beijing. Mahananda left enough kilos of posh seed mix
with a tenant to get all the goldfinches in north London
through the winter, and on the same day that my name
was at last entered on the Roll of Solicitors of England &
Wales we boarded the Eurostar at Kings Cross.

Our first stop was Krakow. Mahananda lived in the
shadow of his mother's ordeal, which began there. He
showed us the hotel window where Zosia and her husband
had lived for a short spell, hiding their identity from the
Nazis. They ended up tenanted in another family's home.
The warning sign was a flower pot on the window sill. If
the pot was out, the agreement was to walk on by and not
come in. Coming home one day, Zosia saw the pot. She
could see people inside, officials. Assuming the game was
up, Zosia went in anyway to take the blame, to save the
family who had allowed them to live there. It was a brave
thing to do and a terrible mistake. The officials were there
on unrelated business. Their cover was blown and she never
saw her husband again.

We sauntered around town with Mahananda, being
chided for our measly knowledge of modern architecture.
Something as plain as a factory wall or building facade, a
young woman on a tram all made up for work, or a waiter

smoking in a back alley, could reduce him to tears of sadness or joy. His mother's Auschwitz number – 63565 – had been tattooed on her forearm. He told us how children of camp survivors feel protective towards their parent, responsible for them, burdened by the unspeakable past. When he was a boy his mother buried his pet budgerigar in a neighbour's back garden before little Andrew got home from school, to protect him from the fact of death. Little Andrew was furious, but the family rule was to keep schtum.

Andrew was 18 when his father died. Zosia was stoic, talented; she managed the family business on her own. Her son was homosexual and would never repopulate the family. She cut out photos of his female friends and arranged them suggestively on the fridge. She enraged him in a hundred different ways, but she had suffered so much. It was just the two of them. He wrote about her traumatic past, painted it, visited it. One day, in his forties, the grief, fury and guilt burst out in her kitchen, in a hail of eggs, flour and china plates. Maitreyabandhu gave Andrew a new name at his ordination ceremony. He wept with joy on hearing it. It was new identity, a new story, which promised something beyond his dark and messy personal history and the horror of the Holocaust. He donated money to help turn a second-hand clothes shop in the old Jewish quarter into Krakow's – if not Poland's – first Buddhist Centre.

Our visit was timed to coincide with the opening ceremony. Bhante was there in his Afghan hat, looking older, walking with a stick, but beaming with delight as he cut the ribbon. This was the same person who'd met my mother in the breakfast room in Cheam forty-five years earlier. My mother's spiritual aim was a happy family life away from her father. Bhante had no interest in family life, wishing only for the spiritual life in its fullest form. I was somewhere in the middle. Bhante had given me a koan: what more is there than this little life to which you cling?

We set off by train towards Siberia.

Joanna refused to be impressed by the fairy tale domes of St Basil's in Moscow. For fifty years Russia had bled Poland dry of its produce, so in revenge we scrumped apples in the Kremlin gardens. Later we descended down a dark marble stairway in Red Square, into an airless underground chamber. Rounding the corner we saw, still lying in state eighty-five years after his death, the figure of Lenin in a black suit, face unearthly pale, one hand clenched into a fist.

'There are soldiers lurking in the gloom,' Mahananda said, clutching my arm. 'I want one of their hats.' He was taking surreptitious pictures of them from a camera held at his hip.

'Shhh, you'll get us arrested,' Joanna said.

'He's in bed,' I said.

'It's not a bed, it's a catafalque!' I knew nothing about ballet, architecture and now catafalques.

Joanna was brought up Catholic. Her culture taught her there is the spiritual reality behind things, whereas my culture told me things is all there is. A big difference. As a teenager she did four long pilgrimages from Warsaw to the shrine of Black Madonna in southern Poland. Then the other Madonna grabbed her interest and she went west to London, marrying a Portuguese man at twenty. They soon split up. She battled her way through A Levels, then read law at university, rising all the way to the Bar at Inns of Court. In Yekaterinburg she dyed her hair blonde to fit in with the Russian girls, the way she used to have it. I wouldn't have got a look-in during her period of leather mini-skirts and Michael Jackson concerts. The Head of Chambers was after her, and other guys with boats. I had to wait for her spiritual phase. She insisted I was getting the best bit.

Our train ride was a long route to Wat Pa Nanachat, a temple in Thailand founded by Ajahn Sumedho under the guidance of his Thai teacher. Ajahn Chah was a famous forest renunciant, a small and mischievous man, whose direct, Zen-like teachings were widely loved. He had a koan about spiritual progress being 'not forwards, not backwards, and not standing still'. He died in the 1980s after an illness had him bedridden for ten years, unable to move or speak. His monastery was part of the Theravada, a tradition older than the Catholic Church, tracing a direct line back to the Buddha. Joanna said she was able to go deeper with the teachings of Ajahn Chah than she'd been able to do in 'my' Buddhist group. After just four retreats with Ajahn Sumedho, she exuded confidence in the Dharma.

'Do you think Ajahn Chah is better than Bhante?'

'Holding to ideas of better and worse is a cause for more suffering,' she said.

I was pretty easy to outflank. There was hubris in the way I'd taken up Bhante's teachings. No doubt he was an exceptional figure, a spiritual genius, a sort of cross between William Blake and Rudolph Steiner. I borrowed his genius and mistook it for my own. Joanna spoke about Bhante with affection. She sent him birthday cards and once went to visit him to express her gratitude. Whatever else he was, he was also a person with feelings. Joanna treated everyone like that, nice and evenly. She was always giving stuff away, sometimes stuff I considered my stuff.

We began the long haul east from Moscow on the Trans-Mongolian, trundling through the birch forests which rose over the gentle watershed of the Urals. In towns full of big shiny cars and Versace advertisements we visited museums about displacement and starvation. Mahananda led us round back streets, teaching us to distinguish Deco from Bauhaus from the international style. Chugging again through endless forest, we played travel scrabble over pot noodles and borsch, taking turns to collect water from the samovar, an intimidating contraption at the end of each carriage.

At Lake Baikal I finally felt the freedom of being lost mid-journey. Joanna and I ran along the tracks of the old Trans-Mongolian route which fringes the southern shore in exultant mood. We were five thousand miles and six train days from London. Far enough away from the law firm to let go of the sting from occasions I'd been wrongly blamed – or rightly blamed – for some error. The sun sparkled on one quarter of the world's fresh water. Mahananda ambled behind chatting to our guide, a blond-haired botanist who told us about the nerpas, freshwater seals indigenous to the lake. The lake was cold, he warned us, though according to legend a dip adds twenty-five years to life.

The others stood on the shingle while I stripped off.

'I'll wager he doesn't make it in,' said Mahananda.

'He's got plenty of blubber. He looks like a nerpa,' Joanna replied.

Mahananda was usually first in an open body of water to cool off like a hippo, but the botanist was making him shy. He was 'in the closet', we later heard. My swim was a nano-second of wild splashing.

Then on to Mongolia. We meditated in our cabin, Joanna wrapped in a shawl against the breezes that Mahananda was desperate to allow in. I wasn't meditating much, and the less I meditated, the less I wanted to meditate. Travelling was tiring and often there was nothing obvious to sit on. Meditating in a chair didn't appeal to me. The less I meditated the more I made of whatever was my instant mood. A minor sense of weariness plus a poorly laid out museum display betokened a meaningless universe. A beggar gnawing a piece of chicken gristle I'd seen him pull from a pile of rubbish reinforced my sense of the hopelessness of spiritual practice. Then, just because the sky was blue or we found somewhere with a proper coffee machine, the overall meaning of things seemed to cheer up again.

In a copper mining town in Mongolia we appeared on live television to tell the residents about Western Buddhism. The local abbot, at whose request we were there, cut in to say that meditation wasn't possible without many years training as a monk and studying Buddhist philosophy. Meditation was only for a specialist monk. Our friend and translator, a Mongolian woman who'd been to the London Buddhist Centre, disputed this with the abbot, live on TV.

We thought the issue was more simple: everyone in Mongolia, the abbot included, was constantly distracted by their mobile phones and answered them as a priority over whatever else was happening. In a monks' quarters in Ulan Bator, Mahananda and I were offered a pinch of snuff by some friendly young aspirants. They laughed when we told them our room in a Buddhist community was even messier than theirs. They came from poor backgrounds. Now they had food, shelter, education and respect. None of them meditated, or so it seemed.

Some young people in Mongolia become Christian to get away from the Buddhist mumbo jumbo of their grandparents. Tibetan-style Buddhist temples didn't inspire me much either. I wanted an English Buddhism with oak leaves and the green man. 'Then grow your beard more,' Mahananda suggested. By now his beard was wild and hoary. The contrast with his bald pate caused several children to burst into tears. I felt I could relate more to Jesus than the Buddha. Evensong in a cathedral is much more uplifting than those dreary mantras. 'Jesus was a good man,' Joanna said.

The finches in Phnom Penn

On our way to a famous monastery in the mountains of middle Mongolia our driver got us lost in a blizzard. As darkness fell, a nomad appeared and agreed to lend us his yurt. We ate something to do with yak and slept under yak blankets at minus ten. A nighttime pee meant braving the Tibetan mastiff at the door.

The next morning we went on horseback to visit the high monastery, which overlooks a vast forest. I found myself imagining the distant future moment when pilgrims from the East visit famous Buddhist caves and rocky ledges in the Cairngorms or the Sierra Nevada, at a time when the Dharma has washed through Western culture, leaving only a popular Buddhist culture and the memory of bygone meditators, those great Western masters who are with us now and yet to come. Some say the heyday for the Dharma in the West is right now, before the hoi polloi get in on the act. Will we have to suffer government-sponsored Buddhism and army top brass bowing at lavish shrines, like they do in Thailand? Sainsbury and Unilever paying for golden meditation halls? Serious practitioners will have to run for the hills to get away from Buddhism, as did the forest monks of Thailand and Burma and the hermits of China.

Traditionally lay Buddhists concentrate on making merit for a better life in the future, either later in this one or in the next one. Merit is gained through good acts, like giving. So far so good. *One good deed a day*, as the scouts say. The more we give, the more inner abundance we feel. Buddhists even imagine giving away the merit gained rather than hoarding it for oneself. This leads to more merit, and hopefully better marriages and better business.

On a boat on the River Yangtze, a local government worker told us the Communist Party had recently unbanned religion, acknowledging that social improvement alone didn't bring happiness. The State itself was now making merit by restoring temples it had once destroyed and installing despondent looking Taoist caretakers. Monks were still not allowed to preach in towns. Office workers came to make offerings, looking ill at ease around a shrine, a bit like some Westerners do when they make offerings at the London Buddhist Centre.

In the Chinese mega-city of Chongqing we were looking for a Starbucks to get away from China when we came upon something more hopeful. The Arhat Temple, hidden between high-rise office blocks, was busy with sculptors working by lamplight on hundreds of life-size statues of Buddhist figures. They included one of Xuanzang, the seventh century monk who had made an epic and dangerous journey on foot around the Himalayas to bring Buddhist teachings to China from India. A terracotta army of Buddhas was being chipped back to life. In a hall underneath, people were chanting a mantra I recognised. I was relieved. I was beginning to think Buddhism may be dead and buried – although our ad hoc survey was far too small for such grand statements.

Throughout our trip we enjoyed new foods, motorbike adventures, stunning scenery and brief friendships. In a third-class carriage in Vietnam an almond-eyed little girl with beautiful young parents became entranced by Mahananda, who duly back-combed his beard into a huge hive for her amusement. They played peek-a-boo through the wooden slatted seats as we rattled past paddy fields towards Hanoi.

Death followed us around too, you couldn't shake it. Every place we passed through was underwritten with a history of war. Down the long curve of Vietnam we saw people with bodily malformations brought about by Agent Orange, the herbicide spread by US bombers to kill the Vietnamese and their forests. Museums displayed graphic shots of exploded carcasses, carpet bombing and napalm. In Cambodia it had been even worse. A woman on the pavement opposite our hotel cradled a young child with large splayed eyes set in an enormous, smooth and hairless head. A land mine victim tried to sell us photocopied classics while we breakfasted on sweet milk and rice. I chose *The Quiet American* and bumped his two stumps with mine in recognition.

Whatever becomes of Western Buddhism, I hope it never includes the practice of bird-freeing. Outside a Buddhist temple in Phnom Penn we saw worshippers paying to free finches from a cage in an act of compassion designed to swell their store of merit. The flaw in the scheme was that the starved creatures hardly had the strength to make it off the ground before they were re-netted and re-caged. Their only escape from the cycle was dropping dead. With the rage of Jesus in the marketplace, I recited the Buddhist precept on non-violence in the original Pali for the bird-caging man's moral education and noisily poured water on a dehydrated bird I found in a bush, well aware that any merit gained by me thereby would be heavily circumscribed by my pomposity. And moan though I did about popular Buddhism, in these parts of the world the secular creed of communism hardly left the air alive with rose scent. If only Pol Pot had wished for social betterment by setting a few birds free, instead of trying to create merit by ordering families to be torn apart or bludgeoned to death with the back of a shovel.

Four months after setting out, we reached Bangkok. We also hit the buffers of tolerance of each other's habits. I was fed up being the details man. Mahananda was fed up with travelling with a couple. Joanna was fed up with two giant babies for company. After a stay on the beach, we headed north to Joanna's monastery and Mahananda flew home to Primrose Hill and his well-fed goldfinches.

A week after we got back to London, Joanna and I went over for dinner. The magnolia was out and winter's detritus cleared from the garden. A friend we made in Vietnam, a Dane, was staying in the spare room. He was fascinated by the weird and wonderful objects decorating Mahananda's flat – a 1950s dentist's chair, wooden mannequins, ancient radio equipment, a collection of plastic biscuits with bite marks in them. Over spring greens and corn on the cob we laughed about our moodier moments holed up in train carriages.

'Spie dobrze, dzieci,' Mahananda said as we left.

Sleep well, children, in Polish.

Next morning, the Danish friend was uncertain about what to do when Mahananda failed to appear for the slow-cooked porridge he had made. There has been some stumbling-about sounds in the night. Eventually he decided to knock and enter Mahananda's bedroom. Mahananada was on the bed, writhing and making incoherent noises. By the time we got to A&E he was completely unconscious on a trolley bed. The doctor said blood was leaking deep into his brain and the surgeons were deciding whether to operate.

Joanna went into a ward toilet and fainted. I heard her calling out and pushed the door open to find her on the floor. She was horribly white and unable to get up. A nurse said she couldn't be treated in A&E because she was a visitor, though I was welcome to carry her out and back in if I liked. I appealed to a passing doctor and he arranged a trolley bed so Joanna could be wheeled into the cubicle next to Mahananda.

The rest of the world dropped away. I made rational decisions, moving back and forth between my two travelling companions. Mahananda squeezed my hand, but the doctor said it was only a reflex, like a squeeze from a baby's hand. Then back over to Joanna. She looked dreadful, but her ECG machine showed improvement and soon her vital signs were restored. Back to Mahananda and a different doctor holding up some x-rays.

This moment had arrived so abruptly. When Maitreya-bandhu got to the hospital all three of us met the surgeon, who looked at Mahananda's pupils and concluded that he didn't want to operate. Surgery would leave our friend in a vegetative state at best. He would die naturally in a few hours. The surgeon left and we sat quietly taking it in.

Mahananda did die a few hours later, after a bout of choking, heaving breaths. Many friends had gathered and we began a Buddhist chant, quietly, as the rest of the ward was getting off to sleep. The nurses wedged the white bed sheet tightly under his arms and across his barrel chest. His bare shoulders soon became cold to the touch and before long our travel companion was taken down to the hospital vault.

IN THE BARDO

The body was pointed headfirst towards the Buddha, the bald, blotchy scalp resting on a cushion of blue silk. The coffin lid was propped against the wall behind the shrine. Mourners came in quietly and crept across the squeaky wooden floor in their socks, and stood there for a while, just looking. He looked a bit squeezed in. This square shrine room at the London Buddhist Centre, once home to Victorian fire trucks, had been Mahananda's spiritual home and it was mine too. Many hours had been spent sitting here, a few feet from the spot he now lay. As people crammed in for the ceremony I sat with my eyes closed, thinking over what I was going to say.

Maitreyabandhu busied with last adjustments to the shrine. Mahananda's Indian puppets and old teddy bear were positioned among the Buddha figures, along with the bag his mother had carried from the concentration camp on the day she was liberated. Jnanavaca, soon to become the Centre chair, entered and bowed. The morning after the death he had driven Joanna and me up to Mahananda's flat. Joanna and I had made Wills before we left to travel and I'd cajoled Mahananda into doing the same. He had no family and a valuable house. We met in a pub and he wrote his wishes on the back of a beer mat. Later I drafted a Will and emailed it to him. He promised to get it executed and to leave it in the safe at the Buddhist Centre, but I'd never checked he actually did it, and it wasn't in the safe.

A mysterious arc of events was crystallising on this moment. The stakes felt very high. I had left the Buddhist Centre to study law. That study had resulted in me bring able to write a Will for Mahananda, which he otherwise would not have written. The London Buddhist Centre was set to inherit the house. The Krakow Buddhist Centre would get a substantial legacy. I wasn't thinking of our legacy, though there was that too. As I searched, Joanna stripped the soiled sheets and Jnanavaca opened the curtains. Here I was again with Jnanavaca, searching around a room for money. This time it was not three thousand but three million pounds at stake. I wanted to find a way back to our friendship again like before and in some bizarre way that possibility was intersecting with this moment. So long as there was a Will.

On the bedroom desk was a half-empty bottle of Leffe and Mahananda's spectacles set down next to a postcard. The writing had tailed off and slurred on the address, a sign of a stroke. He must have gone to bed without realising what was happening. I was rigid with tension leafing through his filing cabinet. I had a sinking feeling. Mahananda hated administration. If he hadn't done the Will I would blame myself forever more. I would never recover. Everything would go to Mahananda's 'mad' fifth cousin in Krakow, the one he hated, or the UK government. I pulled out a brown folder. Inside was an envelope. Inside that was the Will, Mahananda's final piece of paperwork, duly executed. I dropped down on the carpet sobbing.

The shrine room was crammed with friends sitting knee to knee on the floor: old boyfriends, East Enders he'd befriended on the respite retreats for carers he enjoyed leading, his dentist was there; the check-out staff at John Lewis would have come if they'd have known. Mum loved him too. She sat at the back on a chair as the puja unfolded, listening to the rejoicings in his life, joining in his favourite Yiddish folk song, and watching people light incense and scatter orange, white and gold flowers on the floor around the coffin. It went on for three hours. Mum said Maitreyabandhu led it beautifully and that she would like an uplifting funeral like that. Buddhism got one thing right: not birthdays, but funerals. She was glad there was no talk of going to heaven and I felt proud of Buddhism's lack of dogma and theology.

So where was Mahananda now? When death is close it seems possible to believe more than usual. According to the Tibetans he was in the bardo, an intermediate state between one life and the next. The bardo teachings point out how life is continual change, from dreaming to waking, from everyday wakefulness to deep meditation, from one identity to another. This life itself is a bardo, an intermediate state. We are never the settled and finished article. Tibetans practice to meet death with a clear and open heart, and see it as an opportunity to make great spiritual strides.

The idea of consciousness surviving or continuing in other forms no longer seemed wholly implausible to me, or merely a wishful fantasy. In the final part of the ceremony a friend and I screwed down the coffin lid, pausing for a last look at the waxy form, soon to be burned down to granules at the crematorium. When the anchor of the body is gone they say one needs great love and fearlessness to embrace whatever appears in the bardo state and recognise it as your own mind. A few days later Joanna and I brought Mahananda's ashes back on the Central Line, neatly packed into the small rucksack he'd used on our trip for gherkins and Russian sausage. We placed his urn next to his mother's still un-scattered ashes on our window sill.

A month later Joanna decamped to her monastery and I was left on my own to grapple with Mahananda's administrative reality, the Goldwasser on hand for when it all got too much. Tenants were reassured, deals done with Swiss banks, bullion shifted about. Big shirts went to big Buddhists, watches and family wedding rings foisted on his close friends. Tax was paid, probate was granted and the house transferred to the Buddhist Centre. As the weeks went by his possessions appeared to deflate, almost visibly, as though he was draining out of them.

Mahananda's death had reduced the tension between Jnanavaca and me and given us something to talk about. I attended a talk he gave about Manjushri, a Bodhisattva who wields a sword of discriminating wisdom. He conjured a vision of intrinsic emptiness and transcendent love so powerful that I worried newcomers to the Buddhist Centre would flee in fear. That's what I felt like doing. I wanted to bow to Jnanavaca and the radiant gem of truth which sparkled in him and which I'd always found alluring.

Joanna loved life at the monastery. She had a tiny bedroom with a window onto a meadow, around which she walked in the early morning mists, sometimes finding mushrooms to dry on the retreat centre radiators. Ajahn Sumedho had given her a Buddhist name: Niccalā (pron.

nitchalah). It means Eternal, a synonym for the Deathless 'state' attained by the Buddha. The monks and nuns got new names when they were ordained and used them exclusively. Lay people were more flexible with names, so Joanna stayed Joanna, mostly, though she was also Niccalá

I went on a retreat at the monastery. Maybe I wanted to join them instead, Maitreyabandhu wondered?

'I'm not a Thai Buddhist,' I complained to Joanna.

'Why don't you just tell them why you want to join the Order?'

'The West may be fucked up but it's my kind of fucked up.'

'But why do you actually want to join?'

Ratnaghosha thought ordaining me now would give me the confidence I needed to move forwards. Maitreyabandhu and Jnanavaca wanted me to demonstrate this confidence before I was ordained. My ordination process had been going on for nine years. Someone said I could be 'peevish'. I pretended to be cool about it, but any criticism and I'd tighten up in the stomach, then in the neck, then in the brain. No amount of awareness seemed to achieve much. I'd pinball around my mind for a while between familiar landmarks of comparison and blame. The best result was to walk away without an outright argument. I could rack up a score when no-one was around to answer back. I had to choose what my story was, rather than shrink back into crappy ideas about myself or boring, boring doubt. The only good thing about my doubt was that it ran so deep I ended up doubting it. And because of that I kept coming back, just like patiently coming back to the breath, again and again in the mindfulness of breathing exercise, the first meditation I learned. Keep coming back. Keep wearing out the mind's negative patterns.

Meanwhile life went on. My story refused to magically resolve itself. I took an interview and was offered a post as a government lawyer at the Department for Environment, Food and Rural Affairs. Before I could sign the contract, the Tories came to power and slashed the environment budget, sparing me a decade in the civil service.

Days later I landed a six-month contract at an environmental NGO, with a team of lawyers paid to bring cases to defend the Earth. With no prior knowledge of environmental law, I hurled myself into the world of fishing quotas, types of tackle and fishing-relevant articles in the European Union treaties. I spoke (for thirty seconds) to the European Fisheries Minister at an Aberdeen fishing conference about regionalised fishing policy in the Mediterranean and North Atlantic sea basins. A week later we flew to Denmark for three days of aggregated fish statistics. It was my perfect job – ethical, legal, environmental, well paid – and I hated it. It was more competitive than one of Dickinson's deals, plus you had to save the Earth. I was outmanoeuvred, regularly adrift from any useful purpose, like discarded by-catch. I've never wanted to be a lawyer enough to suffer it and that makes me not especially good at the job. If saving the Earth meant twelve hours a day in front of a computer then someone else would have to do it. Colleagues flew around the depleted Earth in search of a beach to recover from the strain.

Joanna and I went to Tunisia. When the Arab Spring started a month later, just down the road from our hotel, Joanna said my negativity may have tipped the balance.

One small thought got through to me, though, as I sat on the balcony of our hotel room. It connected to a dream I'd had. I was at the top of a hill looking at many rivers and streams criss-crossing and flowing down to the plains below. Why do I have to make sense of my life and make it all add up? I gazed under drying trunks and over palm trees towards the sea. I thought: this is my life and no-one else is responsible for it. No-one can do it for me. Not my mother, not Joanna, not Ratnaghosha. I was entirely free to struggle with self-doubt, doubt about the Order, doubt about anything, for as long as I liked. Or not. I could trust the current of energy that had got me started in the whole thing, get ordained and see where that took me. I had true friends on the path, the likes of which my definitely peevish grandfather had never found. And, for heaven's sake, it wasn't such a big deal. I wasn't deciding the fate of the universe.

Ten years after I posted my request at the letter box in Kathmandhu, a letter dropped on my doormat inviting me to attend the next ordination retreat in Spain. It's done then, I thought. I went back to bed and read through the kit list, feeling a surge of relief that I'd never have to deal with the question of my readiness for ordination ever again. There'd be twenty of us in all, incommunicado in a mountain valley for four months. All being well, halfway through we'd be ordained and given new names.

I told my parents all about it.

Mum's verdict: 'Worse than Siberia.'

23

DEATH AND REBIRTH

Parting from Joanna was hard. We wouldn't see or talk to each other for four months. In the middle of the night, she in her thick pyjamas, we hugged on the doorstep and I got in a taxi. She was good at loving and letting go. My retreat was a retreat for her too and she planned to stay at the monastery more full time.

On a train up the coast from Alicante I called my parents to let them know I was safely on my way. Dad had been bemused that I wouldn't be hearing the news for four months, an indecency verging on the immoral; our liberty guaranteed only by the quiet army who listen to headlines on Radio Four several times a day. Mum was worried I'd be forced to do things I didn't want to do, bad things against common sense. I'd have to shave my hair and become thin.

'Just tell us one person among your friends who has been on this retreat and come back normal,' she said. 'Mahananda was nice, but he didn't go on this retreat.' She said the whole premise of the retreat was wrong. I didn't need to change as I was already perfect. Joanna snorted.

Two-week retreats were ignorable, but not four months. How could they explain that to their friends? However I put it, it sounded like a glorified spell of navel-gazing. Death and re-birth are ancient and rather pretentious-sounding themes and not ones that soothed my parents. In our last phone call we talked awkwardly and tenderly about the weather and practical things I might need up in the mountains. This was their way of blessing my endeavour. Retreats are when I most feel grateful to my parents. The Buddha called it the debt that cannot be repaid. I knew I wasn't going there to destroy my personality or shun my family, or Radio Four.

Half a dozen ordinands had already gathered at a beach-side restaurant for the pre-retreat ritual of pizza and chips. Afterwards Satyaraja, the retreat leader, a muscular and intense man in his fifties, who could have led a platoon in another life, forged ahead into the navy-blue waters. I thrashed about until my skin adjusted to the chill and looked up towards the mountains. We'd be able to look back to the sea from between the rocky crags.

The last rite before lugging our rucksacks to the taxi stand for the last leg of the journey into the mountains was to visit the cafe known in ordination folklore for its churros and chocolate. Legend has it that once an ordinand went a bit far in his quest for last worldly pleasures and arrived at the ordination retreat after a bout of heavy drinking. Three nights on the lash in Benidorm didn't bode well for four months' abstinence, and he was very put out when they told him to go home.

I looked out of the taxi window taking in details of the towns and villages, texting Joanna, chatting to my companions, speculating about this and that. I called Joanna, then called her again. I wasn't ready for the last call. I kept calling until she got fed up. At a climbers' refuge we dumped our bags and walked the last few miles to the retreat centre. At each turn in the track a different vista of mountain and pine opened up. A light breeze took the edge off the afternoon sun. The limestone ridges of one valley merged into another, or split off to form different valleys, edged by sharp cliffs which jutted out of the earth like the spine of a sleeping dragon. Along the valley floor smaller lines of rocks thrust out of the pine.

The topmost valley was Guhyaloka, the Hidden Realm. It consisted of a few basic huts dotted around a thousand acres of pine forest. In the kitchen block the first of many paellas was being served. I met Gabe from California, Jari from Helsinki, Andreas from Stockholm, Ross from Sydney; sixteen retreatants in all and four team members including Maitreyabandhu. After dinner we walked along the narrow paths through patches of holm oak on a tour of compost loos and outdoor wash stands. It was Spring and the bushes were busy with insects and the rocks were still giving out the stored warmth of the day. I sat on one overlooking the forest stretching down the valley towards the blue horizon and felt a touch of fear. This retreat was eight times longer than any I'd been on.

The next morning the retreat manager's briefing was military in tone.

'Wash your bed linen once a fortnight at least . . .

'There's cheese in the fridge. Don't touch it unless given permission by me. I weigh it. Seriously, I do . . .

'There may be scorpions under rocks but do not go looking for them. Leave the rocks alone . . .

'Oh yes, and please note there are no lions in the valley. Someone once swore blind he saw two young lions. We have ibex, pine marten, boar, snakes and owls, but no lions. If you're bitten by a snake walk calmly down to the manager's cottage.'

Satyaraja had led this retreat twice before. He suggested we'd all do well to let go of pettiness, so I checked an urge to question the methodology of the guy who'd started a temperature chart at the back of the kitchen block. Satyaraja also recommended we open our hearts to every aspect of the routine, and try not to pick and choose. I had already been calculating which of the retreat chores left most scope for 'me-time'.

The first thing to open my heart to was tinnitus, which became louder the quieter it got. At night the only sound was a toad croaking in the shrubbery. The tinnitus thrummed like a generator running further up the valley with a high beep chiming in over it. I'd been to my GP and explained about the retreat, how there was to be some silence every day and in total a whole month of full silence.

'For tinnitus you must avoid the silence,' he said.

'It's supposed to be in silence, that's the point.'

'Take a radio, that should mask it.'

When the nightingale in the holm oak behind the shrine room stopped singing during morning meditation, the tinnitus faded back in. This would surely drive me bonkers. I decided to actually practise the teaching and let the sound be. Having given in to the sound, I realised there were also periods of time which passed without me noticing the sound. When I didn't notice it, that was the same as it not being there. When I did notice it, it was there. Part of the conditions for it arising and ceasing was my attention. Not picking and choosing whether it was there helped me relax and give my attention to other things, which increased the sense of it not being there. Soon days passed without me thinking about it, which meant it was hardly there at all, although it was.

Our lives were getting simple. The mood was harmonious and excited. I felt happy. Last letters went out to family and friends and the valley was ritually closed. We shaved each other's heads, apart from one guy who had a thing about his locks, and tried out our blue robes, which looked a bit like long dressing gowns and needed careful gathering up around the pee-pits. I was sharing a small, pitched hut with a neat middle-aged Frenchman called, for the time being, Christian. We balanced our few books on a plank of wood and stuck some postcards on the wall. Christian was kind and considerate, always thinking of something I might need or tidying the hut. I decided to copy him by trying to offer to wash his robe before he could get in with an offer to wash mine.

Learning to paint

Maitreyabandhu was coming up to his fiftieth birthday, grey haired and a little thinner, but still with his beaming, clownish smile. In the mornings he sat outside his hut reading poetry, black-rimmed glasses perched wonkily on his ears. One morning I went to his hut with a tray of watercolour paints.

'Please tell me what to do with these, you've been to Goldsmiths,' I said.

'That doesn't imply any ability to paint.'

He selected some transparent colours and suggested a view into the woods below.

'Just concentrate on seeing where things are and putting down colour. Like Cezanne, be as faithful to perception as possible.'

I hadn't painted or drawn a thing since school. A day later I ferried the results back.

'Is that branch actually there?' he said.

'Yes,' I said.

'I don't think it is.'

'How do you know, you haven't been there?'

'Surely it should be here,' he said, brushing his finger across the foreground. 'Try not to draw an idea of where things are.'

I went back and discovered he was right. Getting things roughly where they are was a more rigorous process than I'd expected. My next subject was a rock a hundred metres high, nicknamed locally the Whale. It changed in shape and girth as you walked down the valley. Maitreyabandhu gave feedback in between silence periods.

'Look carefully, make a mark,' he said.

Choughs nested high up in crevices, staining the white rock below with strands of orange and blue. I looked carefully and made a mark. The sun dried the paper quickly. Each new attempt layered in some unexpected richness, then suddenly a few careless flicks and the Whale was right there on the page. I dashed back to Maitreyabandhu, who confirmed it was my first finished painting.

'You get luck like this if you keep trying,' he said.

I knew nothing at all about painting, which made me a good student. If I looked and made marks, things came through. It was a thrilling discovery. I apologised to Maitreyabandhu for harmful things I'd said to him or about him in the past. Confessing and apologising freed up energy, for painting and meditation.

Every morning, mid-morning, afternoon and evening we sat facing each other in two rows on opposite sides of the shrine room on the cool polished floor. One meditation involved visualising the Buddha in order to evoke in our imagination the qualities of the Enlightened Mind. Even though the painting had filled my mind with colours, I still struggled to visualise things. The tarantula-like spider on the shrine room ceiling taught me that I didn't need to literally 'see' things in my mind order to imagine them. Someone said spiders like to drop to the ground. He had nineteen bald pates to choose as a helipad, from Andreas the Swede down to Jari the Finn eight cushions away. If he landed on me I resolved to remain mindfully alert and allow the beast to wander down my neck, shoulder, arms and away. I'd feel the touch of each foot and the drag of its underbelly as pure sensation and nothing more. Ideally, this act of heroism wouldn't go unnoticed so maybe I could make just a small noise so everyone looked my way. The danger was losing control of my senses and flinging it onto the person next to me who might deal with things more coolly. Due to this intense visualisation, more engrossing than my attempt to visualise the Buddha, my scalp was prickling as if the monster had already landed.

After a few weeks I was aware of the world in an easy, broad and pleasurable way. Having integrated our energies, we entered the spiritual death phase of the retreat where we let go as much as possible of old, encumbering ideas about who or what we are. Satyaraja, bolt upright and vigorous, led us through a silent and intense fortnight meditating on the six elements. One reflects on how all the basic elements of experience are 'not me, not mine, not myself'. Spiritual death starts with loosening of the belief in a fixed, unchanging self.

As I walked every day to fill up my water bottle at a natural spring I reflected that there was water outside me, water inside me. I added a sense of 'me' and 'not me' to the water element. The water was not me when it flowed into my bottle, sort of me when it flowed past my lips and into my stomach. When it formed the cells in my body I thought of it as me. When released into the pee-pit, not me again. The water never changed. Bodily heat, air, sweat, food, thoughts, moods; they all flow in and out, and on reflection it's clear that no owner of experience is to be found. Letting things through without getting tangled up in them was joyful.

About halfway through this silent period, Satyaraja warned us that however we had been so far, Mara was likely to stage a fightback right about now. In Buddhist tradition, Mara personifies the unconscious or habitual forces of the mind. I first noticed Mara flexing his muscles at the dinner table. He suggested we stuff our faces with carbohydrates. I saw one fellow grappling a sandwich into his mouth made from two thick slices of bread and a whole jacket potato as filling. The cook reported a rise in evening cocoa consumption and in the morning, porridge bowls were filled to the brim, as though we were readying for the battle of Culloden Moor.

Mara was like a door-to-door salesman. If I shut the door in his face, he'd just drop the holiday brochure onto my doormat knowing I had plenty of time to flick through it later. Why have I never been to Vancouver? Everyone says it's so bloody great. Do they have trains going across Canada? I can't wait to hear what Joanna thinks. Mara wasn't picky about the type of distraction. I spent several meditation sessions resetting numbers from the musical *Oh What A Lovely War*. I came up with a stirring version of 'When This Lousy Retreat is Over' and regretted not being able to put on a performance.

At a one-to-one meditation review Satyaraja recommended asking questions of persistently stuck states of mind. 'It may be the best of you in there,' he said. My smokescreen mode throws up anything to prevent me experiencing boredom, unease or tiredness. If I embrace those states directly the distractions stop and newer creative energy invariably appears. Satyaraja said I sometimes gave away my positive states too easily. I had a lot to offer, he added, which moved me to tears.

One night I accidentally kicked a toad. I'd stepped out of our hut for a pee. The moon had clouded over so I didn't spot the mottled green-grey toad camouflaged on a slab. My flip flop pushed him half a yard. The toads were out for a drink and I worried about them. The ground was bone dry and cracking up. Clouds had rolled through for the past few days but there had been no rain. He was unharmed, but in the fright he appeared to have pee-ed himself. I poured some water on him to say sorry.

The next day I felt moody and dissatisfied. For a few more days low mists continued to scud through the valley, but still no rain came. I was less communicative, privately listing things that were wrong with other people or the programme or how I could arrange it better. There was still a long time to go and the end wasn't in sight. Johnny, a Venezuelan in his forties, slept fitfully in the hut next door. A few years ago he had played Sangharakshita some songs on his banjo. He was feeling it too.

'Imagine we bad people, had to stay here for twenty-five years. Now we only three months to go,' he said.

The valley reminded him of the landscapes of his childhood. Nothing like pancake flat Cambridge where he had lived in Buddhist community for the last few years.

'Thing I don't get . . . tell me . . . English people put names on the food in the fridge. It's crazy, man!'

Every morning he'd sit in the sun philosophizing while covering himself in baby oil:

'I went to two lectures about the universe at Cambridge. I was going to look for a pillow to buy first. I went in Tesco, you know, but couldn't get one. Then I went to the lecture. The woman was pointing out the black parts of the universe we don't know anything about. I almost cry. I can't think about my pillow now. It's stupid really . . . we so small.'

One afternoon Johnny came running into my hut, panting, with a look of wild alarm.

'What's the matter?' I said.

'She wearing a bikini, hiking in a bikini, man! She ask me for directions. What could I say? I just want to eat her.'

I laughed until it hurt.

One afternoon we were clearing up after lunch when the limestone escarpments started to rebound with tremendous claps of thunder. The rain was a relief. It eased me back into a feeling of brotherhood with things around me. I sat under an awning talking with the cook who had plenty of good stories about rockfall, lizards and wild pigs. Later, while meditating, the impression arose, quite suddenly, that I was floating in amniotic fluid. It was a pleasant liquid sensation until I realised I was about to be born. Then there was alarm and chaos, people panicking and running about. I was watching and wanting to say to everyone, 'It's okay folks, it's just a baby . . . it's okay, he's fine.' Was this a trace of my actual birth moment or the birth to come? That night I dreamt a baby crawled onto my chest and slept.

Satyaraja's best piece of advice, about six weeks in, was to spend more time doing nothing. Every morning after breakfast I sat with my coffee watching geckos darting out of the shadows around our hut and ants trailing through a scrubby bush. Spring had changed into early summer, and new flowers had emerged for new flies, beetles and butterflies. I thought looking at nature would get a bit samey after a while, but day by day my fascination for the miracle of it increased. Nature was relief from self-concern. It was not me or mine. Perhaps Christians would call this opening to the mystery of creation as a revelation of the immanence of God. I became familiar with the crackling sound one bird made after its whistle and the other-worldly swoosh from the edge of a peregrine's wing as it pulls out of a downward plunge. For many hours I sat by the scrubby bush by my hut with its sub-world of red-winged insects, wasps and hummingbird bees, desisting from gainful activity for longer periods than I'd previously managed.

The practice of relaxed awareness was carving a niche in the present moment. Breakfast was porridge, tomatoes and onion on bread, which we baked ourselves. I kept having an inexplicable thought about how this is the one porridge I will ever have. I stopped salting it with thoughts about tomorrow and yesterday. Routine, relaxation, awareness: brushing teeth, slooshing out in the bushes, crouching over a compost toilet. I kept layering on the watercolours – looking, marking, scrubbing out, seeking Maitreyabandhu's counsel. The routine, regular effort opened things up. Suddenly I might sense the depth down the path through the pines. I can't say what it is that happens as awareness unfolds. It's as if the heart of the matter is momentarily found, then lost again in the mists.

Making up a better story

A week before the ordinations, Ratnaghosha arrived in the valley along with the other preceptors. In blue robes he looked the same as ever, bright and cheerful with a quiff of silver hair. His confidence had given me the confidence to get to this point. Decades of simple living and Dharma practice had given him time to read broadly and think clearly. Although I trusted Ratnaghosha to choose my new name, for the avoidance of doubt I'd given him a list of names I disliked or didn't want. For example, the Sanskrit words 'naga' (a mythical snake dragon) and 'sukha' (happiness or bliss) mean 'naked bitch' in Polish. He assured me that the name he'd chosen (six years ago, he said ruefully) was not on my list.

I was to be ordained on the same evening as Jari, a vegan Finn with a body builder's physique. We were nervous and a bit giggly all day and kept passing each other on the way back and forth to the compost loo. The night before, my dreams had been violent. Morgan Freeman played a reformed gangster who was torn apart by a Mexican gang in a blood vendetta. He lay dying while I held his hand. In the afternoon Mara appeared with some undisguised doubt: this whole thing is made up; you're stuck up a mountain playing swallows and amazons in a dressing gown! But it was too late to roll out the red carpet for doubt.

Before the ceremony I asked Ratnaghosha for feedback so we could get it out of the way.

'What feedback?' he said.

'You must have been storing it up all these years.'

'I have no feedback.'

An hour before the ceremony the clouds were gathering. I sat out on the rocks gazing down the valley thinking about how good and evil are both definite possibilities for any human being. Most of the time I'm about middling, neither very good nor very bad, hoping the cards of life fall my way.

Evening came with the rainclouds that had threatened all day, finally conquering the sun, so we started the ceremony inside a hut rather than outside by the stupa. Jari and I sat on cushions opposite our two preceptors. Each line of the puja, whose words I'd heard many times before, weighed more than normal. I roused my energy and sat upright.

Ratnaghosha left to prepare the small white ordination stupa, which was nestled in a secluded spot in a glade of pine trees. I was to follow five minutes later. We had to walk to the stupa on our own to symbolise that the step is made of our individual free will.

When I got the nod, I started out with purposeful strides. The rain had turned the paths to mud and I almost slid into a spiky bush. The stupa had to be entered like an igloo, on hands and knees. Going in, I was giving up my old identity. At that moment I realised I hadn't thought about this moment, and I didn't know anything about it.

Inside was small – and vast. Ratnaghosha and I sat opposite each other. He said some things and I said some things back. He gave me a string of beads called a mala and a name. When I crawled out the sky had cleared to a single cloud gently reddened by the sun from below the horizon.

For a few days the routine slackened. Ratnaghosha and I hiked around the valley. We told each other our life stories in minute detail. Some post-modern authors in the twentieth century did away with storylines because life isn't a story, it's a series of moments. Yet as soon as we describe these moments, they inevitably turn into a story or part of one. Ratnaghosha told his story for ten hours in all, as we walked, sat on rocks, ate sandwiches and admired the view. Stories capture meaning and we need better stories, for ourselves and for our civilisation. Without better stories we are doomed. Ordination connected to a story of what it means to be human, beyond the consumer story, the individualist story, the materialist story, the socialist or capitalist story. When I'd finished telling my story, I asked Ratnaghosha for the negative feedback he kindly hadn't given me when I was anxious before the ordination, now that I was more relaxed. He said he didn't have any.

My name had slipped into my body as easily as a bird finds its nest. It was known only to me and Ratnaghosha until ten days later when everyone met for the public part of the ordination ceremony, passages of which were repeated in the six European languages spoken by the retreatants.

There was a buzz of excitement and anticipation as one by one our new names were announced. When it was my turn, Ratnaghosha stood up:

'David Waterston has become Satyadasa, which means "He who is a servant of the Truth". The truth in this context is synonymous with the Dharma. He who serves the Truth, serves the Dharma. I have given him this name as from early on in his involvement I had the sense the Dharma had caught him, had captured him even, and even if he tried he couldn't escape. He was the servant of the Dharma and the Dharma is Truth – Satya.

'The second reason is to give him a clear direction in life. His vocation is simply to serve the Truth, to serve the Dharma. This is, of course, a challenge. In order to serve the Truth you need to know the Truth, or at least be in touch with it. You need to be aware of the Truth – that will be the challenge for Satyadasa.

'The third reason is to encourage Satyadasa to serve the Truth in the context of the Order and through the medium of the Community. Our Community and Order are vehicles for Truth.

'And, finally, he is Satyadasa, a servant of the Truth, because Truth cannot be mastered. We cannot be masters of the Dharma, only servants. Even the Buddha looked up to and revered the Dharma. Please welcome Satyadasa to the Order.'

Satyaraja, my public preceptor, put a kesa round my neck, a silk strip embroidered with the Three Jewels encircled by a flame, symbolising the three precious refuges and the possibility of transformation.

I loved my name, both the sound and the meaning,

although at first it was weird to hear someone say 'Satyadasa' and realise they were expecting me to reply. Old names popped back, although by the time the July sun had burnt away the last of the spring flowers, they had mostly evaporated too. Before the trip home we were offered a choice of three day trips to aid our reintegration. Prasadhacitta (formerly Gabe) and I chose the outdoor swimming pool trip with a few other guys. I was gleeful as a child as we walked out the top of the valley and all the way down to the small tourist town five miles away. The pool attendant mopped around the diving board, with six pairs of eyes on her. She was an actual woman. From our pool-side recliners Prasadhacitta called his wife in California and I called Joanna.

'Hello, it's me.'

'Hello you.'

It was a pleasant enough town, full of silly things to buy. In the end I was happy when the time came to walk back to our huts in the valley.

On the final morning I skipped meditation to say a goodbye to the young tree I had painted and the scrubby bush by my hut. The flowers had all dried now and the stalks thinned. I watered it once more, sorry not to be seeing it through the rest of the year.

Back in our civilian clothes we walked down to the climbers' refuge, from where a coach took us straight to the airport. After sixteen weeks of whole foods, sunshine and steep walks we were as lean as mountain goats. Without news feeds to sap our strength we had become shining counterparts of our pale city-dwelling selves. Suddenly we were queueing in a line of tourists on the way back from

Benidorm. It wasn't very shocking. It was what it was: advertising, neon, makeup – lives lived on the basis of a different set of stories. Someone brought me up to date with the news in just four words. 'They shot Bin Laden'. We made our way through departures still suffused with the scent of pine and the high mountain air.

24

LINEAGE

Traffic at the Buddhist Centre has doubled since the financial market turmoil. The slow-moving apparatus of peer-reviewed science has cautiously validated the benefits of mindfulness and put something in the *New Scientist* to that effect. GPs refer patients to the Buddhist Centre's secular health project for help with stress and depression. Now that meditation officially works, it's socially acceptable for bankers, lawyers and civil servants to tell colleagues they're going on retreat. Shoes in the Centre cloakroom have changed: Uggs are up, Birkenstocks down. Before the scientific pendulum swings back the other way, showing no net gain against the placebo, Maitreyabandhu seized the moment and devised a new course mingling mindfulness with daily life, art, philosophy, poetry and Dharma. I did the cushions again.

It's six years since my ordination. Someone once asked me if I was Enlightened. It's hard to know where to start with that one. Makes me want to run away. For me, there's still a long way to go, I hope. There's a magic to having a new name for the journey. It allows for different things to happen.

It took a while, though, to find my feet as Satyadasa. Sometimes, especially outside the Buddhist context, I felt awkward about it and reverted to David. Along with my hand here was a second reason to seem a bit strange. Joanna took to the name straightaway. Mum and Dad steered clear. I was grateful when an old friend gave it a go. Nowadays there are people who've known me only as Satyadasa. It's not such a big thing in my mind and I find sticking to one name leads to less confusion.

I met a friend who walks barefoot around the country. Satyadasa was a good name and I'd taken a step in the right direction, he said, but all names are limiting identities. True enough, I replied. Having given up the worldly conventions of shoes and cars, to keep things simple, he'd now given up having a name as well. We've since lost contact.

This year I led a retreat at our purpose-built retreat centre in Suffolk, designed and constructed from the proceeds of the sale of Mahananda's house. Before we bought the farm Ratnaghosha had stood in the front garden telling the farmer how we'd be there for at least fifty years. I thought he was exaggerating, but his prediction now looks on the conservative side. The straw-bale shrine room and ramshackle outbuildings have been replaced by a large light-filled meditation hall, surrounded by courtyards of flowers and trees, an ornamental pond and facilities for sixty retreatants. In season the rapeseed in the surrounding fields encircles the centre on all sides with a band of gold. At the opening ceremony, the main stupa had been consecrated with the ashes of Bhante's teacher, Dhardo Rinpoche, after which I lowered in a small pot of Mahananda's ashes. His family line has ended with the creation of a communal place for tens, maybe hundreds of thousands of people to enjoy. What

better end to a story which began in the dark hour of
the Holocaust.

While leading the metta practice one afternoon, I
suggested we cultivate metta by imagining it's already
there, just like the golden flowers in the fields around us.
This approach works well for me. If I look within too hard,
grasping at experiences, sometimes there doesn't seem to be
much there. Another evening I gave a talk about *prapanca*,
the tendency to proliferate thoughts and stir emotions,
ruminating on them in an unaware and unhelpful way.
In ambiguous situations, such as when someone doesn't
reply to an email, we make up stories about why and turn
our thoughts into facts. Then we mind-spar them to death
only to discover they forgot to turn on the out of office. A
disability, too, creates an ambiguous situation. While giving the talk I was aware of my stump gesticulating away in
an imprecise and carefree sort of way. I tried to rein it in a
little, wondering about the impression it made, but maybe
I should just let it be. After all, missing a hand is a big part
of what has made me who I am. Writing and talking about
it has helped make an obvious fact obvious to me.

I grew up telling myself that I have a practical problem
which I overcame in a variety of oddly impressive ways,
insisting that it should not, must not, make a significant
difference to my life. The story ensured a kind of silence.
Nothing to see here, folks. But of course there is. Watch
me put up a curtain and you'll probably be impressed. I like
that. You don't have to say anything, I don't need that. I do
things well and you quietly admire it, that's the deal. This
odd silence allowed me to function happily, just to one side
of my feelings about it all.

The original story was so clear it became a kind of forcefield which stopped anyone asking me about it. On rare occasions a brave adult would broach the topic in a straightforward manner. Must be pretty tough, they'd suggest. Not really, I'd say. I get on fine, thanks. True and not true. A deflection, a story. As I have picked my way through this story, making it more conscious, I realise that the place I am headed for is the one I fear most: a feeling of weakness. Meditation rarely gets me to that place. It's too well guarded. I'm too scared of it. Helpless, ungainly, inept, weak: ghastly feelings I hate.

Walking round the park with Maitreyabandhu I start telling him I want to completely drop that silly old story, that it didn't affect me or hold me back in any big way. In reality it altered the course of everything: my career, love life, hobbies. . . And, I exclaim, I'm just not that super at doing stuff, which was supposed to make up for any deficit. I'm very average at most things. I can't even pick up a spade or a hammer and blast away for hours any more. So much riding on a few functional fingers and a stump with absurdly tiny tendons. I'll be done for if the right hand packs up. Maitreyabandhu wonders if my missing hand was a necessary glitch, giving me an extra dollop of difficulty to bring out the good stuff. With nothing to restrain my sharp mind and its sharp thoughts, the two-handed version of me might have been less likeable and less happy. Joanna says that too.

On reflection, I think I'll keep the original story too: having one hand doesn't matter in the slightest.

Leading a retreat is hard work. The moody thoughts you're entertaining get amplified. You have to double down on practice. No good nursing irritabilities for too long or getting stuck on how the retreat *should* be going and how people *should* be behaving. Twenty years of retreats has been good training and I know things will work out. I've been bringing Tara to mind, to remind me to trust things more. A Tibetan lama was once asked by a Western student if Tara *actually exists*. His answer: 'Tara knows she doesn't exist.'

It was Jnanavaca who introduced me to the Green Tara practice after my Ordination. We went through it in his room underneath his painting of Manjushri, the Bodhisattva of Wisdom. The figure emerges out of a star nebula just as Jnanavaca, ex-physicist, had requested the artist draw it. From a fiery sun, orange Manjushri emerges, wielding a flaming sword. The blue book held to his heart is bound like a Western book rather than a traditional scroll. I understand the Tara practice as a way of expanding my imagination. She's taken over a vestigial belief I've sometimes had in guardian angels. Up to now the angels might have been sticking around for free, but now I'm in my forties it occurs to me that if I don't consciously honour the angels, the Bodhisattvas, or something higher, they'll rightly desert me. Leonard Cohen gave me that idea.

I'm more capable of returning Jnanavaca's friendship these days. Bhante taught that friendship is a relationship where values and meaning can flourish. Friendship is an intersection for positive qualities, truth and beauty. Where else are we going to find them? Ratnaghosha and I remain steady friends. He recently gave me a new gnomic utterance to consider on one of our walks. He said he'd reached the point where any notion of him personally striving to make spiritual progress, however subtle, had become a block. The future is not built on the past in a linear sort of way, he added, so things rarely happen as we imagine they will. He's started learning Spanish, apropos of nothing.

Goodbye for now

On the edge of a village in the Malvern Hills, a former oil company headquarters has been transformed into a headquarters for the Order. The airy library, once used for laying out exploratory maps of the North Sea bed, now houses Bhante's enormous book collection and volumes of correspondence and writings. I booked a week-long retreat there, led by one of our community's elders, the same man who wrote the pamphlet on communication exercises forty years ago, the one Nanna found for me among Grandpa's papers. After the evening meditation I stood by a duck pond fringed with trees. I thought the mallards would be peaceful at this hour, but they were still scudding across the water at each other in low-beaked lunges of love and war.

Behind me was a conservatory, annexed to the main house. The lights were on and I could see Bhante sitting in his armchair with hands pressed together below his chin. He can't read any more due to macular degeneration, so someone was reading to him from a Kindle. After twenty years of soul searching about communal attitudes towards families and relationships, doubts about people's spiritual attainment, gender politics and concerns about some things that went on in the past, one might have expected the Order to have settled down peacefully, but it hasn't. It seems there's no escaping the messiness of human affairs.

The next day a handwritten note with my name on it appeared on the board next to the retreat timetable. Bhante would like to see me today. It was the chance I'd hoped for. At the appointed hour his carer showed me through the hallway to the annex where he lived, warning me that Bhante ran out of energy easily so the meeting would probably last only ten minutes. As I entered the room Bhante pushed himself up and greeted me with a broad smile. I wanted to bow and I did bow, I couldn't stop myself, even though it meant I was directing homage to the back of the armchair which stood between us. A full floor-length prostration would have been merited, though it may take a while longer before such a gesture comes naturally to me.

We shook hands. He seemed a bit off-colour, though his hair was brushed out in waves to one side in a regal way. The room was extremely overheated, so I took off my jumper. He asked what I was up to. I told him about the things I do at the Buddhist Centre, and the legal work. And how is Joanna, he asked? Joanna had left the monastery to study acupuncture and functional medicine. I'm her human pin cushion. Thinking of Joanna, Bhante said he was sorry he wouldn't be able to go to Poland again. He spoke slowly and less clearly than before.

I reminded him about his visit to the Cheam Eastern Philosophy Group, a small and forgettable event by anyone's reckoning.

'I have a vague memory,' he said.

'It must have been hard for you when you came back to the Buddhist scene in the UK. If it was anything like Cheam it must have been very heady and intellectual, especially at the Buddhist Society.'

'Not just at the Buddhist Society, some of the monks at the Hampstead Vihara had some strange ideas . . . . Still, people have been straightened out now, or some of them anyhow,' he said, breaking into smile. 'By the way, I think it must have been 1965, not 1964, the visit to your grandfather. I have a vague memory. I was still in India in 1964. It should be noted in my diary. They're all in the new library. We can look for the entry next time.'

He faded out a little.

I told him about the study I lead with a group of men at the London Buddhist Centre each week.

'Sometimes you don't know what you've been given until you try to teach it,' he said, perking up.

Before I could get round to properly expressing myself he suggested I had better get back to the retreat.

'Thank you Bhante,' I said, leaning forward and shaking his hand again. I wanted to say more but it felt self-indulgent.

'Until next time,' he said.

'Yes, indeed, bye for now.'

Afterwards I wandered up the nearby Oyster Hill to gaze out over a panorama of English and Welsh farmland. It was the first warm day of the year and the sodden clay earth had half-caked over. A pair of buzzards circled and veered away beyond the trees over the brow of the hill. I sat on a bench listening to a tractor somewhere below. A passing retreatant pointed behind me back in the direction of the retreat centre towards the full rainbow that had appeared.

Gratitude welled up in me. The blue sky seemed to welcome big thoughts. Just as long ago some figures were foremost in taking the Dharma from India to Tibet, or from

China to Japan, Bhante had spent sixty years hacking away at a bramble patch of ideas and beliefs to give space for a new flower to grow in the West. With uplifted imagination and vigour he had posed and re-posed the great koan of life to many eager hearts and minds.

But has Bhante managed to pass on the flame? Allen Ginsberg said he wept on hearing Bob Dylan sing 'Hard Rain', because he knew the fire of the Beats had been passed to a new generation. With Bhante gone, will Order members find ways to pass that vitality on, or will the energy fizzle out, the whole thing soon consigned to a bookshelf or a straggle of institutions existing just because they exist? The greatly inspired first generation of Western Dharma teachers is dying away; and statistically, so I once heard, new spiritual traditions more often fail than burgeon. It's all so young in the West and, as that wise old Chinese man once told me, there's such a long way to go. Joanna would call all this one of my 'pointless speculations'.

Grandpa un-thumbed and unvisited

I marked the centenary of Grandpa's birth with a trip on the District Line to East Ham, to the Duke of Bedford pub where he was born, 'between the four-ale and the saloon', as he liked to say. Nowadays it's a grocery cum off-licence covered in Lycamobile adverts. Inside I looked around at the predictable assortment of packaged food, hardly what the word grocer conjures up. I picked something to buy and went up the counter. The manager, a Tamil, grinned at my story and relayed it to a man stocking up. I showed them a pre-war photo of my great grandfather standing outside.

'Yes, pub, I know, still there's room for taking the beer underneath,' the manager said.

I didn't know what I was expecting from this encounter. I bagged up my water, Tetley teabags and a Snickers bar.

'It's a Punjabi now who owns here,' the manager went on. 'He won the lottery and bought the house. He bought 110 houses, and he bought the ticket right here in the shop.' I looked at the lottery machine. There was an €80m Euromillions draw on so I bought a ticket.

Continuing my pilgrimage, the next day I went to the British Library and signed on as a reader. For some reason I doubted the library staff would be able to locate a copy of Grandpa's book, or else it would have been condemned to deep storage somewhere in the provinces. I found the catalogue number and ordered it up to the Humanities Reading Room. In less than thirty minutes it was in my hand. Feeling moved by the mysterious inner processes of the British Library and proud to be British, I turned it over to see Grandpa with his wavy white hair, corduroy jacket and paisley tie. His head slightly cocked, his gaze serious and keen. Back at my desk I looked for stamps or marginalia to see if anyone had ever wanted to read *An Existential-Ontological Approach to Contemplative Experience*. It looked wholly un-thumbed. The corrigenda chit as thin as confetti was still tucked in.

'[on p.468, line 9, for 'authentic Ontonescience' read '*in*authentic Ontonescience'].'

Even with two call-ups per decade that chit would have fallen out by now.

I flicked through. Although it's outmoded and abstruse there are some great sections and reading them makes me feel sad. I'm not able to rescue the book from oblivion.

The following Saturday I completed my melancholy meanderings with a trip to Grandpa's grave at a cemetery in south London. Unless the *other woman* or a faithful old student still came by, the grave of Donald Henry Huckle Martin was unvisited. A flower circle cut in the marble slab had filled up with gravel. Grandpa was developed in some ways and lacking in others. Meditating in his study didn't heal the rift. It's hard to imagine people can be like that because we get dazzled by their brilliant side. I try to sympathise with contradictions in others by seeing them in myself, how I espouse ideals but want to stay comfy and small; or lacking initiative and courage, I pass off my fear as common sense. I kicked around his grave for a bit not knowing if I should say something or wish something for him or apologise for writing about him.

At the end of the summer Joanna and I went up to see Nanna. She was very frail, now 97, though her hair was still coppery and thick. She was prone to bouts of doom and gloom, according to Mum, but never when I was around. She kissed my hand, like she always did, as though Jesus had come to see her. The Cheam house had finally been sold and Nanna had moved to a cottage next door to my parents in Norfolk. Henry the tortoise came with her, roaming a new patch of garden, living on the same mulch of tomato, lettuce and milky brown bread.

During the last census I had asked Nanna what religion I should put her down for. She'd raised a bent forefinger to her lips and searched her conscience. As it was the government asking, it deserved a serious response. No-one had asked her about *her* religion as the focus had always been on Grandpa's stance.

'Church of England.'

'But Nanna,' I said, 'why then did you tell me to study the Mahayana, then Zen, then finally the Tao That Cannot Be Named?'

She gave me a sheepish grin and giggled.

Despite reading dozens of books, not a single word of Eastern religion had made the slightest impact on Nanna. If Grandpa had been into Voodoo she'd have advised me to get into that.

A couple of weeks after our visit she had a fall and stopped eating. She crinkled like a leaf into the utmost reaches of old age. Her last words to Mum were 'Thank you dear.' Just after she died Mum and Howard both swore independently that they saw her bedsheets rippling, a phenomenon they later searched for on Google.

A week later at the local crematorium the hearse pulled up, its doors opening and shutting with soft clicks. The undertaker's polished shoes sounded so clear on the gravel that a faint dread of reality came on me. We followed behind the coffin, seven family members in a room that could hold three hundred. My last grandparent was gone and now all four of them are equal before my mind's eye. How good it would be to have them back, for a cup of tea and a chat.

Afterwards we went back to my parents' house. Mum warmed some food in the Aga. She was now 'Granny' to my sister's children. We sat around the long slender oak table in the kitchen. As it often does, talk turned to the Cheam house and what to do with the last of Nanna's furniture, including the old breakfast table, which might or might not exist. I suggested Mum and Howard smash it up and have a bonfire.

It didn't take long for sadness to give way to hunger. Mum dished out some fresh scones and I wrestled with a pot of blueberry jam, twisting the lid while clamping it steady against my shirt. As usual the pot wasn't as clean as it looked. I hoped the stains would come out in the wash.

AUTHOR'S NOTE

A few characters in this book are disguised and/or have names changed. Changing Sanskrit names would have left me in a muddle, re-ordaining people who ordained me, so I was grateful for permission to use all of them as they are. One character, Adam, is a composite character, to whom I give the role of two or three friends. This device seemed necessary for brevity of exposition and did not seem to damage the truthfulness of the account. Truth in memoir means a commitment to factual truth, consulting memory and diaries as honestly as possible, and a commitment to the inner truth of the story. Anyone who has produced a book from 'real' life will know that it's not so much about penning an account of things that objectively happened but which merely lack the writing down, as unfolding a new story as you go.

WINDHORSE PUBLICATIONS

Windhorse Publications is a Buddhist charitable company based in the United Kingdom. We place great emphasis on producing books of high quality that are accessible and relevant to those interested in Buddhism at whatever level. We are the main publisher of the works of Sangharakshita, the founder of the Triratna Buddhist Order and Community. Our books draw on the whole range of the Buddhist tradition, including translations of traditional texts, commentaries, books that make links with contemporary culture and ways of life, biographies of Buddhists, and works on meditation.

As a not-for-profit enterprise, we ensure that all surplus income is invested in new books and improved production methods, to better communicate Buddhism in the twenty-first century. We welcome donations to help us continue our work – to find out more, go to windhorsepublications.com.

The Windhorse is a mythical animal that flies over the earth carrying on its back three precious jewels, bringing these invaluable gifts to all humanity: the Buddha (the 'Awakened One'), his teaching, and the community of all his followers.

Windhorse Publications	Consortium Book Sales	Windhorse Books
38 Newmarket Road	& Distribution	PO Box 574
Cambridge	210 American Drive	Newtown
CB5 8DT	Jackson TN 38301	NSW 2042
	USA	Australia

info@windhorsepublications.com

THE TRIRATNA
BUDDHIST COMMUNITY

Windhorse Publications is a part of the Triratna Buddhist Community, an international movement with centres in Europe, India, North and South America and Australasia. At these centres, members of the Triratna Buddhist Order offer classes in meditation and Buddhism. Activities of the Triratna Community also include retreat centres, residential spiritual communities, ethical Right Livelihood businesses, and the Karuna Trust, a United Kingdom fundraising charity that supports social-welfare projects in the slums and villages of India.

Through these and other activities, Triratna is developing a unique approach to Buddhism, not simply as a philosophy and a set of techniques, but as a creatively directed way of life for all people living in the conditions of the modern world.

If you would like more information about Triratna please visit thebuddhistcentre.com or write to:

London Buddhist Centre
51 Roman Road
London E2 0HU
United Kingdom

Aryaloka
14 Heartwood Circle
Newmarket
NH 03857
USA

Sydney Buddhist Centre
24 Enmore Road
Sydney NSW 2042
Australia

Entertaining Cancer: The Buddhist Way
Devamitra

You're diagnosed with an aggressive cancer – what do you do?

Devamitra – English actor and Buddhist teacher – describes the discomforts and indignities of being treated for prostate cancer. He draws on the deep well of his Buddhist practice to work with his mind and meet fear, uncertainty and frailty with resolve.

'Devamitra has written a compelling book about his cancer journey that straddles a wide range of emotions: gruelling, funny, poignant and uplifting. You are drawn into his world as he undergoes particularly challenging treatment, whilst always maintaining a uniquely wry, even amused, perspective on life and death.' – **Vidyamala Burch**, co-founder of Breathworks, author of Living Well with Pain and Illness and Mindfulness for Health

'This is a remarkable book – honest, lucid, unflinching, funny and radical in its willingness to confront the facts of life and death. Devamitra tells the story of prostate cancer, and how his Buddhist practice met the challenges of diagnosis and treatment, even how cancer led to the deepening of his practice and his love of life.' – **Maitreyabandhu**, author of Life with Full Attention and The Journey and the Guide

'Quite often stories about cancer are framed in terms of a battle. This isn't always helpful, as it implies that disease progression means defeat or failure. Devamitra frames his account with interweaving themes of struggle, victory and setback, but also of calm and insight. We hear this story flavoured with his deep engagement with Buddhist teachings and practice, and his devotion to his teacher.' – **William Stones**, Professor of Obstetrics and Gynaecology and researcher in global health

'Who would have thought that having cancer could be so instructive, and at times so amusing? Devamitra writes of his experiences with a style unique to him: beautifully crafted, engaging, witty, poignant, reflective and always disarmingly honest. Devamitra faces his test as a Buddhist, but he wears his Buddhism lightly, even though it is Buddhism that guides him through it.' – **Subhuti**, author of Mind in Harmony

ISBN 978 1 911407 88 1 | £12.99 / $18.95 / €14.95 | 224 pages

Cyberloka: A Buddhist Guide to Digital Life
Prajnaketu

Prajnaketu takes us into the world of the cyberloka – the online realm in which so much of our lives now take place. In this short, punchy, and often funny book, Prajnaketu offers deep Buddhist insights that help us manage and flourish in the digital age of hyperavailability, superstimulation, and social media.

'Prajnaketu has written a deeply thoughtful, nuanced contemporary account of how Buddhists can relate to their digital life. Rather than offering simple solutions based on a now vanished, pre-Internet past, he accepts that the digital landscape is an inescapable part of our lives in the twenty-first century, and offers a wide-ranging critique of how we can best navigate this new world.' – **Vidyamala Burch**, author of Mindfulness for Health and Mindfulness for Women, and Co-Founder of The Breathworks Foundation

'Prajnaketu knows from experience the deep, restorative value of awareness and positive emotion when it comes to facing the new kinds of challenges inherent in an online world. His non-judgmental, unfailingly kind, and witty engagement with the thornier aspects of the Web promotes open-ended dialogue with the reader.' – **Candradasa**, Founding Director of Free Buddhist Audio and The Buddhist Centre Online, and author of Buddhism for Teens

'An engagingly personal dialogue between Buddhism and how to survive life in the metaverse. Read it and be enlightened!' – **Robin Dunbar,** Professor, University of Oxford

'Prajnaketu offers a clear-sighted and refreshing Buddhist critique of our digital lives, free from dogma and moralizing. Besides this, we now have a new sutta – the Facebook Sutta *– to guide us.'* – **Shantigarbha**, activist, mediator and author of The Burning House: A Buddhist Response to the Climate and Ecological Emergency and I'll Meet You There: A Practical Guide to Empathy, Mindfulness and Communication

Prajnaketu, 'he who holds a lamp of wisdom', was ordained into the Triratna Buddhist Order in 2014. He currently directs the Urgyen Sangharakshita Trust and teaches meditation and Buddhism in Oxford.

ISBN 978 1 911407 92 8 | £11.99 / $16.95 / €13.95 | 200 pages